Exploring Post-crisis Trajectories of European Corporate Governance

T0366788

Edited by

Alan Dignam and Michael Galanis

WILEY Blackwell

This edition first published 2014
Editorial organization © 2014 Cardiff University Law School
Chapters © 2014 by the chapter author

Blackwell Publishing was acquired by John Wiley & Sons in February 2007. Blackwell's
publishing programme has been merged with Wiley's global Scientific, Technical, and
Medical business to form Wiley-Blackwell.

Editorial Offices
350 Main Street, Malden, MA 02148-5020, USA
9600 Garsington Road, Oxford OX4 2DQ, UK

For details of our global editorial offices, for customer services, and for information about
how to apply for permission to reuse the copyright material in this book please see our
website at www.wiley.com/wiley-blackwell

Registered Office
John Wiley & Sons Ltd, The Atrium, Southern Gate, Chichester, West Sussex PO19 8SQ.

The right of Alan Dignam and Michael Galanis to be identified as the authors of the
Editorial Material in this work has been asserted in accordance with the Copyright, Designs
and Patents Act 1988.

Library of Congress Cataloging-in-Publication Data
Library of Congress Cataloging-in-Publication data is available for this book.

A catalogue record for this title is available from the British Library.

ISBN: 978-1-1188-3260-8

Set in the United Kingdom by Godiva Publishing Services Ltd
Printed in Singapore by C.O.S. Printers Pte Ltd

Contents

JOURNAL OF LAW AND SOCIETY
VOLUME 41, NUMBER 1, MARCH 2014
ISSN: 0263-323X, pp. 1–5

Introduction: Exploring Post-crisis Trajectories of European Corporate Governance

ALAN DIGNAM* AND MICHAEL GALANIS**

This special issue comes at a time of particular complexity for the 'so far' successful integration project that is the European Union. After over half a century of unprecedented cooperation and unification efforts by an expanding number of states that have been willing to surrender sometimes small and other times larger parts of their sovereignty for the common purpose of safeguarding prosperity and, more importantly, peace in a continent with a long history of war and misery, the project seems to have reached its first existential crossroads. Shortly after its most decisive unification initiative, the Economic and Monetary Union of some but not all member states, a private and, in turn, public financial crisis unfolded that has set the stage for a political choice between two totally antagonistic trajectories: a return to increased state sovereignty and protectionism[1] or further economic (and therefore further political) unification.

The crisis has signalled an imperative need for a realistic reassessment of economic regulation and single market structure more generally. This cannot leave corporate governance unaffected and therefore relevant policy and institutional elements need re-evaluation to deal with recent structural failures. Uncertainty about the efficacy of economic governance and corporate governance specifically is particularly pronounced in Europe due to its institutional peculiarities as a union of (semi-)sovereign states and fragmented private sector governance systems. This not only makes the EU an interesting case study, but also renders the re-evaluation and coordination

* School of Law, Queen Mary, University of London, 67–69 Lincoln's Inn Fields, London WC2A 3JB, England
a.dignam@qmul.ac.uk
** School of Law, University of Manchester, Oxford Road, Manchester M13 9PL, England
michael.galanis@manchester.ac.uk

1 For an interesting selection of essays on the interactions between European protectionist tendencies and corporate governance see U. Bernitz and W.-G. Ringe (eds.), *Company Law and Economic Protectionism: New Challenges to European Integration* (2010).

1

of corporate governance even more imperative than if its central governance issues were present at the national level. Is there or should there be a unified corporate governance trajectory in the EU? If so, should it be reoriented totally or would an upgrade of current misfiring arrangements be sufficient? Which agents should be responsible for formulating policy in this area and how? In other words basic but important questions need answering.

Prior to undertaking the role as guest editors for this volume and following a series of common projects where we developed our own approach to corporate governance as a structurally determined function, we felt the economic and political conditions are such in the crisis-stricken EU that they deserve a closer specialist examination in the field of corporate governance. We thus gathered a list of distinguished academics of divergent and dissenting standpoints in a one-day workshop on 'Post-crisis Trajectories of European Corporate Governance', supported by the *Journal of Law and Society* (for which our thanks), where ideas about the way forward for European corporate governance were debated, at times quite intensely, proving the complexity of our current social, political, and economic situation. This special issue reproduces, we hope, a large part of the intellectually stimulating debate of that workshop by drawing out the themes within the papers not only of the reforms required in basic areas of EU corporate governance, but also of the interconnected desirability of EU structural change generally.

Beginning with this latter point, *Johnston* persuasively demonstrates how precarious and costly it can be to leave structural reform to the forces of market contracting. He shows how the European Commission performed a dramatic pendulum-style readjustment from contractual self-correction to decisive prescriptive intervention in the heated field of bankers' pay within a very short period of time. Similarly, *Avgouleas and Cullen* tackle the problem of banks' corporate governance by advocating a decisive sector-wide intervention that would simplify, or rather segregate, banking and financial markets. There are contractual and regulatory failures of the significant type, but intervention in the micro-structure, they argue, would not suffice if banks' governance is to be meaningfully and effectively reoriented. Their approach is similar to our own perspective of corporate governance, emphasizing the interaction and interdependence between micro-level governance arrangements and diverse institutional structures that seem to mainly lie outside the corporate organization, such as modes of regulation concerning financial markets, competition, foreign trade markets and capital movements, labour markets, and macro-economic policy.[2]

---

2 A. Dignam and M. Galanis, *The Globalization of Corporate Governance* (2009); A. Dignam, 'The Role of Competition in Determining Corporate Governance Outcomes: Lessons from Australia's Corporate Governance System' (2005) 68 *Modern Law Rev.* 765; M. Galanis, 'Vicious Spirals in Corporate Governance: Mandatory Rules for Systemic Rebalancing' (2011) 31 *Oxford J. of Legal Studies* 327.

On the other hand, *Villiers* explores the interactions between corporate governance and the labour market structure in the EU and more widely, but, although her starting point is also the systemic nature of corporate governance, she takes issue with the view that the medium of restructuring should necessarily be in the form of prescriptive regulation. The embeddedness of current institutional arrangements in a particular (neoliberal) type of socio-economic organization is such that conventional reform channels are incapable of bringing about the changes required without the radicalization of interests that are disadvantaged by current corporate governance structure. A more Marxian perspective is better suited, Villiers would argue, to determine and explain the deeply rooted changes required for a more balanced governance and general socio-economic system.

To add even more complexity to this debate about the appropriate mechanisms of reform, *McCahery and Vermeulen* warn us about the perils of over-regulating corporate governance, such as the asphyxiation of innovation before it is even born, not only in micro-economic organization but also more generally. *Eckardt and Kerber* distance themselves even further from the pro-regulatory perspective of corporate governance. They discover significant added value in a more enabling corporate law that offers increased choice for European companies, with regulatory competition assisting as a secondary mechanism of developing efficient rules at least for SMEs and start-up companies. *Magnier* adopts a more moderated middle-ground approach to regulatory reform that moves away from hard-law interventionism. She suggests that, given the complexities created by institutional diversity among member states, soft-law approaches accompanied by external corporate governance audit and greater shareholder information rights are the appropriate general reform solution for European corporate governance.

On the other hand, as far as corporate governance 'ideology' is concerned, the lessons seem to be a bit clearer and more consistent, with a virtual consensus emerging from the various analyses and perspectives offered herein. More specifically, it seems that, following the financial crisis, faith in market-led light-touch regulation has had its day, at least in academic quarters. The moral-hazard effect of government-backed financial markets however, seems to still be with us. The financialization[3] of the economic system that brought to the forefront and led to the establishment of the often mythologized concept of shareholder value maximization as the guiding norm of good governance has had an instrumental role in the enormous social cost the crisis caused by the market failures of the late 2000s continues to create.

---

3 E. Stockhammer, 'Financialisation and the Slowdown of Accumulation' (2004) 28 *Cambridge J. of Economics* 719. See, also, M. Galanis, 'The Impact of EMU on Corporate Governance: Bargaining in Austerity' (2013) 33 *Oxford J. of Legal Studies* 475.

3

Thus, the ideological shift away from shareholder value is clear in Johnston's analysis of the causes of bankers' pay extravagance. He explains how the combination of the shareholder norm's prevalence with the reliance on contractually determined managerial incentive mechanisms led to disastrous choices in the banking sector. Aligning executive pay with short-term shareholder returns, which become a well-established demand of the markets in recent decades, now has to be reversed, given the devastating consequences it has had in the financial sector. Villiers provides another dimension to this need for an ideological shift in corporate governance, by treating the dominance of the shareholder in corporate governance as the outcome of a working class defeated and dispersed by the current form of capitalist organization and the power of financial capital in particular. Nonetheless, Magnier is a bit more optimistic, in that shareholder pressure via soft-law governance may under certain conditions influence corporate behaviour even if the dominant ideology remains largely unchanged. In a somewhat similar effort to rework corporate governance and mitigate the destabilizing effects of dominant governance norms without undoing them completely, *Mukwiri and Siems* propose that the malaise of short-termism could be resolved by distinguishing between 'good' and 'bad' shareholder interests and privileging the former.

On the other hand, and from a very different standpoint, McCahery and Vermeulen seem to agree that the exacerbated influence of financial capital through the adherence to shareholder supremacy can have a subverting impact on innovative companies. Regulators' efforts to enforce this shareholder-oriented norm by imposing it through accountability-focused governance on every company, irrespectively of its particular needs, damages the growth prospects of companies who need to protect those stakeholders they really need. This disrupting effect may have even wider consequences as those companies who could otherwise be the most dynamic ones are undermined or even prevented from flourishing. However, these entrepreneurial companies are instrumental in the regeneration of capitalism,[4] as envisaged by a Schumpeterian process of creative destruction,[5] and current regulatory perspectives seem to stifle this process when Europe probably needs it more than ever before. This is a problem that cannot easily be tackled by prescriptive regulation, as prescription clashes directly with the attributes of organizational dynamism required to achieve this economic regeneration. This is perhaps the point where the need for a choice of regulatory mechanisms and wider organizational goals codified through governance ideology begin to interact with and complicate each other.

---

4 S. Wennekers and R. Thurik, 'Linking Entrepreneurship and Economic Growth' (1999) 13 *Small Business Economics* 27.
5 J. Schumpeter, *Capitalism, Socialism and Democracy* (1942).

Policy makers both at EU and state level,[6] however, seem to have missed not only that an ideological shift in corporate governance away from shareholder-oriented norms, may be necessary, but also that paving the way out of the crisis may require something more than just better accountability mechanisms. There is a need for these bigger ideolological questions to be tackled, if policy is to deliver sound results. Given the on-going European crisis, answering these questions is even more imperative as corporate governance structures form part of the wealth-creation processes and wealth-distribution channels necessary for recovery. These problems, unless resolved, will continue affecting the legitimacy of the project of a unified Europe, even if the current financial problems – extremely complex themselves, given the institutional structure of the EU – are resolved. We hope that the ideas contained in this volume are a contribution that could throw some light on our effort to find a direction in the current socioeconomic gloom of Europe.

---

6 For example, see 'Shareholder Rights' Directive 2007/36/EC, OJ L 184. However, the recent European Commission, 'Action Plan: European company law and corporate governance – a modern legal framework for more engaged shareholders and sustainable companies' (COM(2012) 740 final) seems to diverge slightly from the blind adherence to shareholder supremacy since; although two of its three objectives concern investor protection and shareholder engagement, it demonstrates some scepticism about the negative side effects of short-termist shareholder activism and securities markets.

JOURNAL OF LAW AND SOCIETY
VOLUME 41, NUMBER 1, MARCH 2014
ISSN: 0263-323X, pp. 6–27

Preventing the Next Financial Crisis? Regulating Bankers' Pay in Europe

ANDREW JOHNSTON*

This article offers a critical appraisal of the way in which executive pay in financial institutions is regulated in the European Union. Despite the widely acknowledged role of executive pay in causing the financial crisis, regulators and policy makers were reluctant to intervene because of the ideology of shareholder primacy and an unjustified belief that this was a matter for companies and their shareholders alone. As a result, the original regulatory scheme which was introduced was very weak. The European Parliament responded to these developments by capping executive pay. The article argues that, while this cap is a crude instrument, it can be justified on economic grounds because it considerably reduces the likelihood of a future financial crisis, with all the social costs that would entail. If it also results in much higher fixed pay, that is a matter of concern for shareholders alone, and might even force them into the activism so long expected of them.

INTRODUCTION

This article offers a critical appraisal of the European scheme that regulates executive remuneration in financial institutions. This scheme is an important part of the wider response to the financial crisis, and an essential complement to the ongoing reforms to the Basel system of banking regulation, because remuneration schemes provide the most important incentives for bank executives to 'innovate' in ways which get around banking regulation. Before the crisis, innovations such as wholesale off-balance-sheet financing of loans and the use of complex derivatives increased bank profitability by creating risks which were not visible to regulators or other actors, and undermined the financial stability goal of the Basel system. While the recent revisions of the Basel system specifically target some of these practices,

* School of Law, University of Sheffield, Bartolome House, Winter Street, Sheffield S3 7ND, England
Andrew.Johnston@sheffield.ac.uk

regulation of remuneration is still required to prevent as yet unidentified practices leading to future financial sector instability.

The main obstacle to the necessary far-reaching reforms is the ideology of shareholder primacy, which insists that increases in shareholder value within the law can be equated with the common good. This ideology continues to dominate policy debates about corporate governance, despite recent failures, such as Enron, which resulted in massive costs for both shareholders and employee stakeholders, or the various bank failures which led to the current financial crisis, which imposed huge losses on shareholders and taxpayer stakeholders. The driving force behind both of these economic disasters was the practice of paying executives for increasing the share price or return on equity, a practice justified by the ideology of shareholder primacy. Even though this practice has repeatedly led to enormous social costs, and has been widely identified as a central cause of the crisis, key policy makers remain in thrall to shareholder primacy and are reluctant to introduce the regulation which appears necessary. As this article will show, they were happy to leave remuneration primarily to bank boards and shareholders, while the national regulators, who failed to even notice the massive expansion of credit and risk that preceded the crisis, were charged with the impossible task of identifying when remuneration schemes give executives incentives to take 'excessive' risks. Policy makers even recognized that this regulatory scheme would be likely to fail. This was unacceptable to the European Parliament, which forced a more prescriptive regulatory scheme into the Capital Requirements Directive, maintaining the requirement that national regulators oversee remuneration schemes, but against the backdrop of a quantitative cap on variable remuneration.

This article argues that the cap is a vital addition to the regulatory scheme. In a broader sense the cap demonstrates an important shift in the debate about whether markets or regulation should shape corporate governance. For the first time, policy makers have recognized that prescriptive regulation may be required to prevent companies setting pay in ways that produce unacceptable social costs. This is a significant intervention into an area which has, to date, been left to corporate boards (under the constraints of soft law alone), a policy justified by the assumptions of shareholder-primacy ideology.

The first part of the article examines the contribution of executive pay to the crisis. The second part offers an overview of the original regulatory scheme, while the third part critiques it. The fourth part outlines and evaluates the cap, and a brief conclusion follows.

EXECUTIVE REMUNERATION AND ITS CONTRIBUTION
TO THE CRISIS

It is widely recognized that the practices and structures of executive pay played a central role in the financial crisis, although there is less consensus on its exact contribution. The de Larosière report concluded that 'Remuneration and incentive schemes within financial institutions contributed to excessive risk taking by rewarding short-term expansion of the volume of (risky) trades rather than the long-term profitability of investments.'[1] The European Commission noted a 'broad consensus that compensation schemes based on short-term returns, without adequate consideration for the corresponding risks, contributed to the incentives that led to financial institutions' engagement in overly risky business practices.'[2] Elsewhere, it noted that executive pay was 'one of five driving forces of the financial crisis', along with credit rating agencies, and regulatory and supervisory failures.[3] These views are echoed in numerous other reports.[4]

What is lacking from these policy documents and reports is any explanation of *why* remuneration came to be a problem and *how* it contributed to the crisis. Remuneration practices were justified and driven by the ideology of shareholder primacy, which assumes that, in order to increase social wealth, executives should be prevented from imposing 'agency costs' on shareholders.[5] The most important means of ensuring that executives will further the interests of shareholders is to pay them for doing so. Other interests are assumed to be fully protected by regulation, and it is assumed that regulation is not undermined by pay practices. These arguments were applied to banking without regard for the peculiarities of the sector.

The core function of banks is to issue short-term liabilities to pay against long-term promises to pay from borrowers. Risk taking is inherent in banking. Minsky notes that 'commercial banks are the prototypical speculative financial organization' because they engage in the 'short financing of long positions'.[6] Unlike normal industrial companies, banks are able to increase the riskiness of their balance sheets very quickly in ways which are not observable by outsiders, including regulators and shareholders. Increases in risk taking make banks vulnerable to changes in the economy which affect borrowers' ability to pay, and to changes in financial markets which affect

1 See J. de Larosière (chair), *Report of the High-level Group on Financial Supervision in the EU* (2009) para. 24 (de Larosière Report).
2 Commission Communication accompanying 'Recommendations on Executive Remuneration' (COM(2009) 211 final, April 2009).
3 'Impact Assessment', Commission Staff Working Document accompanying European Commission, 'Commission Recommendation on remuneration policies in the financial services sector' (SEC(2009) 580, April 2009).
4 See, for example, the Financial Stability Forum (FSF), *Principles for Sound Compensation Practices* (2009); the conclusions of the OECD Steering Group on Corporate Governance, *The Corporate Governance Lessons from the Financial Crisis* (2009) 12; and the Parliamentary Commission on Banking Standards (PCBS), First Report, *Changing Banking for Good*, HL 27 (2013–14) HC 175, particularly at Vol. II, para. 836, noting that 'Remuneration lies at the heart of some of banks' biggest problems'.
5 For critical overviews, see A. Johnston, *EC Regulation of Corporate Governance* (2009) ch. 2; L. Stout, *The Shareholder Value Myth* (2012).
6 H. Minsky, *Stabilizing an Unstable Economy* (2008) 231.

8

their ability to obtain short-term liquidity to discharge their liabilities. Assuming willing borrowers, there are two main limits on the otherwise virtually unlimited expansion of bank balance sheets.

First, individuals and businesses must be willing to be creditors of banks (that is, hold banks' liabilities). The effectiveness of this first limit is significantly reduced because, in order to ensure the stability of the financial system, the state guarantees bank liabilities through explicit and implicit deposit-guarantee schemes, and acts as lender of last resort to banks. Unlike normal companies, banks cannot be allowed to become insolvent and default on their liabilities. Second, as guarantor of the banks, the state introduces banking regulation to limit balance-sheet expansion and risk taking, which is absolutely crucial to protecting the public interest because guarantees remove the incentive of bank creditors to evaluate the riskiness of banks.

Shareholder-primacy ideology glosses over these matters of regulation and insists that bank executives should be incentivized to maximize returns to shareholders, just as they are in other types of company. Accordingly, senior executives in financial institutions were remunerated with stock options, which allowed them to purchase shares in the parent company,[7] and bonuses linked to return on equity (RoE). When translated to the banking context, these forms of remuneration encouraged bankers to 'seek bigger and riskier bets'.[8] As Haldane shows, by increasing leverage, banks could increase RoE even while return on total assets remained the same. The other side of those returns was an increase in risk. Executives sought to increase leverage and risk in any way which was not explicitly prohibited by regulation, encouraging bank employees to make riskier loans to meet revenue targets, their conventional concern that borrowers would repay their loans overridden by their 'high-powered incentives'.[9] The effect was to neutralize the best means of controlling risk: bankers are better placed than any other actor (including regulators) to ensure that lending practices are prudent.

The existence of these powerful incentives to increase leverage and risk made banking regulation even more critical. The adequacy of bank capital is regulated internationally by the Basel Accords.[10] Their stated aim is to 'further strengthen the soundness and stability of the international banking system'[11] by controlling risk taking by individual banks. Banks are required

---

7 L. Bebchuk and H. Spamann, 'Regulating Bankers' Pay' (2010) 98 *Georgetown Law J.* 247, at 258.

8 A. Haldane, 'Control Rights (and Wrongs)' (2012) 32 *Economic Affairs* 47, at 50–1.

9 See for example, FSA, 'Final Notice to Peter Cummings', 12 September 2012, concluding at 4.32 that in HBOS 'staff were incentivised to focus on revenue rather than risk' and at 4.48 that 'under Mr Cummings' [executive] direction all areas of the business focused on revenue generation'.

10 See Basel Committee on Banking Supervision (BCBS), *International Convergence of Capital Measurement and Capital Standards: A Revised Framework* (Comprehensive Version) (2006) (Basel II).

11 id., para. 4.

to hold a ratio of capital to risk-weighted assets of 8 per cent.[12] Different types of loans are accorded standardized risk-weightings. For example, under Basel II, loans secured against residential mortgages are risk-weighted at 35 per cent,[13] so banks have to hold capital amounting to 8 per cent of 35 per cent, that is, 2.8 per cent, of the total loan. While this allows banks to make £100 worth of loans against £2.80 in capital, which is a leverage ratio of over 35, it does prevent unlimited expansion of balance sheets, and so places some limit on risk taking.

Yet even this was considered too prescriptive, and Basel II permitted national regulators to authorize larger banks to use the 'Internal Ratings-Based Approach' (IRB) and determine risk weightings for themselves, using their own internal models. For example, if an IRB-authorized bank used a model which placed a lower risk weighting on residential mortgages than the standardized 35 per cent, then they would be able to back those loans with even less capital.[14] Relatively little is known publicly about banks' internal models – and their risk weightings, in particular – because, despite their central role in this system of public interest regulation, they are considered proprietary. This is problematic because the IRB method creates a number of risks: first, that the credit risk assumptions made by the banks might turn out to be inaccurate; second, there is 'potential for intentional distortion of model inputs'; and third, there is a 'dearth of useful historical data' on which to base the risk models, making it difficult to backtest the models.[15] As Satiyajit Das presciently noted, the IRB approach created the 'illusion of precision', whilst in reality 'most of the inputs were either unavailable or difficult to verify'.[16]

It is not known whether banks deliberately manipulated their models to allow them to take on more risk. What is clear is that executives had employment contracts which gave them powerful incentives to increase return on equity by taking on more risk, which would be easier if their banks' internal models indicated that their operations were less risky than the standardized approach. Northern Rock's response to the FSA authorizing it to use the IRB Approach is an interesting example. The House of Commons Treasury Committee concluded:

12 id., para. 40.
13 id., para. 72. In Basel I, residential mortgages were risk weighted at 50 per cent: see Basel Committee on Banking Supervision, *International Convergence of Capital Measurement and Capital Standards* (1988, updated to April 1998) 18, Annex 2.
14 There were *de minimis* provisions which applied to banks' models and prevented them from concluding that their loans were risk free. For example, banks were not permitted to assume a probability of default of below 0.03 per cent (Basel II, op. cit., n. 10, para. 331).
15 D. Tarullo, *Banking on Basel: The Future of International Financial Regulation* (2008) 153.
16 S. Das, *Traders, Guns & Money* (2006) 159–60.

Northern Rock was told by the FSA that its application for a Basel II waiver had been approved ... Due to this approval, Northern Rock felt able to announce ... an increase in its interim dividend of 30.3%. This was because the waiver and other asset realisations meant that Northern Rock had an 'anticipated regulatory capital surplus over the next 3 to 4 years'.[17]

In his evidence to the Select Committee, Chief Executive Applegarth said that Northern Rock's IRB approval 'saw our risk weighting for residential mortgages come down from 50% to 15%. That clearly required less capital behind it, so that links to why we were able to increase the dividend.'[18] He confirmed that executives' 'salaries incentives were linked to profit growth and total shareholder returns.'[19] As they were intended to do, these incentives encouraged executives to increase the dividend, and with it, their remuneration.

More generally, remuneration schemes encouraged banks to take advantage of the inevitable lacunae and gaps in the Basel Accords. For example, Basel II did not prohibit banks from moving loans off their balance sheets into bankruptcy-remote entities such as conduits and structured investment vehicles. This 'shadow banking system' freed up regulatory capital to back fresh loans, thereby increasing return on equity. It doubled in size between 2002 and 2010,[20] yet 'regulators seemed only vaguely aware of what the banks were really doing.'[21] Crucially, however, banks still bore a – difficult to quantify – measure of residual responsibility for these formally separate entities through the provision of lines of credit, guarantees, and 'liquidity backstops', which committed them to bring the assets back onto their books in the event of financial difficulties. These devices were binding either legally or for reputational reasons.[22] Similarly, banks used credit default swaps (essentially insurance) to reduce or even eliminate the need to hold any capital against securitized loans.

This shadow banking system was the locus of a massive build-up of risk outside the scope of the Basel Accords. The motivation to establish these complex structures was provided by executive remuneration schemes that rewarded increased return on equity. Whilst formally complying with Basel II, banks could increase the riskiness of their operations, and with them, interdependence and systemic risk. The Basel Accords were not the only

---

17 See House of Commons Treasury Committee, Fifth Report, *The Run on the Rock*, HC (2007–08) 56, paras. 43–4, at <http://www.publications.parliament.uk/pa/cm200708/cmselect/cmtreasy/56/56i.pdf>.

18 id., response to question 689.

19 id., response to question 540.

20 European Commission Green Paper, 'Shadow Banking' (COM(2012) 102 final, March 2012) 4.

21 G. Tett, *Fool's Gold* (2010) 116.

22 R. Hetzel, *The Great Recession: Market Failure or Policy Failure?* (2012) 181; G. Gorton and N. Souleles, 'Special Purpose Vehicles and Securitization' in *The Risks of Financial Institutions*, eds. M. Carey and R.M. Stulz (2007) 551.

aspect of banking regulation that failed. As noted, national regulators failed too, doing nothing about the massive build-up of leverage and risk in the banking system, or the exponential growth of the shadow banking system. The FSA concedes that 'many aspects of [its] approach to the supervision of systemically important firms in the pre-crisis period were inadequate.'[23]

The Basel Accords are undergoing revision to deal with some of the shortcomings revealed by the crisis,[24] requiring banks to hold more capital against off-balance-sheet exposures, and more high-quality liquid assets. In the United Kingdom, responsibility for prudential supervision has been reallocated to a newly constituted subsidiary of the Bank of England, the Prudential Regulatory Authority. However, these essential reforms must be complemented by regulation of remuneration because the new rules address the causes of the *last* crisis, and will inevitably contain gaps. Without regulation of remuneration, the same incentives will remain to exploit those gaps, increase complexity, and take on more risk wherever this is not explicitly prohibited.

The ideology of shareholder primacy, coupled with a belief that market-correcting regulation cannot be justified, creates powerful pressure on policy makers not to intervene in pay, even though pay practices incentivized behaviour which created enormous social costs. Indeed, policy makers have not even attempted to quantify the costs to taxpayers of bank bailouts and compare it with the benefits to social wealth in the form of returns to shareholders. However, the IMF estimated in 2009 that the British government's support to the banking sector would total some 81.6 per cent of 2008 GDP, with an upfront cost of 18.9 per cent.[25] Even excluding the wholesale destruction of shareholder primacy wrought by the financial crisis, these costs to the state are surely many times higher than total shareholder returns during the boom years.[26] In any other area where the past social costs of a

---

23 Financial Services Authority (FSA), *The Failure of the Royal Bank of Scotland* (2011) 29.

24 See BCBS, *Basel III: A global regulatory framework for more resilient banks and banking systems* (2010, revised June 2011). A non-risk-weighted leverage ratio of 3 per cent should come into force in 2018, restricting banks to maximum leverage of 33 times equity. Most banks had leverage below this level when the GFC began, with even Lehmann Bros only at 33.7 times equity.

25 See IMF Staff Position Note, 'Fiscal Implication of the Global Economic and Financial Crisis', 9 June 2009, 7. There are 'significant uncertainties' about the medium-term net costs of the support for the banking sector, which will depend on whether assets recover their pre-crisis values; the IMF estimated that, for the advanced economies of the G20 which on average spent 5.8 per cent of GDP on supporting financial institutions, the average medium-term cost of the crisis was likely to be some 2.5 per cent of GDP. However, the United Kingdom's costs would be likely to be considerably higher than this, given that its upfront spending was much higher.

26 Discussing the 1982 banking crisis, which was dwarfed by the current crisis, Taleb notes that 'large American banks lost close to all their past earnings (cumulatively), about everything they ever made in the history of American banking – everything.'

practice so far exceeded its benefits, there would be a prima facie case for prohibiting the practice entirely. However, policy makers continued to resist this conclusion, framing the issue of pay in financial institutions as the technical one of 'optimal contracting', that is, aligning bankers' incentives with the long-term interests of shareholders,[27] an interest which is never articulated in corporate governance processes, but the pursuit of which has repeatedly resulted in enormous social costs.

OVERVIEW OF THE ORIGINAL REGULATORY SCHEME

1. *Background to the EU initiatives*

The most important policy documents display a marked reluctance to consider prescriptive regulation, and an astonishing willingness to contemplate the failure of their weak regulatory proposals, despite the enormous social costs this would entail. The de Larosière Report[28] reflects the dominant aversion to regulatory intervention, emphasizing the need 'to re-align compensation incentives with shareholder interests and long-term, firm-wide profitability', but stressing the importance of not 'impinging on the responsibility of financial institutions in this field'. It concluded that 'supervisors should oversee the adequacy of financial institutions' compensation policies', and should require boards to reassess them where they conflict with 'adequate risk management or are systematically encouraging short-term risk-taking'.[29] Similarly, the Financial Stability Forum (FSF) began by emphasizing the 'theoretical' role of 'stock-based compensation' in motivating employees 'to act in the interests of the firm's shareholders'.[30] Despite the clear failure of both boards and shareholders to control risk taking in the build-up to the crisis, the FSF insisted that remuneration schemes should remain primarily the responsibility of the board, whilst shareholders should also contribute to effective governance. In their view, the perennial corporate

---

See N. Taleb, *The Black Swan* (2007) 43–4. Similarly, it has been estimated that the pay of the top bankers in Iceland amounted to around ISK6bn, some 0.1 per cent of the total losses to Iceland (five times its GDP, or ISK7trn).

27 See, similarly, PCBS, op. cit., n. 4, which recognizes that 'unbalanced incentives ... pervade banking' but seeks to correct them with ex-post remedies such as enforcement schemes and deferral of bonuses (vol. I, paras. 167 and 234), even whilst admitting that 'risk and remuneration are subjective'. It insists that 'individual rewards should be primarily a matter for banks and their owners', and 'encourages shareholders to take a more active interest in levels of senior remuneration' (vol. I, paras. 208 and 180), yet later admits that 'it would be a mistake to expect greater empowerment and engagement of shareholders to lead to the exercise of profound and positive influence on the governance of banks' (vol. II, para. 666).

28 de Larosière, op. cit., n. 1.

29 id., paras. 118–20.

30 FSF, op. cit., n. 4, p. 10. This body is now known as the Financial Stability Board.

13

governance problem of shareholder passivity can be overcome merely by disclosure of the 'general design philosophy of the system'; the scheme's risk adjustment provisions; and the way the scheme links compensation to performance over time.[31] While 'rigorous and sustained' supervisory review of compensation practices is essential, 'the industry must experiment' with risk adjustment.[32] The FSF openly acknowledges that risk takers will still be able 'to boost short-run performance' by concealing tail risks, and accepts that risk adjustment will only work 'if the tail risks the employee or business unit takes are measured well'.[33] The challenges that tail risks, and uncertainty more generally, pose for prudential oversight of remuneration are discussed below.

2. The Commission's recommendations

In its March 2009 Communication, 'Driving European Recovery',[34] the Commission responded by announcing that it would issue two recommendations and propose legislation to include 'remuneration schemes within the scope of prudential oversight'.[35] Those recommendations provide 'principles and best practices' addressed to member states to ensure that companies implement 'pay policies which reward long-term sustainable performance', and emphasize the need for 'culture change in the businesses concerned'.[36] The accompanying Impact Assessment demonstrates that the crisis has not changed the Commission's operating assumption that remuneration should be understood in shareholder-primacy terms.[37]

The Commission's 'Recommendations on remuneration policies in the financial services sector'[38] claims that it will 'increase the likelihood' that risk management and control systems will become effective.[39] Member states should ensure that financial institutions have remuneration policies which promote 'sound and effective risk management' and do not 'induce excessive risk-taking'.[40] Bonuses should be deferred, with the deferred

31 id., p. 14.
32 id., p. 9.
33 FSF, *Implementation Standards* (April and September 2009) 12 and fn. 9.
34 EC Communication, 'Driving European Recovery' (COM(2009) 114 final, March 2009).
35 id., pp. 7–8.
36 id., p. 2.
37 'Whether, and the extent to which, an executive director, will fully pursue shareholders' interests depends on finding an appropriate way to motivate the executive director', with agency theory suggesting that 'the performance-based pay contract, which links pay to the company's wealth via performance indicators, is the most appropriate way': European Commission, op. cit., n. 3, p. 7.
38 id. (The second Recommendation (C(2009) 3177, April 2009) deals with remuneration in listed companies generally and is not considered further here.)
39 id., para. 5.
40 id., para. 3.1.

14

element 'tak[ing] into account the outstanding risks associated with the performance'; boards should determine remuneration, relying on members with 'relevant expertise and functional independence from the business units they control'; and national competent authorities should monitor whether these principles are followed.[41]

Like the FSF Principles, which it implements, this recommendation offers no meaningful guidance on how regulators are supposed to ensure that remuneration schemes identify and 'take into account the outstanding risks associated with the performance'.[42] We will see below that a good deal of guidance has been published since the recommendation, but it too fails to address this question.

3. *Reform of the Capital Requirements Directive*

The most important aspect of the original regulatory scheme is the amendment of the Capital Requirements Directive (CRD III),[43] to implement the de Larosière and FSF recommendations.[44]

(a) Information disclosure

CRD III requires financial institutions to disclose certain information about remuneration to the national regulator, which should then transmit that information to the Committee of European Banking Supervisors (CEBS),[45] which is to use it to benchmark remuneration practices at EU level.[46] Institutions are also required to make public disclosure of information on an annual basis about remuneration policies and practices for staff 'whose professional activities have a material impact on its risk profile'.[47] The hope is that shareholders will take a more activist approach in relation to matters of remuneration than they have in the past.[48]

---

41 id., paras. 4.4, 6.4, and 10.
42 id., preamble, para. 14.
43 See Directive 2010/76/EU amending Directives 2006/48/EC and 2006/49/EC as regards capital requirements for the trading book and for re-securitizations, and the supervisory review of remuneration policies (OJ L 329/3). The CRD implements the Basel Accords in the EU.
44 In turn, in the United Kingdom, the FCA's Remuneration Code implements the prudential oversight requirements of CRD III.
45 Such is the pace of change that the CEBS has been superseded by the European Banking Authority.
46 Art. 1(3)(b) of Directive 2010/76/EU inserting Arts. 22(3)–(5) into Directive 2006/48/EC.
47 Article 15 is added to Annex XII of Directive 2006/48/EC.
48 Directive 2010/76/EU, preamble, paras. 17–18.

15

(b) Prudential oversight of remuneration schemes

CRD III requires national competent authorities to ensure that financial institutions have 'robust governance arrangements', including 'remuneration policies and practices that are consistent with and promote sound and effective risk management'.[49] Supervisors are to 'assess whether those policies and practices are likely to encourage excessive-risk-taking',[50] with member states giving them 'power to impose financial and non-financial penalties or other measures'.[51] Annex V sets out a number of principles, requiring, amongst other things, that remuneration policies do not 'encourage risk taking that exceeds the level of tolerated risk of the credit institution'; that at least 40 per cent of variable remuneration should be 'deferred over a period which is not less than three to 5 years' and 'correctly aligned with the nature of the business, its risks and the activities of the member of staff in question'; and that remuneration should only be paid or vest 'if it is sustainable according to the financial situation of the credit institution as a whole, and justified according to the performance of the credit institution, the business unit and the individual concerned.' These principles reflect both the FSF Guidelines and the Commission's Recommendation, while the more detailed components, such as the deferral requirements are taken straight from the Basel Committee on Banking Supervision's *Compensation Principles and Standards Assessment Methodology*.[52]

The CEBS was charged with drawing up guidelines to assist national supervisors, and delivered its *Guidelines on Remuneration Policies and Practices* in December 2010. The most important section of the *Guidelines*, headed 'Specific Requirements on Risk Alignment',[53] advises national regulators to ensure that institutions 'take into account both current and future risks that are taken by the staff member', 'whether on or off balance sheet',[54] and that their risk adjustment measures include 'difficult-to-measure' risks.[55] Regulators should ensure that institutions 'consider the full range of current and potential (unexpected) risks associated with the activities undertaken', including 'severe risks or stressed conditions' and make ex-ante risk adjustments which take account of them.[56] The *Guidelines*

---

49 id., Art. 1(3).
50 id., preamble, para. 16.
51 id., Art. 1(4).
52 BCBS, *Compensation Principles and Standards Assessment Methodology* (2010).
53 CEBS, *Guidelines on Remuneration Policies and Practices* (2010) 37–69.
54 id., pp. 49, 51.
55 id., p. 51. The *Guidelines* strongly echo the BCBS, op. cit., n. 52: see, for example, paras. 40–1.
56 For example, at id., p. 52, the *Guidelines* discourage the use of profits, volume, share price, total shareholder return, and other measures which 'do not incorporate explicit risk adjustment and are very short-term', and so 'are not sufficient to capture all the risks of the staff member's activities'.

16

recognize that ex-ante risk adjustments may fail 'due to uncertainty',[57] making ex-post adjustments of remuneration, such as 'malus' or clawback,[58] 'absolutely necessary' to allow financial institutions 'to adjust ... variable remuneration as time goes by and the outcomes of the staff's actions materialize.'[59] Accordingly, regulators are encouraged check that 'ex-post risk adjustments are defined and detailed'.[60]

The difficulty with reliance on ex-post adjustments is that, if institutions and regulators fail to identify risks before hand, and those risks materialize causing banks to fail, various stakeholders, including states, and ultimately taxpayers, will be exposed to losses. While ex-post adjustments are a useful means of aligning executive incentives with the shareholder interest, they do nothing to protect stakeholder interests if excessive risk taking results in bank failure. This point is discussed in more detail in the next section, which assesses the CRD III regulatory scheme.

The CEBS was also required to lay down 'specific criteria' for determining the ratio between fixed and variable pay. The *Guidelines* note that 'the higher the possible variable remuneration, the stronger the incentive will be to deliver the needed performance, and the bigger the associated risks will become.'[61] The CEBS recommended that policies set out 'explicit maximum ratio(s) on the variable component in relation to the fixed component'[62] but declined to 'decree one optimal relationship between the fixed and variable components'.[63] In so doing, the CEBS left identification of an appropriate ratio almost entirely to the discretion of individual financial institutions.[64] This put the onus back on national regulators to determine the appropriateness of those ratios from a prudential perspective.

The Impact Assessment which accompanied the original proposal justifies this approach, blaming the 'lack of express requirements to supervise risks arising in connection with remuneration policies' for the 'insufficient supervisory oversight' of remuneration before the crisis.[65] In other words, it

---

57 id., p. 59.
58 Malus 'operate[s] by affecting the vesting process and cannot operate after the end of the deferral period', while clawback 'typically operates in the case of established fraud or misleading information'. These measures should be 'based on both quantitative measures and informed judgment' (id., pp. 67–8).
59 id., p. 66
60 id., p. 69.
61 id., p. 45.
62 id., p. 46.
63 id.
64 Para. 23(l) of Annex V of Directive 2010/76/EU states that 'Credit institutions shall set the appropriate ratios between the fixed and variable component of the total remuneration.'
65 Commission Staff Working Document, Impact Assessment (SEC(2009) 974 final, July 2009) 18. It notes that investment firms were arguably already obliged 'to ensure that remuneration policies and practices do not expose the firm to unmanageable risks that exceed the level tolerated by the firm', but that these obligations were 'insufficiently explicit'.

assumes that, if prudential regulators had been explicitly instructed to ensure that remuneration did not create incentives for excessive risk taking, they would have been able to achieve this and demand appropriate changes. A perfunctory cost-benefit analysis simply assumes the scheme will be effective and head off:

> the risk that systemic shocks of a similar scale [occur] in the future ... subjecting a wide range of stakeholders, including bank creditors (e.g. depositors), shareholders, employees, borrowers and taxpayers, to unprecedented economic costs.[66]

The 'most material expected benefit' of the scheme is the 'containment' of banking losses in the future, and this 'by far outweighs the costs' of the scheme. Comfortingly, the scheme will not create a danger of a 'drain of talent abroad' which may 'impact on the supply of talent to the industry'.[67] The crucial assumption here – which is questioned in detail in the next section – is that regulators will be able to identify incentives for excessive risk taking. For now, it is worth noting that, without that assumption, the same cost-benefit analysis could be used to justify an absolute ban on bonuses in financial institutions.

In summary, then, CRD III assumes that preventing remuneration from contributing to the next financial crisis requires only that prudential regulators be given a clear instruction to ensure that financial institutions do not incentivize excessive risk taking. This neat and unintrusive solution will allow banks to attract talent and continue to generate shareholder value with the least possible interference. As we will see in the next section, there are considerable doubts about whether this regulatory scheme would be likely to prevent enormous social costs in the future.

ASSESSMENT OF THE CRD III REGULATORY SCHEME

This regulatory scheme is wholly inadequate. It depends on national supervisors identifying incentives for 'excessive risk taking', and then making appropriate adjustments to remuneration policies to correct those incentives. This section will argue that policy makers gave national supervisors an impossible task.

Its first main weakness is that it depends on regulators being less deferential to the practices of banks than they were before the crisis. For example, the House of Lords Economic Affairs Committee noted that 'supervisors and regulators were very reliant upon risk assessments provided by credit ratings agencies, or created by banks using their own mathematical

66 id., p. 20.
67 id., p. 32.

18

risk models.'[68] For its part, the FSA accepts that it offered 'insufficient challenge to management assumptions and judgements', as well as failing to address obvious risks arising from RBS's dependence on 'non-sterling short-term wholesale funding'.[69]

A number of explanations have been advanced for the various pre-crisis regulatory failures. The first is (cognitive) regulatory capture.[70] Regulators internalized the models put forward by banks and believed the story that financial markets were allocating risk away from the banking sector towards those who were willing to hold it.[71] The second focuses on information asymmetry and cognitive limitations. The banks' operations were simply too complex for regulators to grasp and control effectively.[72] The third emphasizes implicit and explicit political considerations. Implicitly, there are powerful political pressures not to intervene in a banking boom, because credit growth drives asset prices and GDP upwards, creating wealth effects that benefit incumbents. Explicitly, at least in the United Kingdom, the regulator was instructed to have one eye on the competitiveness of the financial sector in discharging its regulatory function.[73] The dynamics of the integrated European market probably increased the political pressure on national regulators not to intervene because banks respond to even a hint of unilateral regulatory intervention with threats to relocate.

A more fundamental weakness of the CRD III scheme is that, even if they are willing, it is very unlikely that regulators will be able to distinguish

---

68 Select Committee on Economic Affairs, Second Report, *Banking Supervision and Regulation*, HL (2008–09) 101-I, para. 18.

69 FSA, op. cit., n. 23, pp. 27 and 23.

70 This expression appears to have originated with Willem Buiter in 'Lessons from the global financial crisis for regulators and supervisors' (2009), at <www.lse.ac.uk/fmg/workingPapers/discussionPapers/fmgdps/DP635.pdf>. See, also, J. Kwak, 'Cultural Capture and the Financial Crisis' in *Preventing Regulatory Capture: Special Interest Influence and How to Limit It*, eds. D. Carpenter and D.A. Moss (2013) 71.

71 See E. Engelen et al., *After the Great Complacence: Financial Crisis and the Politics of Reform* (2011) ch. 2 and 178–9, arguing that 'regulation develops within broader frameworks of understanding, where narratives frame what is possible or necessary'. Even by 1986, Minsky (op. cit., n. 6, pp. 51–2) was remarking on the influence of neoclassical economics, noting that 'fashionable economic theory argues that markets are stable and efficient', which puts the regulators 'under pressure to allow financial practices to evolve in response to "market forces"', notwithstanding their 'right and responsibility' as lender of last resort and insurer of the financial system to 'control and prevent business practices that tend either to create or to worsen financial crises'.

72 Select Committee on Economic Affairs, op. cit., n. 68, para. 18.

73 FSA, op. cit., n. 23, p. 29, noting that the FSA operated in a context 'which entailed … a strong focus on the importance of the "competitiveness" of the UK financial services sector and so of avoiding "unnecessary" regulation', a focus which 'reflected in part' section 2(3) of the Financial Services and Markets Act 2000, which instructed the FSA to 'have regard to' the proportionality of benefits and burdens, and the possible adverse effects on competition of its activities.

between remuneration which encourages 'normal' risk taking, which is the core business of banks that fund long-term assets with short-term liabilities, and remuneration which encourages 'excessive' risk taking. First, regulators must obtain sufficient current information about the activities and exposures of banks. Gathering this information will be expensive: the complexity and interdependence of the existing financial system, with special-purpose vehicles, securitization, tranching of cash flows, and widespread use of derivatives will make tracing the various cash flows and the ultimate allocation of risk very time consuming. Willem Buiter doubts that this is even possible, but adds that, even if it were, the regulator in this scheme would face an almost impossible task:

> Understanding the effect of a heterogeneous collection of individual employment contracts on the risk-return performance of the whole bank is a complex task that may well be beyond the ability of the regulator.[74]

However, the problems run deeper than this: the scheme glosses over the fairly well-known economic distinction between risk and uncertainty. Under uncertainty, the parties can foresee the different possible outcomes but do not know the distribution of probabilities, because 'there is no valid basis of any kind for classifying instances'. Under risk, they know the distribution of probabilities either a priori or statistically.[75] The regulatory scheme emphasizes the importance of including 'difficult-to-measure' risks within the scope of oversight, forcing the issue into a conventional risk-management framework, in which regulators use information about past distributions of outcomes in order to quantify the future risks facing banks. This is entirely unconvincing as regards tail risks, which are ultra-rare but very costly events. Taleb, for example, argues that the rareness of tail-risk events makes it impossible to assess the likelihood of their future occurrence.[76] Is it really plausible that regulators will be able to evaluate the probability of tail-risk events such as closure of securitization markets or the failure of systemically important counterparties to derivative transactions? If it is not, regulatory risk assessments are almost certain to be incorrect.

Going further, Keynes reserved the term 'uncertain' for matters for which there is 'no scientific basis on which to form any calculable probability whatever'.[77] The complexity and opacity of financial markets, the constant quest for 'innovation' in response to incentives, and the interdependence of

---

74 Buiter, op. cit., n. 70, pp. 23, 38. Buiter's preferred solution is a binding shareholder vote on remuneration.
75 F. Knight, *Risk, Uncertainty, and Profit* (2006, originally published 1921) 225.
76 See for example, N.N. Taleb, 'Black Swans and the Domains of Statistics' (2007) 61(3) *Am. Statistician* 1.
77 J.M. Keynes, 'The General Theory of Employment' (1937) 51 *Q. J. of Economics* 209. In a similar vein, see G.L.S. Shackle, 'Economic Theory and the Formal Imagination' in his *Epistemics and Economics: A Critique of Economic Doctrines* (2009) 3–4.

20

financial actors make it impossible even to identify *how* the system might fail, let alone calculate the probability of this. Past data is not merely insufficient to identify the likelihood of tail risks; it is irrelevant in light of the constant changes in the institutional structure of markets. Before the last crisis, the massive increase in securitization, the rise of the credit default swap, and changes in the risk weightings of various assets under the Basel Accords created unidentifiable dangers for the stability of the financial system.[78] As we saw above, these developments were driven by remuneration practices, which incentivized executives to evade regulation and increase return on equity.

If financial markets are characterized by uncertainty, regulators cannot distinguish between 'normal' and 'excessive' risk taking. Minsky divided loans into 'hedge finance', where the parties expect the cash flow from the assets to service interest and repayment obligations, and 'speculative and Ponzi finance', where the parties do not expect adequate cash flow and will be dependent upon access to financial markets to fund principal and interest payments respectively. While this scheme is fundamental to understanding the causes of financial instability, it cannot be used as the basis for regulation. The category to which a particular loan is assigned will change over time, being based on the expectations of the parties, which evolve in line with the broader productive economy, which itself is strongly influenced by the lending activities of banks and their effect on the supply of broad money. As Minsky puts it, 'the risks bankers carry are not objective probability phenomena; instead they are uncertainty relations that are subjectively valued.'[79] Since objective probabilities cannot be assigned to the chances of default on particular loans, the regulator's assessment of whether risks are 'excessive' will be as subjective as those of the bankers who made the original loan. Accordingly, the factors which led to regulatory passivity in the build-up to the crisis are likely to come back into play, leaving banks very broad scope to determine how executives are to be remunerated.

We saw above that, in their technical documents, policy makers recognize the difficulty of making ex-ante adjustments for 'difficult-to-measure' and tail risks, and that these issues should be addressed by means of deferrals and ex-post adjustments instead. For example, the BCBS recognizes that 'ex-ante risk adjustment is less likely to work effectively' where risks are 'difficult to measure, to model or are simply not known at the time of the award', but suggests hopefully that 'deferral *could* help reduce incentives to take such risks'.[80]

---

78 Zalm, for example, argues that the creation of the securitization market amounted to a 'regime change' in which 'all the statistics of the past become irrelevant', but which was 'overlooked by investors and risk-managers': G. Zalm, 'The Forgotten Risk: Financial Incentives' (2009) 157 *De Economist* 209, at 210.

79 Minsky, op. cit., n. 6, p. 267.

80 BCBS, *Range of Methodologies for Risk and Performance Alignment of Remuneration* (2011) para. 37, emphasis added.

In other words, the BCBS recognizes that some risks cannot be prevented by ex-ante risk adjustment, and that deferral and ex-post adjustments to remuneration will be required. Ex-post adjustments and deferral certainly accord with notions of justice, and realign the interests of risk takers with those of shareholders. However, they will not prevent banks from becoming insolvent if risk takers take excessive risks that are not picked up on by regulators. Nor will they help if moral hazard leads risk takers to decide to take the chance of an ex-post risk adjustment in order to benefit from the massive upside of a particular action, knowing that their losses will not exceed their bonus. This is a grave weakness from the perspective of preventing social costs: if, as seems likely, ex-ante risk assessment is incomplete, and those risks eventuate and imperil the financial system, deferral and ex-post adjustment will do nothing to change this.[81]

Recent events highlight the limitations of a regulatory scheme that relies on ex-post adjustments. The *Financial Times* reported that remuneration committees in financial institutions are imposing more ex-post adjustments to 'strip staff of awards they received for past performances that no longer look so favourable'. Over the last three years, 'big European banks ... have enforced clawback dozens of times' in relation to excessive risk-taking which ultimately produced losses, such as J.P. Morgan's massive losses on a credit derivatives position, as well as in relation to frauds of various kinds, such as the LIBOR-fixing scandal or pension mis-selling, and for breaches of money-laundering regulations.[82] None of these risks were picked up by bank remuneration committees, or by regulators who were overseeing the banks' remuneration schemes in line with the CRD, yet the actions which led to these losses were arguably incentivized by remuneration schemes. It is fortunate that J.P. Morgan's derivative losses did not bring down the bank, because if they had, enforcing clawback on the errant traders in question would have done nothing to protect taxpayers and other stakeholders from further catastrophic losses.

The reluctance to intervene prescriptively in remuneration is best explained by reference to the ideology of shareholder primacy, which assumes that it is possible to draft an incentive contract which will perfectly align the interests of executives with those of shareholders; once that contract is written, the common good will be achieved with no need for any

81 The recent recommendations of the Parliamentary Commission for Banking Standards suffer from the same weakness: longer deferral and the threat of ex-post confiscation of bonuses in the event that a bank needs a bail out will not prevent the enormous social costs of a bank bail out should one become necessary (see PCBS, op. cit., n. 4, vol. I, paras. 168 and 245).

82 'Banks ready to claw back more bonuses' *Financial Times*, 27 August 2012. In op. cit., n. 80, para. 21, the BCBS notes that 'most clawbacks are triggered only when the firm learns that information previously provided by an employee was misstated, or when the firm learns that the employee had violated internal policies.' This is not entirely reassuring.

regulatory intervention. This is an aspect of the wider belief and operating assumption of policy makers that markets self-correct and that the social benefits of contracts exceed their social costs, whereas regulation only makes things worse. It is testament to the strength of that ideology that, even after the social costs occasioned by the financial crisis, policy makers preferred explicitly to contemplate the probable failure of ex-ante risk adjustment, rather than consider more far-reaching regulatory intervention. CRD III could have prohibited particular metrics, or even stock options altogether, as the Commission once canvassed.[83] Less prescriptively, it could have required bonuses to be paid in subordinated debt, aligning the incentives of executives with more risk-averse creditors,[84] or in a broader basket of the bank's securities.[85] In refusing to approach bank remuneration practices in a more precautionary way, CRD III created the conditions for the political backlash discussed in the next section.

2013 REFORM OF THE CRD: A CAP ON VARIABLE REMUNERATION

In the event, the flawed CRD III regulatory scheme proved not to be the last word on remuneration in financial institutions. The European Parliament's Economic and Monetary Affairs Committee suggested an important amendment to a proposed directive (CRD IV) consolidating the provisions of the Capital Requirements Directives into a single directive and regulation, implementing certain aspects of Basel III and making changes to risk governance.[86] The amendment provided that:

> in order to avoid excessive risk taking, the variable part of the remuneration should be limited to one time the fixed income. The fixed income should be set in a manner that in case of a claw back, it will still be sufficient to ensure a proper remuneration of the employee.[87]

---

83 European Commission, *Green Paper on Corporate Governance in Financial Institutions and Remuneration Policies* (COM(2010) 284 final, June 2010) 18.

84 F. Tung, 'Pay for Banker Performance: Structuring Executive Compensation for Risk Regulation' (2011) 105 *Northwestern University Law Rev.* 1205.

85 Bebchuk and Spamann, op. cit., n. 7.

86 See Directive on the access to the activity of credit institutions and the prudential supervision of credit institutions and investment firms and amending Directive 2002/87/EC of the European Parliament and of the Council on the supplementary supervision of credit institutions, insurance undertakings and investment firms in a financial conglomerate (COM(2011) 0453).

87 Preamble, para. 48, Report of the European Parliament on proposed directive, 30 May 2012, PE 478.506v02-00 A7-0170/2012. Article 90(2a) then provides that 'The Commission shall come forward by the end of 2012 with a legislative proposal setting a fixed workable ratio between the fixed and variable components of the remuneration in the financial sector.'

The *Financial Times* reported that parliamentary approval at first reading was likely, and that the Parliament was 'in an unusually strong bargaining position', with 'solid cross-party consensus' behind it.[88] It also received cautious support in the Liikanen Report,[89] which recommended that consideration be given to 'further restrictions (for example to 50%) on the level of variable income to fixed income'. It added that a 'clear regulatory cap' on remuneration would 'substantially ease the task of the supervisory authorities in screening out undesirable remuneration policies.'[90]

CRD IV has now become law.[91] For the most part, CRD IV simply transposes national prudential oversight of remuneration policy from CRD III, and sets out the same guidance. It includes a new – albeit less than prescriptive – provision that 'up to 100% of the total variable remuneration shall be subject to malus or clawback arrangements', in particular where 'the staff member ... participated in or was responsible for conduct which resulted in significant losses to the institution'.[92] However, by far the most significant change is the cap on variable remuneration of 'senior management, risk takers, staff engaged in control functions' and certain other employees,[93] which is imposed by law, rather than being left to individual financial institutions under prudential regulatory oversight.[94] CRD IV also draws a functional distinction between fixed remuneration, which is supposed to reflect 'relevant professional experience and organisational responsibility ... as part of the terms of employment', while variable remuneration should 'reflect a sustainable and risk adjusted performance as well as performance in excess of that required to fulfil the employee's job description.'[95]

As under CRD III, institutions are still required to set 'appropriate ratios' between fixed and variable remuneration, but CRD IV then specifies that 'the variable component shall not exceed 100% of the fixed component of the total remuneration for each individual', with member states free to set a lower maximum or to allow shareholders to approve a higher maximum

---

88 'Banks bow to EU over limit to bonuses' *Financial Times*, 13 June 2012.
89 E. Liikanen (chair), *Final Report of the High-level Expert Group on reforming the structure of the EU banking sector* (2012) (Liikanen Report).
90 id., pp. 79, 106.
91 See Directive 2013/36/EU of 26 June 2013 on access to activity of credit institutions and the prudential supervision of credit institutions and investment firms, amending Directive 2002/87/EC and repealing Directives 2006/48/EC and 2006/49/EC [2013] OJ L 176/338.
92 id., Art. 94(1)(n).
93 The European Banking Authority (EBA) is currently consulting on criteria by which to identify categories of staff who 'have a material impact on the institution's risk profile': see EBA, Consultation Paper EBA/CP/2013/11, 21 May 2013.
94 See Directive 2013/36/EU, op. cit., n. 91, Art. 94(1)(g).
95 id., Art. 92(2)(g). Contrast PwC's evidence, cited in PCBS, op. cit., n. 4, vol. II, para. 843, that 'a "bonus" is not an added extra for outperformance. It is part of an employee's expected total pay if they and their business area perform adequately.'

percentage of up to 200 per cent.[96] Detailed rules are laid down regarding the process of shareholder approval. The financial institution should make a proposal to shareholders, which must be justified by reference to information about the number of staff involved and its likely impact on 'the requirement to maintain a sound capital base.' Shareholders must then approve the proposal by unfamiliar (at least to English company lawyers) super-majorities of 66 per cent where 50 per cent of shares are represented, or 75 per cent where less than 50 per cent of shares are represented.[97] The national competent authority must be informed of the proposal and its justification, as well as the shareholder decision. This information can then be used for benchmarking.

ASSESSMENT OF THE CRD IV REFORMS

The decision to cap variable pay in this way has been strongly criticized by financial sector lobby groups.[98] However, the decision can also be justified as follows. It was not acceptable to leave ratios between fixed and variable pay to financial institutions under prudential regulatory oversight because of the difficulties discussed above. The frequency of significant ex-post adjustments since the financial crisis suggests that pay practices are still incentivizing extreme risk taking, and that regulators are not picking up on this beforehand. A cap on bonuses will not prevent financial institutions from giving incentives to their risk takers to increase profitability and therefore shareholder returns; however, it will eliminate the current practice of financial institutions giving their bankers incentives to increase risk indiscriminately in pursuit of ever higher returns on equity and associated personal rewards; to hide risks in complex off-balance-sheet structures; and to game the Basel Accords in other, as yet unknown, ways. This is very important because the financial crisis showed that the hidden risks that accompany these activities cannot be detected by institutional investors, regulators or boards. It is strongly arguable that the best way of eliminating them is to take away the incentive to create them.

---

96 id., Art. 94(1)(g)(i) and (ii). There is also some further flexibility, with member states permitted to allow institutions to apply a discount rate (to be set by the EBA) of up to 25 per cent of variable remuneration as long as it is paid in instruments deferred for at least five years. This may have been introduced in response to the United Kingdom's solitary opposition to the provision: see 'Bonus Cap is a Bad Omen for Britain' *Financial Times*, 18 February 2013.
97 id., Art. 92(1)(g)(ii). Directly concerned staff may not exercise any voting rights they may have.
98 For example, the Association for Financial Markets in Europe warned that the cap created 'a risk of material unintended consequences for the European economy.' See 'Bankers fight new EU cap on bonuses' *Daily Telegraph*, 12 May 2012.

It should also be recognized that these new rules will be likely to result in higher fixed pay, which will eat into shareholder returns in years where profitability is low. The effect of this might be to trigger shareholder activism, something which was strikingly lacking before the crisis and has been ever since.[99] In other words, remuneration would go from being a means to correct for the passivity of shareholders to being a mechanism for spurring them into action. If the European Union is able to agree on the Commission's promised proposal to give shareholders in listed companies a binding say on pay,[100] this would strengthen shareholders' capacity for activism and therefore complement the cap. Finally, the cap will reduce the difficulties facing national regulators when they attempt to identify incentives for excessive risk taking, and will avoid the problem of regulators taking a passive approach and falling back on the ideology of shareholder primacy when confronted with the radical uncertainty inherent in this area. Accordingly, from the perspective of preventing social costs, the Parliament's amendment is to be welcomed.

Finally, proposals to regulate bankers' pay are commonly met with threats to relocate key bankers and even bank headquarters to other jurisdictions.[101] It is unclear whether the threat to relocate headquarters is credible, given the interdependence between banks and states, with states controlling the currencies in which banks' assets and liabilities are denominated, and backstopping banks in the name of financial stability. It is also far from clear that other states with regulatory regimes that appeal to bankers would be willing to backstop the liabilities of banks where they are denominated in foreign currencies.

---

99 Some accounts emphasize the role of shareholders in actually pressing banks to take on more risk before the crisis: see PCBS, op. cit., n. 4, vol. II, para. 665, and de Larosière, op. cit., n. 1, para. 24. Few shareholders avoided the 'herd instinct': see de Larosière, id., para. 112. This would certainly be in line with the incentives provided by limited liability: see Haldane, op. cit., n. 8, p. 49. While bonuses have fallen in the years since the crisis in British banks, total remuneration has not, because fixed pay has risen, and institutional investors have done nothing to challenge this shift, despite the much vaunted 'shareholder spring': PCBS, id., vol. II, paras. 106–10 and 824.

100 Commissioner Barnier stated publicly that he would propose a directive before the end of 2013. At the time of writing, the proposal was unavailable, but some reports suggested that it would give shareholders a power to fix the maximum ratio between fixed and variable pay, and between the highest- and lowest-paid workers in the company: see <http://www.worker-participation.eu/Company-Law-and-CG/Latest-developments/European-Commission-proposal-on-say-on-pay>.

101 See, for example, 'Swiss vote for corporate pay curbs' *Financial Times*, 3 March 2013.

26

CONCLUSION

Minsky emphasized the need for regulators 'to control, constrain, and perhaps even forbid the financing practices that caused the need for lender of last resort activity'; if they did not do this, they would essentially validate the practices that caused the last crisis and create the conditions for the next one.[102] Given widespread recognition that executive remuneration in financial institutions contributed significantly to the financial crisis, it is perhaps surprising that it took so long for regulators to get to grips with the practice of executive pay in financial institutions. This article has argued that the ideology of shareholder primacy, and an associated aversion to regulation, was the principal obstacle to more far-reaching intervention in remuneration practices. Its influence can be seen in CRD III, which gives regulators an impossible task: they have to make ex-ante adjustments to remuneration schemes by reference to dangers that are fundamentally uncertain. It was explicitly recognized in guidance given to regulators that these ex-ante adjustments would be likely to fail, and that ex-post adjustments would be required. The apparent readiness of regulators to contemplate another serious misalignment between bankers' incentives and the public good so soon after the last one is astonishing. The hand of shareholder-primacy ideology is clearly visible here: it conflates protection of the shareholder interest with the public good, two interests which part company when the taxpayer is exposed to the cost of clearing up after another financial crisis. Ex-post adjustments of remuneration can do much to realign executive remuneration with shareholder returns; however, if executives respond to their incentives by increasing bank risk taking in ways which are not apparent to regulators and cause their banks to become insolvent, this will do nothing to protect the taxpayer from catastrophic losses.

Accordingly, the cap on bonuses contained in CRD IV is to be welcomed. It is certainly a crude piece of regulatory intervention, which expresses public outrage at the return of business as usual in banks, and will lead to distortions. However, it also shows that, after the crisis, it is no longer tenable to argue that bankers' incentive contracts are a private matter, which can be left to bank boards, subject only to a fragile system of oversight by under-resourced and pliant regulatory authorities. The cap removes the unlimited upside given to bankers to take and conceal risks, safe in the knowledge that most of the downside will accrue to shareholders and the taxpayer. If, as many predict, it leads to fixed pay moving higher, it may even force large shareholders to take on the activist role that has been expected of them for so long.

---

102 Minsky, op. cit., n. 6, p. 59.

JOURNAL OF LAW AND SOCIETY
VOLUME 41, NUMBER 1, MARCH 2014
ISSN: 0263-323X, pp. 28–50

Market Discipline and EU Corporate Governance Reform in the Banking Sector: Merits, Fallacies, and Cognitive Boundaries

EMILIOS AVGOULEAS* AND JAY CULLEN**

Much contemporary analysis has concluded that the recent financial crisis and bank failures were, among other things, the result of a breakdown in corporate governance regimes and market discipline. In this context, new regulations advocate such market-based remedies as tighter investor monitoring and greater control over executives' remuneration, in order to safeguard financial stability. We argue that this approach largely ignores three very important aspects of modern financial markets that cannot be constrained through market discipline: (i) socio-psychological phenomena; (ii) the epistemological properties of financial market innovation; and (iii) the inherent inability of market participants to predict uncertain risk correlations. Therefore, this article argues that excessive EU focus on corporate governance reforms as a means to improve financial stability detracts attention from much more significant concerns, chiefly, the issue of optimal bank structure.

INTRODUCTION

Building the different blocs of corporate governance over several decades has been a painstaking exercise aimed at curbing the privileges of insider classes and fostering shareholder democracy. Effective corporate governance

* School of Law, University of Edinburgh, Old College, South Bridge, Edinburgh EH8 9YL, Scotland
Emilios.Avgouleas@ed.ac.uk
** School of Law, University of Sheffield, Bartolome House, Winter Street, Sheffield S3 7ND, England
Jay.Cullen@sheffield.ac.uk

The authors would like to thank Charles Goodhart and Marc Moore for valuable comments on an earlier draft of this article.

28

has been placed at the heart of capitalist growth initiatives and is rightly regarded as a key component of a free enterprise economy that wishes to retain its legitimacy in a liberal democracy. As a result, every time that the economy experiences some form of corporate collapse, policy makers and the industry try to upgrade their corporate governance toolkit and legislate for ever-higher standards of governance.[1]

Thus, it is not surprising that in the aftermath of the Global Financial Crisis ('GFC') most commentators' and policy makers' analysis focused on actual and assumed corporate governance failures within big banks. According to this narrative, if reckless bankers were reined in, and market discipline restored, banks would be buttressed against the possibility of failure. A flurry of legislation and legislative proposals has followed, placing sound corporate governance at the heart of regulatory reforms trying to restore health to the banking sector.

While some of these initiatives constitute a marked improvement over the shambolic structures governing banks in the recent past, they are bound to disappoint in terms of effectiveness. The reason for that is not a lack of good intentions on the part of the champions of corporate governance reform, but a number of fallacies in the analysis of the standard narrative. For example, it may be plausibly argued that no corporate governance model can work when the principal actors face severe limitations in their knowledge and understanding of risk due to objective factors, such as complexity, or lack of transparency in financial transactions. The interconnected and opaque structure of banks, the increasing complexity of their operations, and the short-termism of the financial sector – that is subject more than other sectors to fads, herding, and irrational mood swings – place insurmountable obstacles both to a board's capacity to run the bank and shareholders' ability to monitor them.[2] These limitations are compounded by more general cognitive boundaries facing shareholders and directors: so-called 'bounded rationality'.[3]

---

1 A characteristic example, in this context, is the enactment in the United States of the 2002 Sarbanes-Oxley Act in the aftermath of the Enron and WorldCom scandals, which were a combination of insider abuses and accounting frauds.

2 For a discussion of the limitations of market discipline in the banking sector, see E. Avgouleas, 'Breaking Up Mega-Banks: A New Regulatory Model for the Separation of Commercial Banking from Investment Banking' in *Financial Regulation at the Crossroads: Implications for Supervision, Institutional Design and Trade*, eds. P. Delimatsis and N. Helger (2011) 179.

3 Bounded rationality refers to the limited ability of humans to process information because of their limited computational ability and flawed memory. See H.A. Simon, 'A Behavioral Model of Rational Choice' (1955) 69 *Q. J. of Economics* 99. For an analysis of these biases and the contexts in which they tend to appear and decisions that they influence, even when decision makers act under conditions of intense competition and are sophisticated actors, see E. Avgouleas, 'The Global Financial Crisis and the Disclosure Paradigm in European Financial Regulation: The Case for Reform' (2009) 6 *European Company and Financial Law Rev.* 440; E. Avgouleas, 'Reforming Investor Protection Regulation: The Impact of Cognitive Biases' in

29

Lender-of-last-resort facilities and the strong possibility of a public rescue further blunt the disciplining power of the market and provide shareholders and management with a partial shield from business risk, providing incentives for excessive risk taking.[4]

Accordingly, this article argues that a second and more powerful narrative should be added to the standard narrative on which EU legislation and recommendations addressing problems of incentive realignment are based. It suggests that bank size, structure, and complexity were as much responsible for insider rent seeking and inadequate shareholder/stakeholder monitoring. Therefore, EU and international initiatives to improve bank corporate governance may not prove effective in addressing the incentives issue, unless the structure of the banking sector is itself reformed and banks become smaller, less interconnected, and easier to manage.

This article is in five sections. Following this introduction, the second section will discuss EU legislation, proposals, and other initiatives to revamp corporate governance in the banking sector. The third section will cast doubt on the central thesis of these reforms, namely, that corporate governance in big banks can be effective and protect against the risk of systemic failure. The fourth section discusses the potential of structural reform to improve bank governance. The fifth section concludes.

CORPORATE GOVERNANCE REFORM IN THE EU BANKING SECTOR

1. The corporate governance failure rationale

The near-collapse of many European banks, resulting from a number of disastrous corporate and regulatory policies – as well as abysmal board decisions and management control failures[5] – brought into sharp focus corporate governance in the banking sector. Subsequently, a widespread belief that bank corporate governance was in a dismal state in the pre-GFC era has taken hold in academic and policy-making circles,[6] and these views have

---

Essays in the Law and Economics of Regulation in Honour of Anthony Ogus, eds. M. Faure and F. Stephen (2008) 143.

4 F.J. Fabozzi et al., *Foundations of Financial Markets and Institutions* (2007, 4th edn.).

5 For example, see the damning report of the Financial Services Authority into the RBS collapse: FSA, *The failure of the Royal Bank of Scotland: Financial Services Authority Board Report* (2011) 220–50, at <http://www.fsa.gov.uk/static/pubs/other/rbs.pdf >.

6 The potential drawbacks to this view are succinctly articulated by Cheffins, who has urged caution in the face of wholesale corporate governance reform: see B.R. Cheffins, 'Did Corporate Governance "Fail" during the 2008 Stock Market Meltdown? The Case of the S&P 500' (2009) 65 *Business Law* 1.

sketched a clear roadmap towards a safer financial sector. Capital, liquidity, and other regulatory reforms would be augmented by higher governance standards and altered compensation structures in order to enhance board capacity, shareholder monitoring, and eliminate perverse incentives.

During the initial phases of the GFC, attention on bank corporate governance failures was minimal.[7] However, as marked failures of risk management and control were revealed, regulatory focus quickly altered. The de Larosière Report into the financial supervision of European banks conceded that corporate governance was 'one of the most important failures of the recent crisis',[8] as corporate governance systems within financial institutions provided weak incentives for consideration of long-term sustainable investment policies and neglected the interests of bank stakeholders such as government-sponsored deposit guarantors. In the United Kingdom, an independent review of corporate governance at banks was established by Parliament,[9] and the FSA acknowledged that: 'poor governance [whilst] ... only one of many factors contributing to the crisis ... has widely been acknowledged as an important one.'[10]

Moreover, the debate on bankers' remuneration has captured the attention of both the public and policy makers – and, for very good reasons. A small group of insiders was rewarded handsomely for shifting the risk of their actions to society at large. Professor Bebchuk, and others, have argued strongly that remuneration structures in banks were strewn with perverse incentives, which fostered short-termism and excessive risk taking[11] and that, by implication, they were directly causative of the GFC and ensuing

---

7 As noted by Mülbert:
 ... numerous reports, documents and statements published in 2008 dealing with the causes and consequences of the financial crisis do not even mention the corporate governance of banks. This holds true, *inter alia*, for the reports prepared by the (US) President's Working Group on Financial Markets, the Financial Stability Board (FSB) ... the IMF, the Institute of International Finance (IIF), the G-20 Study Group, the Declaration of the Washington Summit of the G-20 proposing the 'Action Plan to implement Principles for Reform', and the German Council of Economic Experts.
 See P.O. Mülbert, 'Corporate Governance of Banks after the Financial Crisis: Theory, Evidence, Reforms', ECGI Working Paper 130/2009 (2010) 7–8 (notes omitted).

8 J. de Larosière (chair), *Report of the High-level Group on Financial Supervision in the EU* (2009) 29, at <http://ec.europa.eu/internal_market/finances/docs/de_larosiere_ report_en.pdf>.

9 D. Walker, *A review of corporate governance in UK banks and other financial industry entities – Final recommendations* (2009), at <http://webarchive.national archives.gov.uk/+/http://www.hm-treasury.gov.uk/d/walker_review_261109.pdf>.

10 FSA, 'Effective Corporate Governance' (2010), at <http://www.fsa.gov.uk/pubs/cp/cp10_03.pdf>.

11 L.A. Bebchuk et al., 'The Wages of Failure: Executive Compensation at Bear Stearns and Lehman 2000–2008' (2010) 27 *Yale J. on Regulation* 257.

31

bank failures. Accordingly, regulation of executive remuneration[12] came to be seen as the most effective path to restoring bank health and the stability of the financial system.

2. The state of reform in the EU

(a) The drive to reform bank corporate governance

Following generalized clamour about corporate governance failures in the banking sector, the EC Commission released a Green Paper[13] on corporate governance in financial institutions in June 2010.[14] The Green Paper noted that:

> although corporate governance did not directly cause the crisis, the lack of effective control mechanisms contributed significantly to excessive risk-taking on the part of financial institutions.[15]

In summary, it highlighted the following functional failures of corporate governance in financial institutions prior to the GFC:

(i) Deficient board oversight and control, driven particularly by a failure to challenge executives, and a lack of expertise amongst non-executive directors. This encompassed weak risk management, attributable to a failure of boards and senior management to comprehend the risks associated with financial products that were traded by institutions (leading to collective overreliance on ratings), and insufficient consideration of aggregate risks that had been assumed across firms.[16]

(ii) Insufficient shareholder control over risk taking, derived from a mismatch between the interests of shareholders and the long-term interests of financial institutions. Structural obstacles to effective engagement between shareholders and management including monitoring costs and voting restrictions, and the limited holding periods of many bank shareholders exacerbated these issues;[17] and

(iii) Supervisory failure to monitor effectively bank governance, a fragmentation of regulatory competence, and potential conflicts of interests between financial institutions and their auditors.[18]

---

12 L.A. Bebchuk and H. Spamann, 'Regulating Bankers' Pay' (2010) 98 *Georgetown Law J.* 247.

13 See European Commission, 'Green Paper: EU Corporate Governance Framework' (COM(2011) 164).

14 European Commission, 'Green Paper: Corporate Governance in Financial Institutions and Remuneration Policies' (COM(2010) 284).

15 id., para. 2.

16 id., para. 3.3.

17 id., para. 3.5.

18 id., paras. 3.6–3.7.

In response to these findings, the Commission recommended in its Green Paper[19] that the following measures be adopted:

(i) Increased independence and skill amongst board members at EU financial institutions to ensure effective monitoring of management. To further this, the creation of a specialist risk supervision committee, within the board of directors and with enhanced status for the chief risk officer, would assist board members in evaluating business strategies;[20]

(ii) A standardized shareholder 'stewardship code' at EU banks, on a 'comply or explain' basis, together with heightened transparency on voting policies. Increased monitoring of both the incentives and conflicts of interests of asset managers ought to be implemented.[21] Further, certain corporate policies – including the remuneration of board members and senior managers – should be subject to a binding shareholder vote.[22]

(iii) Increased national supervisory resources and strengthened pan-European corporate governance oversight and cooperation amongst supervisory colleges. Governance supervisors ought to be given a duty to ensure the correct functioning and effectiveness of boards of directors, and periodically to review the risk management functions within financial institutions.[23]

(b) Regulating executive remuneration

The EC Commission has issued several recommendations[24] in relation to executive remuneration in financial institutions since 2008.[25] Many of the provisions of these recommendations were based on work undertaken by the Financial Stability Board.[26]

The Commission's Recommendation on Remuneration Policies in the Financial Sector[27] ('EC Remuneration Recommendation') invited member

19 European Commission Staff Working Paper, 'Corporate Governance in Financial Institutions: Lessons to be drawn from the current financial crisis, best practices' (COM(2010) 669).
20 European Commission Green Paper, op. cit., n. 13, paras. 5.1–5.2.
21 id., para. 5.5.
22 European Commission Staff Working Paper, op. cit., n. 19, para. 4.1.6. These powers are already provided for by the Shareholder Rights Directive (Directive 2007/36/EC of 11 July 2007 of the European Parliament and of the Council on the exercise of certain rights of shareholders in listed companies [2007] OJ L184/17).
23 European Commission Green Paper, op. cit., n. 13, para. 5.4.
24 Commission Recommendation 2009/384/EC of 30 April 2009 on remuneration policies in the financial services sector [2009] OJ L120/22.
25 In particular, see Commission Recommendation 2009/385/EC of 29 April 2009 complementing Recommendations 2004/913/EC and 2005/162/EC as regards the regime for the remuneration of directors of listed companies [2009] OJ L120/28.
26 Financial Stability Board (FSB), *Principles for Sound Compensation Practices: Implementation Standards* (2009).
27 Remuneration Recommendation, op. cit., n. 24.

33

states to adopt measures in four major areas: (i) structure of the remuneration policy; (ii) governance; (iii) disclosure; and (iv) supervision by competent authorities.[28] Its provisions were designed to apply to staff whose 'professional activities have a material impact on the risk profile of the financial undertaking.'[29] Accordingly, remuneration awards ought to be calibrated to align the 'personal objectives of staff members with the long-term interests of the financial undertaking concerned.'[30] To reduce short-termism, the assessment period of performance on which remuneration is based ought to be between three and five years.[31] Clawback provisions should be used where remuneration is awarded on the basis of financial performance which later transpires to have been based on the adoption of excessive risk.[32] Deferment of bonus payments should be utilized to ensure that any tail-risk in a financial institution's investment strategy has the chance to be winnowed out.[33] To achieve this, the 'actual payment of performance-based components of remuneration [ought to be] spread over the business cycle of the company.'[34]

To enforce the recommendation, the EC Commission has implemented a new Capital Requirements Directive ('CRD IV')[35] which subjects the remuneration policies of financial institutions to supervisory oversight; supervisory authorities must now monitor the implications of remuneration policies for the risk management of financial institutions. CRD IV imposes a mandatory obligation for financial firms to have remuneration policies and practices that are consistent with, and promote, sound and effective risk management, and empowers supervisors to review – and, where appropriate, demand changes to – firm remuneration policies.

Devolution of authority to shareholders in determining executive remuneration was first recommended in the Commission's 2004 Recommendation.[36] The Commission also recommended that, 'Member States should

28 id., paras. 4–12.
29 id., para. 13.
30 id., para. 14.
31 id.
32 id., para. 5.1.
33 id., para. 4.4.
34 id., para. 5.2.
35 Directive 2013/36/EU of the European Parliament and of the Council of 26 June 2013 on access to the activity of credit institutions and the prudential supervision of credit institutions and investment firms, amending Directive 2002/87/EC and repealing Directives 2006/48/EC and 2006/49/EC [2013] OJ L176/338. The Directive recommends that capital requirements under the new Basel III framework be subject to adjustment by supervisors where remuneration policies appear to encourage excessive risk-taking.
36 Commission Recommendation 2004/913/EC of 14 December 2004 on fostering an appropriate regime for the remuneration of directors of listed companies [2004] OJ L385/55.

ensure that the remuneration policy of a financial undertaking sets a maximum limit on the variable component.'[37] There have been many criticisms of the proposal to cap variable compensation; critics have contended that the issue of executive pay is one which must be considered in the traditional terms of effective incentive alignment.[38] These commentators regard greater market disclosure as the basis for improved efficiency in performance contracts and thereby as a solution to the principal-agent issues at financial institutions. However, as subsequent sections of this article will note, these issues are not easily solved through market discipline.

IS EFFECTIVE CORPORATE GOVERNANCE OF MEGA-BANKS A REALISTIC OBJECTIVE?

1. *Introductory remarks*

The authors of this article are sceptical of the ability of corporate governance reforms to achieve their declared objectives. Moreover, we remain fearful that much of the present focus on corporate governance obfuscates the need for regulatory reform of long-term restructuring of the banking sector, at the expense of financial stability. It is therefore appropriate to disaggregate the claims made by those who place corporate governance at the heart of the reform agenda at the expense of other probably more effective measures, such as structural reform. Accordingly, as a first step in our analysis, it is worth considering whether banks are different from other corporations and, if so, why?

Before the advent of the GFC, it was widely acknowledged that banks might require differing corporate governance structures to non-financial corporations, for several reasons.[39] First, banks must have regard to the interests of several sets of stakeholders, which is often not the case in other corporations. Company managements at non-financial firms are usually responsible only to shareholders and creditors. Banks, however, must additionally have regard to depositors, and government-appointed regulators. Secondly, banks perform critical (utility) functions in modern economies and

---

37 Commission Recommendation on remuneration, op. cit., n. 24, para. 4.1. It was clear that most EU members would ignore that plea, and EU-wide bonus caps limiting variable compensation to 100 per cent of base salary have therefore been introduced, to take effect in 2014. See G. Ferrarini et al., 'Executive Remuneration in Crisis: A Critical Assessment of Reforms in Europe' (2010) 10 *J. of Corporate Law Studies* 73. For discussion, see L. Armitstead, 'EU vote clears way for bank bonus cap' *Daily Telegraph*, 16 April 2013, at <http://www.telegraph.co.uk/news/worldnews/europe/9998757/EU-vote-clears-way-for-bank-bonus-cap.html>.

38 Ferrarini et al., id., p. 111.

39 For extended discussion of these factors, see E. Avgouleas, *Governance of Global Financial Markets: The Law, the Economics, the Politics* (2012) ch. 3.

the disruption of their operations can have far-reaching effects. They are central to the payments and clearing systems and control the savings and investments of retail customers and businesses. Their actions therefore affect third parties and losses from financial institutions may quickly spill over into other areas of the economy. Thirdly, banks use high levels of leverage, which are not generally present in non-financial firms. They are therefore particularly vulnerable to liquidity shocks and losses of confidence, which require the provision of (frequently state-backed) deposit-guarantee schemes and a central bank-operated lender-of-last-resort facility.

Moreover, two additional features of banks make them special for the purposes of governance. Banks tend to present much lower transparency of business and income lines, and of contractual relationships and risk exposures, than non-financial companies. In addition, bank size and greater government regulation can make bank management and shareholders rather complacent.[40] We explain in the next paragraphs how bank size, the particular nature of banks as businesses, and government regulations, such as deposit-guarantee schemes, may place considerable restrictions on the disciplining power of the market over big banks.[41]

2. Objective limits to market discipline

Market discipline and its processes are understood (on the basis of intuition rather than precise definition)[42] to include discipline imposed by share-holders and the market for corporate control on bank management and discipline imposed by subordinated short-term creditors, as well as other creditors,[43] by bank customers, and even highly mobile groups of bank employees.[44]

Most of the above are assumed to have the right incentives to monitor bank behaviour in order to avoid being caught in a bank failure and a messy winding up that would bring them large losses. The most important mechanism to facilitate market discipline is thought to be disclosure of accurate information to the market, and the market's ability to process it properly. Further, the mix of debt and equity chosen by a bank is regarded as a strong

---

40 G. Caprio Jnr. and R. Levine, 'Corporate governance in finance: Concepts and international observations' in *Financial Sector Governance: The Roles of the Public and Private Sectors*, eds. R.E. Litan et al. (2002) 17.

41 See Avgouleas, op. cit., n. 2, at 190–1.

42 D.T. Llewellyn, 'Inside the "Black Box" of Market Discipline' (2005) 25 *Economic Affairs* 41.

43 C.W. Calomiris and C.M. Kahn, 'The Role of Demandable Debt in Structuring Optimal Banking Arrangements' (1991) 81 *Am. Economic Rev.* 497; and, for a more realistic approach, see C.W. Calomiris, 'Building an Incentive-Compatible Safety Net' (1999) 23 *J. of Banking and Finance* 1499.

44 Llewellyn, op. cit., n. 42, pp. 189–93.

determinant of the effectiveness of market discipline.[45] Yet, this discipline works only if market actors have sufficient incentives to fulfill their monitoring role and there are no impediments to information signals.[46]

Moreover, at the individual institution level, a number of perverse incentives substantially weaken the strength of market discipline. The first limitation to market discipline is placed by the opaque nature of the financial network, which generates chains of (frequently invisible) claims, increasing institutions' exposure to each other, and which create very strong ties of mutual economic dependence (interconnectedness). Although interconnectedness is an essential element of the financial network, it may also increase its vulnerability, especially because bank collapses are highly contagious and they can evolve, aided by market panic, into full-scale financial cascades threatening the stability of the financial system.[47] Thus, interconnectedness increases the possibility of a public bail out.

Since interconnectedness is a clear obstacle to the resolvability of financial institutions, it amounts to a perverse incentive. Namely, it gives bank management a strong incentive to grow the balance sheet, since the larger the institution becomes and the more interconnected, the more likely it is that its failure will also drag down other interconnected institutions, necessitating a bail out.[48] However, in many cases, unnecessarily growing the bank's balance sheet may be a poor business decision which also makes the bank more fragile, since such expansion is normally based on increased leverage.[49] This is also a convincing explanation of the 1990s drive towards conglomeration in the financial sector, which has resulted in today's megabanks. Size did not only shield banks from the risk of failure,[50] it also

---

45 A.B. Ashcraft, 'Does the Market Discipline Banks? New Evidence from the Regulatory Capital Mix', FRB of New York Staff Report No. 244 (March 2006).

46 M.F. Hellwig, 'Market Discipline, Information Processing and Corporate Governance' Max Planck Institute for Research on Collective Goods, Preprint No. 2005/19 (October 2005).

47 A. Lo, 'Regulatory Reform in the Wake of the Financial Crisis of 2007–2008' (2009) 1 *J. of Financial Economic Policy* 5, at 23; A.G. Haldane, 'Rethinking the Financial Network' (speech delivered at the Financial Student Association, Amsterdam, 28 April 2009) 12–13, at <http://www.bis.org/review/r090505e.pdf>.

48 The Geneva Report 2009 calls this risk the 'interconnectedness spillover'. See M.K. Brunnermeier et al., *The Fundamental Principles of Financial Regulation*, Geneva Reports on the World Economy 11 (2009) 20–1.

49 D.W. Diamond and R.G. Rajan, 'Liquidity Risk, Liquidity Creation and Financial Fragility' (2001) 109 *J. of Political Economy* 287.

50 M. King, speech to Scottish Business Organizations (Edinburgh, 20 October 2009) 3, at <http://www.bankofengland.co.uk/archive/Documents/historicpubs/speeches/2009/speech406.pdf>:

Why were banks willing to take risks that proved so damaging both to themselves and the rest of the economy? One of the key reasons – mentioned by market participants in conversations before the crisis hit – is that the incentives to manage risk and to increase leverage were distorted by this implicit support or guarantee provided by government to creditors of banks that were seen as 'too important to

ensured cheaper funding[51] for years by creditors who charged banks interest rates lower than their risky business would warrant.[52]

Opacity and interconnectedness also place strong obstacles to reforms aimed at enhancing market discipline through resolution regimes that lead to a wipeout of shareholders' equity, or resolution tools – such as the much discussed bail-in instruments – which convert bank debt (including uninsured deposits) to equity.[53] Even if we assume that the possibility of a public bail out becomes much more remote in view of these reforms, thereby eliminating moral hazard, market monitoring by means of shareholder and creditor monitoring would still be insufficient to prevent bank failures and safeguard systemic stability, for three reasons. As mentioned earlier, there is widespread evidence of systematic and often deliberate complexity in the financial sector.[54] The financial network is so complex and opaque[55] that it would be absurd to require shareholders to possess the resources and skill to effectively monitor bank business and discipline boards.[56] In today's markets, there is certainly no private institution that potentially has the ability, resources, and access to information to be able to conduct a risk analysis of all financial institutions, regulated and unregulated.

fail'. Such banks could raise funding more cheaply and expand faster than other institutions. They had less incentive than others to guard against tail risk. Banks and their creditors knew that if they were sufficiently important to the economy or the rest of the financial system, and things went wrong, the government would always stand behind them. And they were right.

51 A.R. Admati et al., 'Fallacies, Irrelevant Facts and Myths in the Discussion of Capital Regulation: Why Bank Equity Is Not Expensive', Rock Center for Corporate Governance at Stanford University Working Paper No. 86 (2010).

52 For example, evidence from the bond markets has shown that bond markets were taking a softer approach to big banks, assuming that they were too big to fail, or they were simply too complex in their structure for the bond market to understand and price effectively. See D.P. Morgan and K.J. Stiroh, 'Bond Market Discipline of Banks: Is the Market Tough Enough?', FRB of New York Staff Report No. 95 (1999).

53 See, for instance, the much lauded EU Commission proposal for a Directive establishing a framework for the recovery and resolution of credit institutions and investment firms and amending Council Directives 77/91/EEC and 82/891/EC, Directives 2001/24/EC, 2002/47/EC, 2004/25/EC, 2005/56/EC, 2007/36/EC and 2011/35/EC and Regulation (EU) No 1093/2010, COM(2012) 280/3.

54 Complexity theory is an interdisciplinary framework used to understand complex systems. It holds that while some systems are too complex to accurately predict their future, they do, nevertheless, exhibit identifiable underlying patterns that can help individuals cope with those systems' complex workings. See, in general, H.A. Simon, 'The Architecture of Complexity' (1962) 106 *Proceedings of the Am. Philosophical Society* 467.

55 S.L. Schwarcz, 'Regulating Complexity in Financial Markets' (2009) 87 *Washington University Law Rev.* 211.

56 M.F. Hellwig, 'Systemic Risk in the Financial Sector: An Analysis of the Subprime-Mortgage Financial Crisis', Max Planck Institute for Research on Collective Goods, Bonn 2008/43 (2008) 59–60.

Another reason relates to the nature of banking business. Due to banks' susceptibility to runs, for business competition reasons, or because of relevant confidentiality agreements, certain crucial data on a bank's business and the performance or profitability of certain business relationships will never be made public on a disaggregated basis. As a result, the effectiveness of monitoring of individual institutions by the market relying on publicly available data becomes less effective, and certainly less important than monitoring by regulators who have access to confidential data.

Finally, there is the flawed concept of market (ir)rationality leading to equilibrium outcomes and systemic stability. First, the rational behaviour of one market actor may not be used as a reliable benchmark to predict the behaviour of all other market actors, and thus of the financial system. Moreover, there is the potential for rational behaviour to lead to dis-equilibrium outcomes.[57] Consider the case of a bank that suffers large losses on some of its loans. The prudent choice for this bank is to sell assets and also reduce its lending activities in line with its smaller capital base. If the bank in question is large, or the losses affect several banks at the same time, the individual bank's attempt to rebuild its capital base will drain liquidity from the system and might even result in panic sales of assets or discounts (fire sales). In addition, less lending by some banks will translate into less funding to other banks which, if other sources of liquidity are not found, might be forced to cut lending levels. Credit restriction will, of course, have an impact on economic growth, lowering output and leading to further decreases in bank asset values, amplifying the deleveraging process.[58]

3. Shareholders as monitors in the banking sector: subjective limitations

(a) Board myopia

Shareholders' agents in the corporation and supposed 'implementers' of their will are corporate boards, since shareholders have no direct directional power over key corporate executives. Yet the cognitive limitations of corporate boards, when measuring risk, especially in an industry as complex as banking, may not be underestimated.[59] These range from bounded knowledge and understanding of their business to 'groupthink'.[60] It has

---

57 Geneva Report, op. cit. n. 48, pp. 20–40.
58 See M.K. Brunnermeier and L.H. Pedersen, 'Market Liquidity and Funding Liquidity' (2009) 22 *Rev. of Financial Studies* 2201.
59 In fact, it has been suggested that these should explicitly be taken into account by the bank corporate governance framework: see J. Dermine, 'Bank Corporate Governance, Beyond the Global Banking Crisis', INSEAD Working Paper 2011/33/FIN (2011).
60 For a good analysis of these biases, see D.C. Langevoort, 'Behavioral Approaches to Corporate Law' in *Research Handbook on the Economics of Corporate Law,* eds. C.A. Hill and B.H. McDonnell (2012) 442.

been postulated that 'the tendency of behavioral biases to interfere with accurate thought and analysis within complex organizations', thus interfering with the acquisition, analysis, communication, and implementation of information within an organization and between an organization and external parties, constitutes intellectual hazard that ought to be seen as a systemic problem in financial markets.[61]

Arguably, where a CEO does not recognize that, for instance, an asset bubble has formed, her compensation arrangements cannot possibly affect the assumption of risk taken by her bank. On the other hand, where a CEO does recognize that a bubble has formed in credit markets, professional and career concerns driven by pressure from (boundedly-rational) shareholders, and market short-termism, may cause her to remain in (or join) a particular market – namely, to herd. This decision will be driven by two connected – and rational – factors: first, by the knowledge that if the CEO does not order her bank to enter an upwardly moving market, she might be replaced, as peers gain from the markets in question; and, secondly, by the concerted hope that her suspicions concerning the bubble in question were ill-founded. Thus, even where it can be shown that there is no overt assumption of risk linked to performance-based compensation awards, the net result will not differ. Naturally, this finding places a limitation on the power of Bebchuk's thesis on the central role of perverse compensation structures in bank failures.[62]

(b) Shareholder short-termism, myopia, and herding

The monitoring problems posed by bounded rationality and cognitive limitations are compounded by the limited investment horizons of most institutional investors.[63] First, institutional investors have very few incentives to engineer takeover bids for firms or to remove poorly performing management.[64] This places an obvious limitation on the disciplining power of the much-vaunted market for corporate control. Investment funds are charged with procuring the maximum return on investment for their beneficiaries and will simply sell their shareholdings rather than engage directly with company management.[65]

61 See G.P. Miller and G. Rosenfeld, 'Intellectual Hazard: How Conceptual Biases in Complex Organizations Contributed to the Global Financial Crisis' (2010) 33 *Harvard J. of Law & Public Policy* 807, at 808.
62 Bebchuk et al., op. cit., n. 11.
63 J.C. Coffee Jnr., 'Liquidity versus Control: The Institutional Investor as Corporate Monitor' (1991) 91 *Columbia Law Rev.* 1277; R.J. Gilson and R. Kraakman, 'Reinventing the Outside Director: An Agenda for Institutional Investors' (1991) 43 *Stanford Law Rev.* 863.
64 G. Jackson, 'A New Financial Capitalism? Explaining the persistence of voice over exit in contemporary corporate governance' (2008) 5 *European Management Rev.* 23.
65 E.F. Fama, 'Agency Problems and the Theory of the Firm' (1980) 88 *J. of Political Economy* 288.

Fund managers are, themselves, in competition with peer fund managers and the performance of their funds is normally benchmarked.[66] They will therefore have very few incentives to actively invoke their ability to discipline management or to launch takeover action and would rather exit a firm than attempt to restructure its governance. In addition, in the United Kingdom and the United States, large investors typically hold their shares for an average of just seven months, producing a relatively short effective time horizon for most institutional investors. This compares with an average holding period of four years 30 years ago, and eight years 70 years ago.[67]

In fact, the assumption of greater short-term risks is a by-product of higher institutional investment:

> compensation and risk-taking are not related to governance variables but co-vary with ownership by institutional investors who tend to have short-termist preferences and the power to influence firm management policies.[68]

Therefore, powerful shareholders will often desire managers who assume risk as opposed to more conservative executives: '[S]hareholders prefer excessive risk taking. So they may have an interest in pay arrangements that encourage risk taking too much.'[69] Many large shareholders will therefore encourage a focus on the short term and certainly cannot be expected to provide a source of extra discipline on management.[70] Herding may be tacitly encouraged by investments which appear to provide commensurate risk-adjusted returns and regulation which requires banks to hold 'safe' capital.[71]

Of course, shareholder short-termism in banks is tempered by the knowledge that any public rescue of their company will invariably mean a dilution of the value of their shares. However, competitive pressure amongst shareholders for returns and the availability of cheap debt, in an environment of low interest rates, which allows banks to maximize leverage-fuelled

---

66 J. Chevalier and G. Ellison, 'Career Concerns Of Mutual Fund Managers' (1999) 114 Q. J. of Economics 389.

67 In addition, computer-driven high-frequency trading ('HFT') has become ubiquitous on global stock exchanges. This may crowd out long-term investors who have the capacity to engage in active monitoring: see A.G. Haldane, 'Patience and Finance', speech given at Oxford China Business Forum, Beijing (2 September 2010), at <www.bankofengland.co.uk/publications/Documents/speeches/2010/speech445.pdf>.

68 I. Cheng et al., 'Yesterday's Heroes: Compensation and Creative Risk-Taking' NBER Working Paper 16176 (2010).

69 L.A. Bebchuk, contribution to 'Governance, Executive Compensation, and Excessive Risk in the Financial Services Industry: A Research Symposium' (2010) 11, at <www4.gsb.columbia.edu/rt>.

70 K. Froot, A. Perold, and J. C. Stein, 'Shareholder Trading Practices and Corporate Investment Horizons', NBER Working Paper No. 3638 (1991).

71 J. Friedman and W. Kraus, Engineering the Financial Crisis: Systemic Risk and the Failure of Regulation (2011).

balance sheet returns, can easily convert shareholders from being risk-neutral to being risk seekers. Shareholders have strong incentives for banks to operate with high leverage.[72] The more a bank lends, the more profit it accrues. Thus, leverage-fuelled returns remove the possibility of a fruitful dialogue between principals and agents and might even crowd out investors who could make a long-term impact on executive behaviour. There is also substantial research to suggest that shareholders may be overconfident in their ability to ride asset bubbles, and 'get out' before a crash.[73] This naturally places limits on the capacity of market discipline to reduce risk taking. Accordingly, it is rather optimistic to expect institutional investors to act as true market monitors and rely on corporate governance mechanisms to restrain rent seeking or to remedy the flawed uses of financial innovation.

Moreover, even if institutional investors had either the incentives – or in an extreme scenario, the obligation – to monitor bank risk, they would still have failed in those duties. First, institutional investors are anything but immune to irrational exuberance and herding.[74] As a result, as soon as good times return, all pretence of effective monitoring will be abandoned in favour of higher returns. Secondly, they are also constrained by the aforesaid bounded rationality and lack of expertise. There is strong evidence that those within financial institutions, who understood the potential of the financial revolution, pushed it to its limits in a rent-seeking exercise, inflating institutions' profits and traders' and managers' salaries.[75] Yet outsiders, mostly institutional investors, did not delve deeper to ascertain the source of financial institutions' strong profitability that generated the hefty dividends and market price appreciation that boosted their returns from financial stocks. They also invariably approved in general meeting after general meeting executive compensations plans.

In fact, it appears that 'owner-controlled' banks had higher profits in the years before the 2008 crisis in comparison to 'manager-controlled' banks, but experienced larger losses and were more likely to require governmental assistance during the GFC.[76] One study after another has shown that firms with higher institutional ownership took 'greater risk in their investment policies before the onset of the crisis.'[77] Coffee rightly argues that:

72 P.O. Mülbert, 'Corporate Governance of Banks' (2009) 10 *European Business Organization Law Rev.* 411.
73 M.K. Brunnermeier and S. Nagel, 'Hedge Funds and the Technology Bubble' (2004) 59 *J. of Finance* 2013, at 2023.
74 E. Avgouleas, 'The Global Financial Crisis, Behavioural Finance and Financial Regulation: In Search of a New Orthodoxy' (2009) 9 *J. of Corporate Law Studies* 23.
75 Avgouleas, op. cit., n. 39, ch. 3.
76 R. Gropp and M. Köhler, 'Bank Owners or Bank Managers: Who is Keen on Risk? Evidence from the Financial Crisis', EBS Research Paper No. 10-02 (2010) 21.
77 D.H. Erkens et al., 'Corporate Governance in the 2007–2008 Financial Crisis: Evidence from Financial Institutions Worldwide' (2012) 18 *J. of Corporate Finance* 389.

Such evidence suggests that even if managers would prefer to avoid high risk and leverage, their preferences can be overridden by shareholders, and that institutional investors in particular can compel firms to accept greater risk and thus cause them to suffer worse losses in a crisis.[78]

It is, therefore, worth exploring further the claim that shareholder greed was at least as culpable as executive greed for high levels of bank leverage and rapid asset expansion in the pre-GFC period, which led to a series of spectacular bank collapses.

4. *Corporate governance failures and risky bank behaviour*

(a) Is there a corporate governance fallacy?

Studies prior to the GFC suggested that relative to manufacturing companies, banks had larger boards and the boards were objectively more independent (a greater number of independent directors). They further found that bank boards had more sub-committees, which met fractionally more frequently, and that directors of bank boards earned considerably less than their counterparts at non-financial firms.[79] These findings would indicate, prima facie, stronger governance levels at banks relative to other companies, even before the GFC.

Bank risk taking is positively associated with comparative shareholder power, suggesting that in jurisdictions which prioritize shareholder supremacy, bank management are encouraged to take more risk.[80] This finding tallies with research which demonstrates that owners with greater voting and cash-flow powers have greater influence over managerial behaviour.[81] Further, it has been demonstrated from research into the performance of banks prior to – and during – the GFC, that banks with shareholder-friendly boards of directors suffered larger equity losses.[82] This suggests that pro-shareholder governance (an indicator of 'better governance') might be inadequate in preventing managerial risk taking in financial institutions.

Institutional ownership does not mitigate these effects. Research conducted into European commercial banks indicates that larger institutional investor ownership of banks correlates with a greater level of risk taking by

---

78 J.C. Coffee Jnr., 'Systemic Risk after Dodd-Frank: Contingent Capital and the Need for Strategies Beyond Oversight' (2011) 111 *Columbia Law Rev.* 795, at 811.

79 R. Adams and H. Mehran, 'Is Corporate Governance Different for Bank Holding Companies?', FRB of New York Working Paper (2003); R. Adams, 'Governance and the Financial Crisis', ECGI Working Paper No. 248 (2009).

80 L. Laeven and R. Levine, 'Bank governance, regulation and risk taking' (2009) 93 *J. of Financial Economics* 259.

81 A. Shleifer and R.W. Vishny, 'Large Shareholders and Corporate Control' (1986) 94 *J. of Political Economy* 461.

82 A. Beltratti and R.M. Stulz, 'The Credit Crisis around the Globe: Why did some Banks Perform Better?' (2012) 105 *J. of Financial Economics* 1.

43

the banks concerned.[83] During the GFC, firms with higher institutional ownership suffered greater losses[84] as did American banks with relatively independent boards (indicated by the amount of money requested through the Unites States' 'Troubled Asset Relief Program'). These findings indicate that ensuring board independence is also possibly an ineffective check on bank risk-taking behaviour.[85] Furthermore, as mentioned earlier, bank shareholders have strong incentives to encourage banks to assume more debt to expand their balance sheet and thus increase leverage. The short-term investment horizons of most shareholders will, of course, be communicated to the board, and managers may be encouraged to pursue risk-laden strategies to boost short-term profits, regardless of the structure of their incentive contracts. It would appear, therefore, that the trust accorded to large shareholders to appoint boards, which will reduce risk taking by executives, is misplaced.

Moreover, there is a convincing line of research indicating that even properly designed compensation contracts, which seek to align principal-agent interests, may be unlikely to work as risk-reducing mechanisms when it comes to very senior executives. Following the GFC, many commentators (most notably Fahlenbrach and Stulz[86]) contend that the incentive arrangements at large financial institutions were not responsible for bank failures or the creation of excess risk within the financial system. Senior management at financial institutions held significant equity positions and suffered substantial paper losses once stock prices began to fall sharply; indeed, banks with CEOs whose interest were most aligned with the interests of shareholders performed worst.[87]

The losses that CEOs suffered in these cases imply that the excessive risks present in the system were related, in addition to rent seeking, to errors of judgment that could not remedied by a realignment of incentives. According to the aforementioned research, senior executives 'managed their banks in a manner they authentically believed would benefit their shareholders'.[88] Senior bankers at institutions which failed did not willingly take massive

83 T. Barry et al., 'Ownership structure and risk in publicly held and privately owned banks' (2011) 35 *J. of Banking and Finance* 1327.

84 Erkens et al., op. cit., n. 77.

85 R. Adams, 'Governance and the Financial Crisis', ECGI Working Paper No. 248 (2009); B.A. Minton et al., 'Do Independence and Financial Expertise of the Board Matter for Risk Taking and Performance?', Charles A. Dice Center for Research in Financial Economics Working Paper 2010-14 (2010).

86 R. Fahlenbrach and R.M. Stulz, 'Bank CEO incentives and the credit crisis' (2011) 99 *J. of Financial Economics* 11. The value of stock and options in the 'average' bank CEO's portfolio was more than ten times the value of the CEO's salary in 2006 and CEO's on average owned 1.6 per cent of the outstanding stock of their bank.

87 The CEOs of Bear Stearns and Lehman Brothers incurred paper losses of $902 million and $931 million, respectively. See Bebchuk et al., op. cit., n. 11.

88 J. Grundfest, 'What's Needed is Uncommon Wisdom' *New York Times*, 6 October 2009, 6.

risks, according to this view. For instance, most of the MBS products purchased by banks were low-yield, and perceived to be low-risk.[89] In addition, it seems that CEOs of firms with relatively high equity stakes in their firms assumed the same level of risk as CEOs of firms with commensurately lower equity stakes.[90] Finally, there were no significant reductions in equity positions amongst bank CEOs post-2006, which meant that they bore heavy losses in the market crash of 2008; in fact, CEO holdings of shares increased on net.[91] This suggests that even as the risk profile of bank investments appeared to change for the worse, bank CEOs did little to hedge their exposure to reduce any potential wealth losses[92] although, admittedly, they cashed in a large number of stock options, which were made highly lucrative by leverage-fuelled bank profits.

Arguably, two conclusions may be drawn from this analysis. First, there is convincing evidence that a number of senior managers were simply boundedly rational. They neither understood the risks that complex securities posed to their firms, nor the extent to which correlations in certain asset markets had been established across banking institutions.[93] Secondly, CEOs complied with shareholder pressure to take risks across the board, irrespective of their individual equity wealth. Neither finding reveals that pay packages were not flawed, fostering excessive risk taking (Bebchuk's thesis). Rather, they point to shareholders' tacit approval for doing so. As Professor Coffee suggests: 'shareholders, as principals, simply found ways to contract with managers, as their agents, to accept greater risk through lucrative compensation formulas.'[94]

But, again, this finding begs a further question: why were shareholders willing to do so? We argue that the main explanation for shareholder behaviour was the supra-competitive returns generated by debt-fuelled balance-sheet expansion, based on the willingness to exploit big banks' cheap funding base.[95] The same practice, of course, meant the assumption of catastrophically high levels of leverage and risk, as bank shareholders

---

89 V.V. Acharya and M. Richardson, 'Causes of the Financial Crisis' (2009) 21 *Critical Rev.* 195.

90 Fahlenbrach and Stulz, op. cit., n. 86.

91 id., p. 26.

92 id., p. 24. According to the sample of Fahlenbrach and Stulz, on average, CEOs lost $31.49 million between 2006 and 31 December 2008. They argue: 'Had CEOs seen the crisis coming, they could have avoided most of the losses by selling their shares. They clearly did not do so.'

93 F. Norris, 'It May Be Outrageous But Wall Street Pay Didn't Cause This Crisis' *New York Times*, 30 July 2009, 31.

94 J.C. Coffee Jnr., 'The Political Economy of Dodd-Frank: Why Financial Reform Tends to be Frustrated and Systemic Risk Perpetuated' (2012) 97 *Cornell Law Rev.* 1019, at 1053.

95 id. 'Based on these expectations, shareholders of major financial institutions could rationally pressure management to accept more risk than shareholders might consider advisable at industrial corporations.'

45

showed no inclination to lobby for a reinforcement of big banks' slender equity bases.

Another factor influencing shareholder attitudes must have been the relative safety provided to them by perceived notions of banks being 'too-big-to-fail', based on (i) bank size; and (ii) bank centrality in the financial network. In the United States and in Europe there is the possibility that these dangers may be somewhat mitigated by the introduction of bail-in regimes that will raise the cost of bank funding and increase creditor monitoring efforts.[96] Also, in the Eurozone, the recent reform to centralize cross-border bank supervision and resolution as part of the European Banking Union will to some extent allow regulators to prevent banks from leveraging their balance sheet beyond a size that is regarded as safe by the single supervisor.[97] However, the bail in is fraught with shortcomings and it remains far from clear whether these reforms will affect individual or collective bank behaviour to such a great extent that banks will assume less risk or will not engage in perilous regulatory arbitrage through asset substitution.

(b) Financial innovation, bank size, and insider rent seeking

Prior to the GFC, market discipline was seen as the paramount tool to control excessive risk taking by financial institutions, and regulators were anchored to the view that risk had been diversified and spread amongst the various units comprising the financial system. Yet it is now clear that homogenization of trading behaviour and risk-management techniques, interconnectedness spawned by financial innovation, and the speed of transmission of shocks from one area of the system to the next, created huge potential for contagion.[98]

One of us has argued elsewhere[99] that, without discarding the multitude of other causes, the best way to understand the GFC is to see it as predominantly the result of uncoordinated risks which came together[100] because of an economic and knowledge revolution that was badly mismanaged[101]

---

96 See s. 5, Art. 37 and following of the Proposal for a Directive on establishing a framework for the recovery and resolution of credit institutions and investment firms and amending Council Directives 77/91/EEC and 82/891/EC, Directives 2001/24/EC, 2002/47/EC, 2004/25/EC, 2005/56/EC, 2007/36/EC, and 2011/35/EC and Regulation (EU) No 1093/2010, Brussels, 6 June 2012, COM(2012) 280, at <http://eur-lex.europa.eu/LexUriServ/LexUriServ.do?uri=COM:2012:0280:FIN:EN:PDF>.
97 Council Regulation (EU) 1024/2013 of 15 October 2013 conferring specific tasks on the European Central Bank concerning policies relating to the prudential supervision of credit institutions [2013] OJ L287/63.
98 Avgouleas, op. cit. n. 39, p. 120.
99 id., chs. 2 and 3.
100 N. Gennaioli et al., 'Neglected Risks, Financial Innovation, and Financial Stability', NBER Working Paper No. 16068 (2010).
101 J. Lerner and P. Tufano, 'The Consequences of Financial Innovation: A Counterfactual Research Agenda', NBER Working Paper No. 16780 (2011).

46

due to ignorance, complexity and opacity, excessive rent seeking by insiders, and an inability to predict the risk correlations that new global trading channels, opened by the financial revolution, would bring about under conditions of widespread panic. Arguably, certain aspects of financial innovation presented a serious breakthrough in knowledge, especially as regards the distribution/diversification of quantifiable credit and project (finance)[102] risk and the revolutionization of the channels available to access finance.

In the past thirty years, financial innovation, technology breakthroughs, and the nearly universal abdication of national capital restriction led to the emergence of a new and poorly understood market landscape. In this landscape, capital flows across borders have been free and have taken place at extreme velocity. These flows have often supported transactions in very complex instruments. As a result, the disparate roots and branches of the global financial system became a tightly-knit and interdependent whole, rendering financial centres, national economies, and individual institutions vulnerable to the volatile winds and moods of global markets. The new market landscape also provided very little room for the untangling of the purpose of individual transactions or for assertion of counterparties' solvency.

Moreover, the enormous insider rents to which information asymmetries generated by the complexity of innovative financial instruments and techniques give rise may only be curbed by controlling bank size and interconnectedness. Individuals within financial institutions have strong incentives to push the boundaries of complexity and obfuscation of product structure and returns.[103] Reducing complexity will therefore lead naturally to superior corporate governance because shareholder and director interests would become better aligned. Corroborating evidence for this assertion is offered in the United States Senate Report on the causes of the GFC, which demonstrates vividly how big American banks forced the boundaries of reckless lending in search of ever-higher returns through the use of complex securitization.[104] Even in the absence of fraud, it is obvious that big banks were taking advantage of their higher sophistication and familiarity with the

---

102 F. Allen and D. Gale, *Financial Innovation and Risk Sharing* (1994).

103 A characteristic example is the Goldman Sachs ABACUS scheme which became the subject of an SEC complaint that was subsequently settled. What was striking about the scheme described in the SEC's complaint (apart from the colossal conflict of interests as per the SEC's allegations) was the extreme complexity of the transactions and the (allegedly) deliberate obfuscation of their true purpose by the investment bank concerned. See 'Who's, Why's & How's of Allegations vs. Goldman' *NYDailynews.com*, 20 April 2010, at <http://www.nydailynews.com/money/2010/>.

104 See Parts II and VI of The National Commission on the Causes of the Financial and Economic Crisis in the United States, *The Financial Crisis Inquiry Report*, Pursuant to Public Law 111-21 (2011), at <http://www.gpo.gov/fdsys/pkg/GPO-FCIC/pdf/GPO-FCIC.pdf>.

complex science of structured finance and were selling to investors (including sophisticated investors) products that were known to be loss-making from the outset.

STRUCTURAL REFORM AS A MEANS OF IMPROVING BANK CORPORATE GOVERNANCE

This article argues that structural reform and other controls on bank size, complexity, and interconnectedness to eliminate the public subsidy,[105] rather than stricter corporate governance framework and executive compensation controls as such, are the keys to curbing insider rents. The great emphasis that contemporary resolution regimes place on shifting losses to shareholders from taxpayers strongly supports the point that proper regulation, rather than corporate governance reform, is crucial to a safer banking sector. By the same token, structural reform may lead to smaller and less interconnected banks and greater competition in the market, improving de facto corporate governance standards.

The reform of the architecture of the banking sector has been widely discussed and, in some cases, acted upon by legislators both in the United States and the United Kingdom.[106] The various proposals and legislative initiatives differ sharply from each other. In addition, some scholars have suggested variations of the Glass-Steagall approach as a model of structural reform.[107] Other commentators have proposed structural reform models that seek to reconceptualize the business of banking.[108] Disagreement on the exact scope of structural reform is important but it should not distract from its urgency and value.[109]

---

105 Coffee, op. cit. n. 94, at 1048.
106 See, for example, the Volcker Rule in the United States, which limits proprietary trading by commercial banks, and the Vickers Report in the United Kingdom, which has provided the basis for structural reform of the British banking sector.
107 The two most prominent academic models of narrow banking are by two well-known economists, Lawrence Kotlikoff and John Kay. See L. Kotlikoff, *Jimmy Stewart Is Dead: Ending the World's Ongoing Financial Plague with Limited Purpose Banking* (2010); J. Kay, 'Narrow Banking: The Reform of Banking Regulation', CSFI Report (2009), at <http://www.johnkay.com/wp-content/uploads/2009/12/JK-Narrow-Banking.pdf>.
108 E. Avgouleas, 'The Reform of the 'Too-Big-To-Fail' Bank: A New Regulatory Model for the Institutional Separation of "Casino" from "Utility" Banking', paper at the 7th Euroframe Conference on Economic Policy Issues in the EU, June 2010, at <http://papers.ssrn.com/sol3/papers.cfm?abstract_id=1552970>.
109 See A.G. Haldane and V. Madouros, 'The Dog and the Frisbee', speech at the Federal Reserve Bank of Kansas City's 36th economic policy symposium, 'The Changing Policy Landscape', 31 August 2012, at <http://www.bankofengland.co.uk/publications/Documents/speeches/2012/speech596.pdf>; L.G. Baxter, 'Betting Big: Value, Caution, and Accountability in an Era of Large Banks and Complex Finance' (2011–2012) 31 *Rev. of Banking and Financial Law* 765.

48

Reform to bank structure to separate proprietary trading and other high-risk activities, and even of wholesale banking from retail divisions will both lead to smaller and less interconnected banks and will enhance corporate governance in the sector.[110] Smaller and more focused banks would be more manageable, making the monitoring of outside 'controllers' such as shareholders and bondholders easier. A further benefit of structural reform, as opposed to solely improving corporate governance, would be a reduction in the widespread conflicts of interests that plague the financial services industry, and the nearly unlimited liability that big banks might incur due to those conflicts.[111] Namely, as the boundaries of banks' contractual relationships increase, for instance, by means of sponsoring high-risk securitization, or other shadow banking deals, attendant exposure may not only be hidden from the board and senior management but also become unlimited, destroying shareholder value.[112] Recommending ever-higher corporate governance and supervision standards in the circumstances may not only prove an exercise in futility, for the reasons explained in the sections above, but also shows an unpardonable unwillingness on the part of policy makers to grasp the true causes of financial market complexity and the risks that this brings to bank shareholders. It follows that smaller and less interconnected banks would be both more visible in their exposures and also run a smaller risk of raking up unlimited liabilities.

CONCLUSION

It is plausibly argued that the grand-scale rent seeking by financial institutions and expert insiders, made possible by the financial revolution, was based on banks' ability to free-ride on public subsidies and the public guarantee. It follows that limiting public subsidies to financial institutions, placing limits on their ability to leverage their balance sheet through the use of debt to fund their asset base, and remedying the 'too-big-to-fail' problem are much better measures in preventing a new crisis than simply regulating bankers' pay and realigning incentives within banks. Naturally, banker

---

110 This was a key recommendation of the recent Liikanen Report on the structure of the EU banking sector. See E. Liikanen (chair), *Final Report of the High-level Expert Group on reforming the structure of the EU banking sector* (2012), at <http://ec.europa.eu/internal_market/bank/docs/high-level_expert_group/report_en.pdf>.

111 A characteristic example of this was the huge losses incurred by one United Kingdom trader at J.P. Morgan, which were caused largely by senior management's failure to understand the complexity and risks associated with the group's portfolio. For a discussion, see J. Kregel, 'More Swimming Lessons from the London Whale', Levy Institute Public Policy Brief No. 129 (April 2013).

112 See A.J. Levitin and W.W. Bratton, 'A Transactional Genealogy of Scandal: From Michael Milken to Enron to Goldman Sachs' (2013) 86 *Southern California Law Rev.* 783.

compensation and corporate governance remain issues of public fascination and part of the quest for justice, given the devastation the GFC has wrought on national economies and peoples' livelihoods. But they are not the only important issues. Thus, it is lamentable that they have stolen the limelight and taken so much of policy makers' time during that rare window of opportunity that existed between 2008 and 2011 to redress the chronic defects in the regulation of the global financial services industry.

Accordingly, it is submitted that the EU should not have sought to reform banking sector corporate governance in isolation from the structural issues affecting governance incentives within large and complex banks. The most effective premise of good corporate governance in the financial sector is competition between smaller, less complex, and less interconnected banks. Industry lobbying power aside, another possible explanation of this logical oversight is that age-old bias affecting policy makers (and, less often, academic commentators) when they need it least: groupthink!

JOURNAL OF LAW AND SOCIETY
VOLUME 41, NUMBER 1, MARCH 2014
ISSN: 0263-323X, pp. 51–72

The Financial Crisis: A Reason to Improve Shareholder Protection in the EU?

Jonathan Mukwiri* and Mathias Siems*

The global financial crisis of 2008 has stimulated the debate on corporate governance and shareholder protection. The intuitive reason for the topicality of shareholder protection is that insolvencies mainly harm shareholders as the companies' residual claimants. In addition, ideally, shareholder empowerment may ensure better monitoring of management and therefore better-run companies preventing corporate failures and benefiting the economy as a whole. Yet, it is not self-evident that shareholder participation has such a positive effect. This article critically examines the discussion about the relationship between the financial crisis, shareholder protection, and law reform. We also develop a central position: while there may be a need to improve shareholder protection, we do not take the view that any increase in shareholder rights is the right way forward; rather, such reforms should aim to encourage shareholder engagement by responsible long-term investors.

INTRODUCTION

Before the 2008 financial crisis, the world economy seemed to be founded on a relatively secure platform, and even at the beginning of the crisis few anticipated its destructive effects.[1] Now, however, policy debates have been

* Durham Law School, The Palatine Centre, Durham University, Stockton Road, Durham DH1 3LE, England
jonathan.mukwiri@durham.ac.uk   mathias.siems@durham.ac.uk

We thank Hatice Kubra Kandemir, Melih Sonmez, and the participants of the Workshop on Post-crisis Trajectories of European Corporate Governance at Leeds Law School for helpful comments.

1 See, for example, B.R Cheffins, 'Did Corporate Governance "Fail" During the 2008 Stock Market Meltdown? The Case of the S&P 500' (2009) 65 *Business Lawyer* 1, at 4: 'Too few regulators, stock market analysts, and journalists ... foresaw the havoc that would follow if and when it burst.'

51

mushrooming, for instance, on matters of bank bail-outs, international financial regulation, economic stimulus, and austerity, but also corporate governance and shareholder protection.[2] Regulators are struggling to place business operations on a more secure basis. Yet, the question remains whether improving corporate governance and shareholder protection is the right answer. In the context of the recent financial crisis and shareholder protection, views are diverse in regard to whether to blame or exonerate corporate governance.[3]

Our examination reveals the issues to be more complex than hitherto understood. The intuitive reason for the topicality of shareholder protection is that increases in insolvencies harm shareholders as the companies' residual claimants. In addition, ideally, shareholder empowerment may ensure better monitoring of management and therefore better-run companies, benefiting the economy as a whole. Yet, it is not self-evident that the crisis actually calls for improvements in shareholder protection. For instance, one can make the point that shareholders of public companies are often only interested in short-term benefits, and that such short-termism was precisely what contributed to the financial crisis.[4]

Specifically, we are interested in the relationship between shareholder protection and the financial crisis in the context of EU corporate governance. Taking the current law as a starting point, it is difficult to say that the EU has 'failed' to align corporate governance with shareholder protection. On the one hand, the EU did address shareholder protection in the past, sometimes directly – namely in the Shareholder Rights Directive[5] – sometimes indirectly in other directives and regulations.[6] On the other hand, the question is whether these rules have really provided shareholders with a strong voice in the corporate governance of public companies.[7] Moreover,

---

2 For the general discussion on regulation and the financial crisis see, for example, S. Konzelmann and M. Fovargue-Davies (eds.), *Banking Systems in the Crisis: The Faces of Liberal Capitalism* (2013); E. Avgouleas, *Governance of Global Financial Markets* (2012); J. Gray and O. Akseli (eds.), *Financial Regulation in Crisis?: The Role of Law and the Failure of Northern Rock* (2011).

3 Similarly, J. Armour and W.-G. Ringe, 'European company law 1999–2010: renaissance and crisis' (2011) 48 *Common Market Law Rev.* 125, at 169 (no consensus whether existing corporate governance is deficient or simply poorly implemented).

4 For details, see the discussion in the following sections.

5 Directive 2007/36/EC of the European Parliament and of the Council of 11 July 2007 on the exercise of certain rights of shareholders in listed companies.

6 Notably through the harmonization of securities law in terms of disclosure and transparency. See, for example, Directive 2004/109/EC on the harmonization of transparency requirements. For a useful overview, see European Parliament Committee on Legal Affairs, *Rights and obligations of shareholders – National regimes and proposed instruments at EU level for improving legal efficiency* (2012) PE 462.463, 21–36.

7 P.E. Masouros, 'Is the EU Taking Shareholder Rights Seriously?: An Essay on the Importance of Shareholdership in Corporate Europe' (2010) 7 *European Company Law* 195, at 196.

52

many topics in shareholder protection have not been harmonized, for example, the enforcement of directors' duties or the rights of minority shareholders. Thus, assuming the need for better shareholder protection, more harmonization could be needed.

The article proceeds as follows. The first section explores the differing views on whether the financial crisis shows failures of corporate governance – or whether its main reasons lie elsewhere. The second one critically discusses the claims that, after the crisis, shareholder empowerment should be strengthened. Third, we look at issues of shareholder participation in corporate governance, and examine investor culture in light of the financial crisis. This forms the basis for our central position, namely, that law reforms should aim to encourage shareholder engagement by responsible long-term investors. For this purpose, this section also provides specific suggestions on how such 'better engagement' may be achieved. Fourth, assuming there is a need to improve shareholder protection, we discuss the right form and level of legal reform, ranging from self-regulation to national, European and international initiatives. The final section concludes.

THE CRISIS: EVIDENCE OF CORPORATE GOVERNANCE FAILURES?

A number of reasons have been suggested as to why the financial crisis occurred.[8] These views include those which argue that corporate governance failed in the crisis, in particular as regards the protection of shareholders. Others take the view that the 2008 financial crisis was not a verdict on corporate governance. We outline these differing positions before reaching the conclusion that it is difficult decisively to exonerate or blame corporate governance for the 2008 financial crisis.

Roman Tomasic and Folarin Akinbami[9] observe that, in the run-up to the banking crisis of 2007–2008, boards and regulators in the United Kingdom did not adequately protect shareholders. They argue that in the banking sector much decision making was left to CEOs who undertook excessive risks without restraint from the boards and regulators. Internal regulation within corporations and corporate networks needs to be backed by net-worked regulation as well as by an effective external regulatory mechanism which imposes some sanction for failure. But the problem was that regula-tors took a ritualistic approach to regulating corporations, and 'government

---

8 See generally, for example, the literature cited in n. 2 above.
9 R. Tomasic and F. Akinbami, 'Towards a New Corporate Governance After the Global Financial Crisis' (2011a) 22(8) *International Company and Commercial Law Rev.* 237. See, also, R. Tomasic and F. Akinbami, 'The Role of Trust in Maintaining the Resilience of Financial Markets' (2011b) 11 *J. of Corporate Law Studies* 369.

regulators seemed to have the role of providing reassurance to market actors rather than effectively sanctioning them.'[10]

Observing the plight of shareholders, Tomasic and Akinbami note that shareholders have traditionally simply voted with their feet and sold their shares, but even that did not seem to affect boards.[11] For shareholders to engage with the boards properly, they argue that companies need to provide more information to shareholders to allow them to act effectively. They observe that under the principle of director primacy, the responsibility to manage and limit risk rests with the boards and CEOs. In that regard, shareholders have much less capacity to influence decision making, and it does not help that the courts have buttressed this under the so-called business judgment rule to support board primacy. Thus, Tomasic and Akinbami call for boards to spend more time on company matters, and for board members to be required to have greater banking related expertise.[12]

A similar focus on boards has been taken in the United Kingdom by the Treasury Committee of the House of Commons.[13] It identified three problems with corporate governance in light of the financial crisis: (a) lack of time devoted by many non-executives to their role, (b) too many non-executive directors within the banks lacking relevant banking or financial experience, and (c) banks drawing upon too narrow a talent pool when appointing non-executive directors to the detriment of diversity of views. With respect to shareholder empowerment, all of this can be read to imply that making shareholders appoint better directors would be an important step in the right direction.

In the literature it has been suggested that the EU should increase shareholder protection in order to restore trust in capital markets.[14] The EU institutions seem to follow this suggestion. The European Commission published a Green Paper in April 2011,[15] and submitted an Action Plan in December 2012.[16] Among other things, the plan suggests that there may be changes to the Shareholder Rights Directive[17] in the coming years.

But the question of 'what went wrong' has also triggered a different response. For example, according to John Coffee, 'the 2008 financial crisis

---

10 id. (2011a), p. 242.

11 id., p. 248.

12 id., p. 249.

13 House of Commons Treasury Committee, Seventh Report, *Banking Crisis: dealing with the failure of the UK banks*, HC (2008–09) 416, 10–11. For further proposals, see Parliamentary Commission on Banking Standards, Fifth Report, *Changing Banking for Good*, HL (2013) 27-II, s. 7.

14 Masouros, op. cit., n. 7, p. 203.

15 European Commission, 'Green Paper: The EU corporate governance framework' (COM(2011) 164 final).

16 Communication from the Commission, 'Action Plan: European company law and corporate governance – a modern legal framework for more engaged shareholders and sustainable companies' (COM(2012) 740 final).

17 See n. 6 above.

54

stands above all as testimony to the error of excessive reliance on broad principles and self-regulation.'[18] He relates this specifically to the regulatory system in the EU and how it applies to American companies. The EU adopted the Financial Conglomerates Directive 2002/87/EC, the main thrust of which was to require regulatory supervision at the parent company level of financial institutions. Yet, major United States financial institutions lobbied the Securities and Exchange Commission (SEC) for a system of 'functional equivalent' regulation to satisfy the EU Directive. This procedure allowed American banks to generate their own risk models, which the banks quickly turned into a process of self-regulation. It also allowed the banks to opt for a relaxed 'alternative net capital rule' instead of the traditional capital adequacy rule that placed a maximum ceiling on debt to equity ratio. What followed, Coffee explains, was a reckless expansion by United States investment banks, characterized by relaxed due diligence standards, to compete for the markets, taking on a greater risk in real estate investment with undiversified exposure to a downturn in the market. When the liquidity from risky acquisitions of sub-prime mortgages hit the market, investment banks were hit the hardest, and this had a negative knock-on effect on the rest of the financial institutions in the global market associated with United States banks.

As one reads the analysis by Coffee as to what went wrong, the implication seems to be that it had nothing to do with corporate governance failure. If there is apportioning of blame, it lies with regulation of securities in the financial market. But even then, it is difficult to say that securities regulation failed to protect shareholders, for shareholders were fully supportive and involved in the seemingly irresponsible practices of financial institutions that led to the 2008 financial crisis. For example, in reviewing the histories of failed British companies, the Kay Review found that many of the bad decisions leading to the failures were supported or even encouraged by a majority of the shareholders.[19] To fully blame securities regulators for what went wrong would be to assign a very paternalistic responsibility to regulators to protect shareholders from themselves.

In a similar vein, Brian Cheffins takes the view that corporate governance did not fail in the 2008 financial crisis.[20] He reaches this conclusion by a

---

18 J.C. Coffee, 'What went wrong? An Initial Inquiry into the Causes of the 2008 Financial Crisis' (2009) 9 *J. of Corporate Law Studies* 1, at 22.

19 J. Kay, *The Kay Review of UK Equity Markets and Long-Term Decision Making, Final Report* (2012) para. 1.28. The general findings of this review were endorsed by the Department for Business, Innovation and Skills (BIS), *Ensuring Equity Markets Support Long-Term Growth, The Government Response to the Kay Review* (2012); House of Commons Business, Innovation and Skills Committee, Third Report, *The Kay Review of UK Equity Markets and Long-Term Decision Making*, HC (2013–14) 603.

20 Cheffins, op. cit., n. 1. A similar study of United States firms is R.B. Adams, 'Governance and the Financial Crisis' (2012) 12 *International Rev. of Finance* 7.

detailed examination of corporate governance practices in the 37 companies that were removed from the iconic S&P 500 index of publicly traded companies during the stock market turmoil of 2008. In these companies, Cheffins found that in various key respects corporate governance operated satisfactorily. Corporate failures that occurred were largely fraud-free; boards of directors generally performed satisfactorily enough to avoid public criticism; and in troubled companies, the directors were far from complacent, as they orchestrated CEO turnover at a rate greatly exceeding the norm in publicly traded firms. In conclusion, Cheffins observes that events occurring during 2008 do not provide a convincing case for radical initiatives.[21] Based on these findings, he also cautions that lawmakers would be unwise to treat the stock market turmoil of 2008 as a justification for sweeping corporate governance reforms.[22]

These divergent views demonstrate the difficulties of exonerating or blaming corporate governance for the recent financial crisis. A possible explanation is that the relevant causes are not independent of each other: for example, if one considers the risks of speculative financial instruments, one interpretation may refer just to the existence of these instruments while another may say that deficiencies in corporate governance allowed managers to make use of them. Moreover, a possible reason for these ambiguities is that considering the relevance of corporate governance as a whole is too abstract. Thus, there may well be lessons to be learnt for more specific topics of company law. It is a question of what lessons and whether that should lead to a stronger empowerment of shareholders, to which we turn next.

SHAREHOLDER EMPOWERMENT: STATUS QUO AND WAY FORWARD

The traditional role of shareholders in corporate governance, mainly reduced to voting on company matters in a general meeting, may explain the difficulty shareholders find in playing an effective role in averting corporate failures. Whereas shareholders may vote in the general meeting on issues that shape the company, the power to manage the company is reserved for the board of directors.[23] If directors manage the company in a manner that causes financial loss, shareholders may be able to file a derivative claim.[24]

---

21 Cheffins, id., p. 61.
22 id., p. 4.
23 For a comparative overview, see M. Siems, *Convergence in Shareholder Law* (2008) 152–3. Specifically for the United Kingdom, see *Harold Holdsworth & Co (Wakefield) Ltd* v. *Caddies* [1955] 1 W.L.R. 352; *Automatic Self-Cleansing Filter Syndicate Co Ltd* v. *Cuninghame* [1902] 2 Ch. 34; *Percival* v. *Wright* [1902] 2 Ch. 421 (directors do not, in general, owe fiduciary duty to shareholders).
24 Siems, id., pp. 212–18 (comparative overview).

But they may also want to intervene earlier: combining a monitoring and disciplinary role, they could aim to remove incompetent directors from office.

Yet, this is not always straightforward. In German law, the management board can only be dismissed by the supervisory board for an important reason, which is presumed if the general meeting withdraws its confidence, and dismissal of supervisory board members is only possible by three quarters of the votes cast, unless an important reason is present.[25] In the United Kingdom, section 168 of the Companies Act empowers shareholders to appoint and remove directors from office at any time. However, for a director with a service contract, even one clearly guilty of wrongdoing, the company may prefer to pay that director to go quietly, rather than insist on dismissing him or her without notice.[26] A director with a service contract may also be entitled to compensation for dismissal.[27] The political necessity to keep the director reasonably well disposed towards the company, if he or she is the only one to be removed and is aware of wrongdoings by other directors, may prove an impediment to removal.[28] In companies with limited number of shareholders, where the company's articles provides for voting arrangements in favour of a director/member being removed,[29] removal would be difficult.[30] The practical remedy may well lie in shareholders simply selling their shares and investing elsewhere. This inevitably reduces the role of shareholders to that of monitoring the market price index for an exit strategy.

In light of the financial crisis, does the answer lie in law reform for greater shareholder empowerment, for instance, introducing binding votes on executive remuneration policy, as recently proposed by the European Commission?[31] William Bratton and Michael Wachter have little sympathy with greater shareholder empowerment as a part of regulatory response to the financial crisis.[32] To them, shareholder empowerment would make it much more difficult for a good board of directors to resist pressures to manage to

---

25 See German Companies Act (*Aktiengesetz*), ss. 84(3), 103(1),(3).

26 P.L. Davies and S. Worthington, *Gower and Davies Principles of Modern Company Law* (2012, 9th edn.) 415.

27 Companies Act 2006, s. 168(5)(a).

28 J. Lowry and A. Reisberg, *Pettet's Company Law* (2009, 3rd edn.) 180.

29 See *Bushell* v. *Faith* [1970] A.C. 1099.

30 D. Kershaw, *Company Law in Context* (2012, 2nd edn.) 227.

31 European Commission, op. cit., n. 16, p. 9. This is in line with recent reforms in the United Kingdom and the United States: see Companies Act 2006, s. 439A, inserted by Enterprise and Regulatory Reform Act 2013, c. 24; United States Dodd-Frank Wall Street Reform and Consumer Protection Act (Pub.L. 111–203, H.R. 4173), s. 951. But see, also, C.M. Bruner, 'Corporate Governance Reform in a Time of Crisis' (2011) 36 *J. of Corporate Law* 309 (for differences in shareholder orientation between the United States and the United Kingdom as they relate to recent reforms).

32 W. Bratton and M. Wachter, 'The Case Against Shareholder Empowerment' (2010) 158 *University of Pennsylvania Law Rev.* 653.

the market. Moreover, incentive-compatible executive compensation and shareholder empowerment are seen as inconsistent goals. They argue that if executive compensation can be fixed by requiring longer holding periods, it is then turned around and unfixed if managers are encouraged to manage the market as a response to shareholder empowerment.[33]

Similar views have been expressed by other academics. Alan Dignam argues that shareholder empowerment as a reform mistakenly characterizes shareholders as willing and responsible owners when in the recent bank failures it was shareholders' activism that was a significant problem.[34] According to Lynn Stout, the 'mantra' that directors are obliged to maximize shareholder value leads to 'reckless, sociopathic and socially irresponsible behaviours', which not only harm the corporation and the public but also individual investors.[35] Andrew Keay too blames managerial short-termism which is seen as a consequence of shareholder pressure and the emphasis on quarterly earnings;[36] Simon Deakin considered the reasons for excessive risk taking, namely, the 'increasing alignment of managerial interests with those of shareholders, through corporate governance innovations such as share options and independent boards.'[37]

Newspaper articles have expressed similar views. According to a column in the *Observer*,[38] regardless of theory, 'a system that encourages the same organisation to pay one person 470 times what another gets will eventually blow up.' But the column does not suggest that therefore incentives should be more closely aligned to shareholders. Rather, the opposite: this trend need to be reversed as the management's first accountability should be to those

33 id., p. 690.
34 A. Dignam, 'The future of shareholder democracy in the shadow of the financial crisis' (2013) 36 *Seattle University Law Rev.* 639, at 688.
35 L.A. Stout, *The Shareholder Value Myth: How Putting Shareholders First Harms Investors, Corporations, and the Public* (2012). See, also, L.A. Stout, 'New Thinking on "Shareholder Primacy" ' (2012) 2 *Accounting, Economics, and Law*. For a similar analysis, see L. Talbot, 'Why Shareholders Shouldn't Vote: A Marxist-progressive Critique of Shareholder Empowerment' (2013) 76 *Modern Law Rev.* 791.
36 A. Keay, 'Risk, shareholder pressure and short-termism in financial institutions: does enlightened shareholder value offer a panacea?' (2011) 5 *Law and Financial Markets Rev.* 435.
37 S. Deakin, 'The Corporation as Commons: Rethinking Property Rights, Governance and Sustainability in the Business' Enterprise' (2012) 37 *Queen's Law J.* 339. See, also, S. Deakin, 'Corporate governance and financial crisis in the long run' in *The Embedded Firm*, eds. C.A. Williams and P. Zumbansen (2011) 30–40.
38 For the following, see S. Caulkin, 'It's time to explode the myth of the shareholder' *Observer*, 9 March 2009, at <http://www.guardian.co.uk/business/2009/mar/29/corporate-governance-moneyinvestments>. Similarly, W. Hutton, 'We need a revolution in how our companies are owned and run' *Observer*, 29 September 2012, at <http://www.guardian.co.uk/commentisfree/2012/sep/30/will-hutton-new-model-capitalism>.

58

who have the greatest power to create or destroy shareholder value – employees, customers, and suppliers.[39]

This relates to the general question of what is meant by corporate governance, in particular in the context of the recent financial crisis. We take the view that corporate governance needs to address 'the basic legal characteristics of the business corporation'.[40] Yet, the tendency has been to concentrate entirely on the protection of shareholders. Corporate governance has been 'increasingly perceived in a narrow sense, that is, pertaining solely to the internal and external control mechanisms between shareholders and managers.'[41] This has led to the managers concentrating on the share/stock market price as a mechanism of aligning shareholders' and managers' interests in order to reduce agency costs. Inadvertently, this has led managers to adopt much risk taking – and major parties in corporate governance have acquiesced in this trend.

It is, however, difficult to blame the financial crisis on corporate governance, even when perceived in its narrow sense. The causes seem to lie in risk management, which is a question of judgement for directors, and not as such a question of shareholders' role in corporate governance. While in its 2009 report, the Organisation for Economic Co-operation and Development (OECD) concluded that 'the financial crisis can be to an important extent attributed to failures and weaknesses in corporate governance arrangements',[42] this conclusion also needs to be understood from the background of an Anglo-Saxon model of corporate governance that is predominantly shareholder oriented. This model concentrates on private aspects of corporate governance, which focuses on internal control mechanisms for aligning interests between shareholders and managers. It places public aspects of corporate governance at the periphery – such that 'public intervention in corporate governance system is only tolerated where it serves to ease market failures.'[43] But it is difficult to see how far simply giving more powers to shareholders could have averted the financial crisis. Yet, this should not be seen as our final word since we also need to examine shareholder engagement in light of possible changes to investor cultures.

---

39 The 'shareholder-stakeholder debate' is also a frequent topic of the academic literature. See, for example, A. Keay, *The Corporate Objective. Corporations, Globalisation and the Law* (2011); M. Siems, 'The Ranking of Shareholder and Stakeholder Interests in Common and Civil Law Countries' in *Company Law and CSR: New Legal and Economic Challenges*, ed. I. Tchotourian (2014).
40 J. Armour et al., 'What is Corporate Law?' in *The Anatomy of Corporate Law: A Comparative and Functional Approach*, eds. R. Kraakman et al. (2009, 2nd edn.) 1.
41 L. Horn, 'Corporate Governance in Crisis? The Politics of EU Corporate Governance Regulation' (2012) 18 *European Law J.* 83, at 94.
42 OECD, *The Corporate Governance Lessons from the Financial Crisis* (2009) 2.
43 Horn, op. cit., n. 41, p. 86.

1. *Short-term versus long-term investment*

Before the 2008 financial crisis, investor culture had shifted from long-term to short-term orientation.[44] Subsequently, this has often been seen as a problem. For example, in the Green Paper on Corporate Governance, the European Commission found 'evidence that the majority of shareholders are passive and are often only focused on short-term profits',[45] and a subsequent Green Paper specifically dealt with the aim of long-term financing of the European economy.[46] Thus, the problem is that corporate governance with its emphasis on shareholder value has enhanced investor pressure for greater returns on short-term investment, and that such short-term investors hardly engage with corporate governance for greater sustainability.[47] For instance, in takeover situations, shareholders often have a short-term focus, as they may have purchased the shares after the bid has been announced in order to make a quick gain, should the takeover succeed, with no interest in the future of the company once they have accepted the offer and exited the company.[48] It also seems fair to assume that since the financial crisis this short-term investor culture has not changed: most shareholders of large public companies only hold their shares to maximize their financial return.[49]

On the lack of shareholder engagement, the European Commission observed that 'it is primarily long-term investors who have an interest in engagement.'[50] We believe the backdrop to this lack of shareholder engagement is the fact that investors who largely contribute to corporate liquidity tend to be short-term investors. Boards of financial firms striving to

---

44 For details, see P.E. Masouros, *Corporate Law and Economic Stagnation: How Shareholder Value and Short-Termism Contribute to the Decline of the Western Economies* (2013) (identifying the breakdown of the Bretton Woods monetary order in the early 1970s as the main trigger).
45 European Commission, op. cit., n. 15, p. 3.
46 European Commission, 'Green Paper: Long-Term Financing of the European Economy' (COM(2013) 150 final). See, also, the 2010 BIS consultation on a 'Long-Term Focus for Corporate Britain', at <https://www.gov.uk/government/consultations/a-long-term-focus-for-corporate-britain-a-call-for-evidence>, which preceded the Kay Review (op. cit., n. 19).
47 This does not imply that long-term shareholders cannot also 'benefit from managers destroying economic value': J.M. Fried, 'The Uneasy Case for Favoring Long-Term Shareholders', ECGI Law Working Paper no. 200 (2013), at <http://ssrn.com/abstract=2227080>.
48 J. Payne, 'Minority shareholder protection in takeovers: A UK perspective' (2011) *European Company and Financial Law Rev.* 145, at 163.
49 A.S. Ginevri, 'The rise of long-term minority shareholders' rights in publicly held corporations and its effect on corporate governance' (2011) 12 *European Business Organization Law Rev.* 587, at 602.
50 European Commission, op. cit., n. 15, p. 11.

keep solvent and therefore in need of liquidity, pushed by stock market price index performance measures, are likely to have little choice but to focus on short-term demands of short-term liquidity providers. Long-term corporation growth is often left to non-financial institutions since 'money growth' and not corporation growth seems the trend in financial institutions.

In addition, the problem is more complex than merely lack of shareholder engagement. In its 2010 report, the OECD found that in both widely-held companies and those with more concentrated ownership, shareholders were ineffective in monitoring the boards, 'neglecting the effect of excessive risk taking policies.'[51] The problem can be traced from the gap between the capital provider and corporation control, leading to a focus by shareholders on the stock market price index to measure board performance. This led to shareholders acquiescing in the practice of short-termism by directors seeking to meet the ostensible appetite of investors for higher and immediate returns. Should the law intervene to reverse this trend and foster a better monitoring and engagement shareholder culture?

On the need for better monitoring of corporate governance, the European Commission is of the view that regulatory authorities should not 'interfere with the content of the information disclosed or make business judgements on the solution chosen by the company.'[52] On the one hand, the law seems handicapped here. On the other, it should not seek to ensure that there are no corporate failures. In other words, the law should not, and cannot, insist on success.[53] Indeed, the OECD observes 'that effective risk management is not about eliminating risk-taking, which is a fundamental driving force in business and entrepreneurship' but, rather, about ensuring 'that risks are understood, managed and, when appropriate, communicated.'[54]

2. Dispersed shareholder structures in particular

For countries such as the United Kingdom and the United States, the further dispersion of shareholder ownership in most public companies[55] makes it difficult for shareholders to engage in corporate governance. In dispersed ownership companies, say where each shareholder holds 1 per cent of the shares, shareholders tend to have little economic incentive to engage in corporate governance, let alone seek to discipline directors. In such structures, shareholders do not have the time and the means to investigate directors' incompetence or excessive risk taking. If the shareholders have

---

51 OECD, 'Corporate Governance and the Financial Crisis: Conclusions and emerging good practices to enhance implementation of the principles' (2010) 24.
52 European Commission, op. cit., n. 15, p. 19.
53 S. Worthington, 'Shares and shareholders: property, power and entitlement (Part 1)' (2001) 22 *Company Lawyer* 258, at 259.
54 OECD, op. cit., n. 51, p. 13.
55 See, generally, F. Barca and M. Becht (eds.), *The Control of Corporate Europe* (2001).

shares in, say, 80 listed companies, holding 1 per cent shares in each, they are only concerned with the share value on the stock market, and if the other company's shares are not doing well, they tend to simply sell the shares and invest somewhere else.[56]

The disciplining of directors in dispersed ownership companies also tends to be left to the market forces – where the assumption is that competitiveness in the market will force management to converge on good and reasonable management, thereby increasing share value. The assumption here is that directors will very much avoid the lowering of share prices, as low share price on the market makes the company vulnerable to a hostile takeover bid, which, if successful, will usually result in the dismissal of the directors. The financial crisis has revealed weaknesses in these economic assumptions, as managing according to stock market prices seems to have increased the appetite for excessive risk taking.

Where, as a result of lack of shareholder engagement, directors take excessive risks, causing loss to shareholders, English company law usually does not provide remedies. In fact, in the context of crises, company law, especially takeover law, may worsen the problem. Company law's response to such problem has often been to give an exit strategy to an aggrieved shareholder – a mechanism of selling shares at a fair price.[57] The most commonly applied relief for aggrieved shareholders is for the court to grant an order that 'the petitioners' shares be purchased by the controllers or the company', which 'gives the petitioner an opportunity to exit from the company with the fair value of his or her investment'.[58] This exit strategy is strengthened by takeover law;[59] yet, the exit strategy in takeovers neither increases shareholder engagement nor disciplines directors, for 'while takeovers might serve an industrial restructuring purpose, they serve no function in disciplining management.'[60]

For years before the 2008 financial crisis, the markets have fostered an increase in short-term-focused investors, as these have contributed to much-needed liquidity. The problem is when those who manage companies fail to know where to draw the line between attracting liquidity and placing business on a sustainable platform. But what choice do managers have if

---

56 For empirical data on shareholder participation, see P. Santella et al., 'Legal Obstacles to Institutional Investor Activism in the EU and in the US' (2012) 23 *European Business Law Rev.* 257, at 262–3.

57 For example, a fair price following a successful petition under the unfair prejudice remedy, – formerly s. 210 CA 1948, then s. 459 CA 1985, and now s. 994 of the Companies Act 2006; see *O'Neill* v. *Phillips* [1999] 1 W.L.R. 1092 for application of this remedy.

58 Davies and Worthington, op. cit., n. 26, pp. 741–2. Such 'exit strategies' are less common in civil law countries, see Siems, op. cit., n. 23, pp. 205–8.

59 Part 28 of the Companies Act 2006.

60 A. Johnson, 'The European takeover directive: ruined by protectionism or respecting diversity?' (2004) 25 *Company Lawyer* 270, at 275.

even the traditionally long-term institutional investors give their mandates through market pressure for greater short-term returns? In dispersed ownership companies, the problem is worse: short-term investors tend to 'invest in thousands of companies, with small stakes in any individual company – it is impossible for any investor to truly understand all these investments.'[61] Accordingly, the focus tends to be on short-term gains without engagement. We therefore observe the well-known problem that for such shareholders 'exit' is just too easily available to make any attempt to exercise 'voice'[62] a worthwhile endeavour.

3. Institutional shareholders and engagement

The lack of shareholder engagement is exacerbated by the fact that today institutional investors often outsource their investment decisions to external asset managers.[63] These asset managers tend to focus on short-term gains based on the market price index, and are usually not interested in engagement with corporate governance. In the words of Jaap Winter, these asset managers, if 'pushed by regulation and codes that require or expect such engagement they will at best engage at what I call a compliance level: engaging because and to the extent they have to.'[64] Should the answer be more regulation? Or should investor culture change? To pursue the former is to seek paternalistically to protect investors, yet the latter is difficult to pursue by legal intervention. Still, there is need for a paradigm shift in investor cultures. Whether this should come via legal regulation or via self-regulation by the markets is the question. According to Winter:

> A key challenge of regulation, in general, but certainly in response to a crisis, is to distinguish which problems can be meaningfully addressed by new regulation and which problems cannot. A bigger challenge still is to act on this distinction and to have the courage not to regulate the latter problems but to seek different avenues of addressing them. Such avenues would typically involve challenging and exposing the world views, beliefs, myths and assumptions underlying the current ways of being and acting.[65]

Whether we seek new regulation to influence a paradigm shift, it seems that EU financial law has often not been helpful in increasing shareholder engagement. Pension and insurance companies have to invest in accordance with the 'prudent person' rule, and this entails assets being properly

---

61 J. Winter, 'The financial crisis: does good governance matter and how to achieve it?', DSF Policy Paper 14/2011 (2011) 7.

62 This refers to A.O. Hirschman, *Exit, Voice, and Loyalty* (1970). See, also, Kay Review, op. cit., n. 19, para. 2.2.

63 J. Winter, 'Shareholder Engagement and Stewardship: The Realities and Illusions of Institutional Share Ownership' (2011) 5, at <http://ssrn.com/abstract=1867564>.

64 Winter, op. cit., n. 61, p. 8.

65 id., p. 14.

diversified in such a way as to avoid excessive reliance on any particular undertakings and accumulations of risk in the portfolio as a whole.[66] Thus, the aim is to avert risk taking by encouraging diversification. However, the result of diversification of portfolio is 'an investment policy that is not focused on an actual understanding of individual companies, but on more or less following the market.'[67] This hardly encourages engagement.

The culture remains that most institutional shareholders are interested in returns on investment, which is monitored via the market share-price index, without need of engagement in the internal governance of the company. Meaningful shareholder engagement will require a shift in the investment culture. In the light of the 2008 financial crisis, investors may need to take John Maynard Keynes seriously:

> As time goes on I get more and more convinced that the right method in investment is to put fairly large sums into enterprises which one thinks one knows something about and in the management of which one thoroughly believes. It is a mistake to think that one limits one's risks by spreading too much between enterprises about which one knows little and has no reason for special confidence.[68]

Thus, there is need to revert to a culture that focuses on the long-term sustainability of companies rather than short-term value gains. Lessons could be learned from the traditional German corporate governance model, which is sustained historically by a notion of long-term commitment between the company and its various stakeholders: with its tenets of not focusing on making money in itself, but on product quality and innovation, it was able to evade price competition and sustain high-growth levels of investment.[69] But this model does not exist in its pure form any more. Especially in the financial sector, a number of global factors have altered the traditional German corporate governance model, making companies more susceptible to hostile takeovers and norms such as shareholder value.[70]

4. Sovereign wealth funds and shareholder activists

In addition, we need to consider the changing composition of investors. Brenda Hannigan argues that 'enthusiasm for shareholder engagement may

---

66 Article 18 of Directive 2003/41/EC on the activities and supervision of institutions for occupational retirement provision. Similarly, Article 132 of Directive 2009/138/EC on the taking-up and pursuit of the business of Insurance and Reinsurance ('Solvency II').

67 Winter, op. cit., n. 63, p. 6.

68 John Maynard Keynes (1883–1946), British economist, Letter to F.C. Scott (15 August 1934), quoted in J. Runde and S. Mizuhara (eds.), *The Philosophy of Keynes's Economics: Probability, Uncertainty and Convention* (2003) 154.

69 A. Dignam and M. Galanis, *The Globalization of Corporate Governance* (2009) 301–2.

70 id., pp. 391–2.

64

be misplaced or at least may be based on unrealistic expectations.'[71] The context of this caution relates well to the increasing Sovereign Wealth Funds (SWF) investors compared with declining domestic investors. A 2012 survey shows a decline of domestic investor shareholding with an increase of foreign investment between 1981 and 2012.[72] Insurance fund holdings declined from 20.5 per cent to 6.2 per cent and pension funds from 26.7 per cent to 4.7 per cent, with foreign holdings at 53.2 per cent in 2012.[73] SWF investments are usually treated with high levels of mistrust and suspicion, especially if these SWF are from government regimes and legal systems not based on democratic principles or not assuming fundamental market liberties.[74] Most of these SWFs are from emerging economies. The call for measures that would avoid potential negative consequences of investments by SWFs is heard louder and louder in the West.[75] Hannigan observes that encouraging engagement by those types of investors is more challenging, not least because they are less susceptible to domestic political pressures to engage.[76]

Beyond SWFs, there has been a growing literature on the possible detrimental effects of activist shareholders. Critics have said that the real problem is now that 'meddling and second-guessing from shareholders' makes it hard for managers to do their jobs effectively.[77] There may therefore be a need to 'protect the autonomy of management' in corporate governance.[78] Yet, one should also not exaggerate the risks of shareholder activism. Following Iris Chiu,[79] it seems plausible to distinguish: while there is no denying that some activist hedge funds may harm companies, other activist shareholders may have a more positive effect. Thus, for example, it

---

71 B. Hannigan, 'Board failures in the financial crisis: tinkering with codes and the need for wider corporate governance reforms: Part 2' (2012) *Company Lawyer* 35, at 36.

72 Office of National Statistics (ONS), *Ownership of UK Quoted Shares, 2012* (2013).

73 Note, though, the survey does not mention the percentage of Sovereign Wealth Funds accounted in the 53.2 per cent foreign shareholdings.

74 J.W.I. Jimenez and A.P. Urena, 'Sovereign wealth fund (SWF) global regulation and transparency: a preliminary private-investment law approach' (2010) 25 *J. of International Banking Law and Regulation* 441, at 446.

75 B. de Meester, 'International Legal Aspects of Sovereign Wealth Funds: Reconciling International Economic Law and the Law of State Immunities with a New Role of the State' (2009) 20 *European Business Law Rev.* 779, at 780.

76 Hannigan, op. cit., n. 71, p. 37.

77 J. Fox and J.W. Lorsch, 'What Good Are Shareholders? (2012) 90 (Jul/Aug) *Harvard Business Rev.* 48, at 50.

78 B. Segrestin and A. Hatchuel, 'Beyond Agency Theory, a Post-crisis View of Corporate Law' (2011) 22 *British J. of Management* 484.

79 I. H.-Y. Chiu, *The Foundations and Anatomy of Shareholder Activism* (2010). See, also, D. Katelouzou, 'Myths and Realities of Hedge Fund Activism: Some Empirical Evidence' (2013) 7 *Virginia Law & Business Rev.* 459 (empirical study not finding activist hedge funds being excessively short-termist).

65

is an open question whether activist shareholders should owe fiduciary duties to the company, as we would need more empirical evidence about the costs and benefits of such shareholder activism.

5. Where do we go from here?

In this section we have seen that the question of shareholder engagement and investor culture remains a challenge. In the United Kingdom, where shareholding in listed companies is mostly dispersed, the market does not encourage shareholder engagement in corporate governance. The structure and regulation of equity markets today overwhelmingly emphasize 'exit' over 'voice' and this has often led to shareholder engagement of a superficial character and low quality. But even with more concentrated shareholdings and stronger employee participation, as in Germany, global factors have long since changed investor culture, making engagement difficult. Thus, the suggested shift towards more companies with family and employee ownership[80] is unlikely to be a solution to all problems of corporate governance.

Yet, more generally, the financial crisis of 2008 may initiate a paradigm shift away from a short-term investment culture towards effective long-term investment and shareholder engagement. Legal reforms can well play a supporting role. These reforms may increase the protection of shareholders – while bearing in mind that just giving shareholders more powers would be unsatisfactory since shareholders too may abuse such an enhanced governance role.

To elaborate, it is suggested that the following measures can be useful tools to encourage long-term value creation. First, legal rules can explicitly reward long-term shareholders. A possible model is the provision of the French commercial code on 'loyalty dividends', namely, that the articles 'may allot an increase in dividends, with a ceiling of 10%, to any shareholder who can show a registered contribution of at least two years' duration.'[81] The EU Green Paper on Long-Term Financing also considers such incentive structures.[82]

Second, following a similar logic, the recent literature has suggested modifying the strength of voting rights according to the duration shares have been held,[83] or even to impose a minimum period in which shares cannot be

---

80 European Commission, op. cit., n. 16, p. 11. For the United Kingdom, see the Ownership Commission, *Plurality, Stewardship and Engagement* (2012), at <http://ownershipcomm.org/> and now the provision on 'employee shareholders' in s. 205A of the Employment Rights Act 1996, inserted by the Growth and Infrastructure Act 2013, c. 27.

81 Code de Commerce, article L232-14, as translated at <http://www.legifrance.gouv.fr/Traductions/en-English/Legifrance-translations>.

82 European Commission, op. cit., n. 46, p. 15.

83 C. Mayer, *Firm Commitment* (2013) 211–12. For previous suggestions by Lord Myners, see Chiu, op. cit., n. 79, p. 164. More generally on the trend away from the

sold.[84] The first of these suggestions could also be used to stimulate entrepreneurship, but this would be different for the second one: thus, it is also clear that encouraging long-term shareholder ownership is not, and should not be, the only aim that company law should pursue.

Third, beyond these direct tools, various other rules of company law play a role. For example, it is frequently suggested that remuneration structures should be designed to reward long-term performance, say, by way of distributing shares to directors that they have to hold until they retire from their post.[85] Another prominent example is disclosure and transparency: here it is increasingly understood that a balance has to be found since, on the one hand, corporate disclosure fosters accountability, but, on the other, excessive reporting requirements foster short-termism.[86]

SELF-REGULATION, NATIONAL, EUROPEAN OR INTERNATIONAL LAW

The previous section concluded with a number of suggestions on how to improve corporate governance. But if these are only taken up in one country, the apparent risk is that international investments would just move elsewhere. Thus, the question is how and by whom these and other regulatory responses can or should be implemented.

Self-regulation in British company law started in the early 1990s following a number of business scandals. Today corporate governance codes are common in many countries.[87] These codes usually follow the British model of the Combined Code in requiring companies to give a statement showing how far they comply with the code ('comply or explain'). Their potential advantages are said to lie in their liberality, flexibility, and effectiveness: if self-regulation works, there is no need to have recourse to the harsher and less flexible means of statute law. It may also be particularly effective regulation because corporate governance codes are usually developed by groups that have special professional and expert knowledge.[88]

'one-share-one-vote principle', see W.-G. Ringe, 'Deviations from Ownership-Control Proportionality – Economic Protectionism Revisited' in *Company Law and Economic Protectionism: New Challenges to European Integration*, eds. U. Bernitz and W.-G. Ringe (2010) 219–40.

84 S. Hockman, 'Can you legislate for responsible capitalism? Yes, here's how' *Guardian*, 2 October 2012, at <http://www.guardian.co.uk/law/2012/oct/02/legislate-responsible-capitalism-miliband>. Apparently, this suggestion goes beyond 'lock-up periods', common for the time immediately after IPOs.

85 BIS, op. cit., n. 19, p. 30.

86 See, for example, the debates preceding the 2013 revision of the EU Transparency Directive, at <http://ec.europa.eu/internal_market/securities/transparency/>.

87 See, for example, at <http://www.ecgi.org/codes/all_codes.php>.

88 See the summary of the discussion in Siems, op. cit., n. 23, pp. 387–90.

In the post-crisis world there are, however, also reasons to be cautious. Generally speaking, self-regulatory tools can be seen as a form of deregulation since companies are given more flexibility. Yet, a lesson to be drawn from the financial crisis is that just leaving everything to market forces may have devastating effects. More specifically, corporate governance codes are based on the idea that shareholders are able to assess properly whether and how companies comply with the codes. But, considering the crisis, this seems a bit naïve since shareholders did not stop excessive managerial risk taking. Moreover, self-regulation can lead to one-sided rules since short-term interests may take preference over the interests of long-term shareholder as well as employees, consumers, and the general public.

But it is also possible that self-regulation can specifically target the lack of responsible shareholder engagement. In the United Kingdom, the Walker Review observed that in the run-up to the financial crisis, board and director shortcomings would have been tackled more effectively had there been more vigorous scrutiny and engagement by major investors acting as owners.[89] This led to the Stewardship Code,[90] which – like the Combined Code – is voluntary, but asset managers are required to report whether or not they apply it. One of its core principles is that institutional investors should monitor their investee companies. In the responses to the EU Green Paper on corporate governance, some suggest that this model may be extended to the entire EU.[91] Given the internationalization of institutional investments, it seems logical to have a code that is not limited to a particular country. Yet, it may also be worth waiting for empirical evidence showing whether the Stewardship Code has a positive effect in practice, not only for investors but also in terms of public accountability.[92]

The general question of whether we need more European harmonization in shareholder law has to start with an assessment of the status quo. The Shareholder Rights Directive[93] has only harmonized some aspects of the

---

89 D. Walker, *A review of corporate governance in UK banks and other financial industry entities – Final recommendations* (2009) para. 5.11 (The Walker Review).
90 Financial Reporting Council (FRC), 'The UK Stewardship Code', revised in 2012, at <http://www.frc.org.uk/Our-Work/Codes-Standards/Corporate-governance/UK-Stewardship-Code.aspx>.
91 See European Commission, 'Feedback Statement – Summary of Responses to the Commission Green Paper on the EU Corporate Governance Framework', Brussels, 15 November 2011, D (2011) 12. European Commission, op. cit., n. 16, p. 8 also refers to the UK Stewardship Code.
92 See I. H.-Y. Chiu, 'Stewardship as a Force for Governance: Critically Assessing the Aspirations and Weaknesses of the UK Stewardship Code' (2012) 9 *European Company Law* 5 (suggesting that these latter aspects should also be considered). On the practical application of the code, see, also, Institute of Chartered Secretaries and Administrators, 'Enhancing Stewardship Dialogue' (2013), at <https://www.icsaglobal.com/assets/files/pdfs/guidance/Enhancing_stewardship_dialogue/icsastewardshipreport.pdf>.
93 Directive 2007/36/EC, op. cit., n. 5.

law, and even there, member states have retained a significant degree of discretion. Other elements of EU company law only indirectly relate to shareholder protection, for instance, if one assumes that rules on capital maintenance[94] may not only serve the interests of creditors but also those of minority shareholders. More extensive harmonization can be found in EU securities regulation, for instance, on prospectuses, transparency, market abuse, and investment services.[95] But these rules are not specifically aimed at the protection of shareholders, since they typically also protect other investors, such as bondholders, or deal with the functioning of financial markets more generally.[96]

Should the EU get more closely involved in the harmonization of core company law, for instance, providing uniform rights to minority share-holders throughout the EU?[97] In general, uniform laws have a number of benefits, such as creating a 'level playing field', reducing transaction costs, and providing legal certainty for cross-border businesses.[98] However, it can also be questioned whether such harmonization is necessary – or even useful. As one of us has shown, in company law legal systems come closer together even without formal harmonization;[99] and as far as such convergence has its limits, it can actually be seen as advantageous, for instance, enabling some experimentation and accommodating different shareholder ownership structures.[100]

But when we turn to more specific measures, the assessment may be more positive. The EU Green Paper asks whether the EU should facilitate share-holder cooperation, for instance, by way of web-based platforms and networks.[101] This is directly relevant in the current context. In the previous

---

94 Directive 2012/30/EU of the European Parliament and of the Council of 25 October 2012 on coordination of safeguards which, for the protection of the interests of members and others, are required by Member States of companies within the meaning of the second paragraph of Article 54 of the Treaty on the Functioning of the European Union, in respect of the formation of public limited liability companies and the maintenance and alteration of their capital, with a view to making such safeguards equivalent.

95 References at <http://ec.europa.eu/internal_market/securities/index_en.htm>.

96 An exception is Transparency Directive 2004/109/EC, op. cit., n. 6, art. 17 (on exercising shareholder rights by proxy and information provided to shareholders in the run-up to the general meeting).

97 See European Commission, op. cit., n. 15, p. 17.

98 See the summary in Siems, op. cit., n. 23, pp. 373–4. In particular, this may be needed for cross-border voting rights: see European Company Law Experts, 'Response to the European Commission's Consultation on the Future of European Company Law' (2012) 9–10, at <http://ssrn.com/abstract=2075034>.

99 Siems, id.

100 See, also, M. Siems, 'The Case Against Harmonisation of Shareholder Rights' (2005) 6 *European Business Organization Law Rev.* 539.

101 See European Commission, op. cit., n. 91, p. 14. See, also, the innovative proposal by E. Micheler, 'Facilitating Investor Engagement and Stewardship' (2013) 14 *European Business Organization Law Rev.* 29.

sections we explained that shareholders are often not interested in the long-term development of their company since they feel that their individual votes would not make a difference. Thus, measures that can address this collective action problem would be useful, though they may not necessarily require formal EU legislation.

Another lesson from the crisis is that relying on national or regional responses is not sufficient. As stated by the European Commission: 'the crisis is global and calls for an international response.'[102] To start with, this requires taking stock of the extent to which shareholder protection and corporate governance have been addressed at the international level. The main source is the OECD Principles of Corporate Governance, which provides, for instance, minimum standards on shareholder rights and equal treatment of shareholders.[103] Yet, these principles are drafted in very general terms, mainly confirming what most developed countries already provide in their company laws.[104] Moreover, the OECD Principles are not formally binding. The same is the case for other international documents related to corporate governance, such as the OECD Guidelines for Multinational Enterprises[105] and the various recommendations by the International Organization of Securities Commissions (IOSCO).[106]

Despite the crisis, it cannot be expected that the international community will be able to agree on a common approach to shareholder protection. Yet, a number of current initiatives aim to provide improved forms of regulation and supervision of international financial institutions and markets.[107] Concerns about financial stability have been on the agenda of the recent G20 summits in London, Pittsburgh, Toronto, and Seoul. For example, at the London summit it was agreed to establish a Financial Stability Board (FSB) in order to monitor the global financial system. With respect to financial institutions, reference needs to be made to the 'Basel III' framework of the Basel Committee on Banking Supervision (BCBS) which raises the capital adequacy requirements on banks. In addition, the BCBS has adopted

---

102 European Commission, 'Restoring the Health and Stability of the EU Financial Sector' (2012) 6, at <http://ec.europa.eu/internal_market/smact/docs/20120206_restoring_health_en.pdf>.

103 OECD, *OECD Principles of Corporate Governance* (2004), at <http://www.oecd.org/dataoecd/32/18/31557724.pdf>.

104 But see, also, M. Siems and O. Alvarez-Macotela, 'The OECD Principles of Corporate Governance in Emerging Markets: A Successful Example of Networked Governance?' in *Networked Governance, Transnational Business and the Law*, eds. M. Fenwick et al. (2014).

105 OECD, *OECD Guidelines for Multinational Enterprises* (2011 edn.), at <http://www.oecd.org/daf/inv/mne/48004323.pdf >.

106 See <http://www.iosco.org/>.

107 See, for example, the discussion in C.R. Kelly and C. Sungjoon, 'Promises and Perils of New Global Governance: A Case of the G20' (2012) 12 *Chicago J. of International Law* 491.

principles for enhancing corporate governance, for instance, specifying obligations for risk management and internal control.[108]

These initiatives show that, as far as corporate governance is concerned, it is specifically the financial sector that may need to be addressed. As Jaap Winter explains, the corporate culture of this sector is precisely what contributed to the crisis:

> A corporate culture of aggressive pursuit of profits with a win-at-all-cost mentality is prone to higher risk-taking and to being arrogant about the risks that are being run. The financial industry seems to have been captured by this culture more than any other business sector, fuelled by substantial and in a number of cases excessive personal gains that could be made by the key players in the industry.[109]

This line of reasoning is also reflected in statements of the EU Green Paper on corporate governance[110] which builds on another Green Paper which explicitly dealt with corporate governance in financial institutions.[111] In the 'Basel' and EU documents on the corporate governance of financial institutions, the core emphasis is not on strengthening shareholder rights. Thus, as is the position in this article, while shareholders play a role, increasing shareholder protection is not seen as a panacea to prevent another crisis.

CONCLUSION

The global financial crisis that started in 2008 has stimulated the debate on corporate governance and shareholder protection. This article has critically examined the discussion about the financial crisis, shareholder protection, and law reform. We started with the question of *what* caused the financial crisis, the answer being that it is not clear that corporate governance was one of the key determinants. This was followed by the question of *whether* post-crisis shareholder empowerment should be on the agenda; again, we could only give a cautiously positive reply. Then, we analysed *how* investor cultures shape the engagement of shareholders. Drawing lessons from the crisis, we took the view that one should encourage shareholder engagement by responsible long-term investors, and we provided specific examples on how this might be achieved. Finally, we discussed *who* should implement such a position. We gave the pragmatic response that a mix of self-

---

108 BCBS, 'Principles for enhancing corporate governance' (2010), at <http://www.bis.org/publ/bcbs176.htm>.
109 Winter, op. cit., n. 61, p. 5.
110 For example, European Commission, op. cit., n. 15, pp. 3, 10–11 (calling financial institutions 'a special case').
111 European Commission, 'Green Paper on Corporate Governance in Financial Institutions and Remuneration Policies' (COM(2010) 284).

regulation, national legislation, and EU and international hard and soft law may be a feasible way forward.

Thus, to address the question posed in the title of this article, simply telling the EU to improve shareholder protection would not be a satisfactory response. First, EU legislation is not necessarily the best tool: changing investor cultures is not primarily a legal question; self-regulation may play some role; and international initiatives may be more relevant than a regional response. Second, we do not take the view that any increase in shareholder rights is the way forward. The lesson learned is that the law should encourage shareholder engagement by responsible long-term investors, thus avoiding excessive risk taking and short-termism.

The EU Green Paper indicated that 'taking into account the diversity of situations, it does not seem possible to propose a "one-size-fits-all" risk-management model for all types of companies.'[112] This is a statement we also endorse. Since the behaviour of financial institutions lies at the heart of the financial crisis, their corporate governance has to receive special attention, for instance, requiring an enhanced involvement of shareholders, financial supervisors, and external auditors.[113] In particular, in regard to financial institutions, where taxpayers may be called upon to bail out financial institution, and to avoid systemic failures, a robust regulatory approach may be justified. Thus, while these details of bank governance and bail-outs go beyond the scope of the current article, they confirm our position that there are no easy answers on how we can prevent a repeat of recent events.

112 European Commission, op. cit., n. 15, p. 10.
113 European Commission, op. cit., n. 111. Specifically on shareholder rights/power see, for example, K. Alexander, 'Balancing prudential regulation and shareholder rights' (2009) 1 *J. of Corporate Law Studies* 61; V. Babis, 'The impact of bank crisis prevention, recovery and resolution on shareholder rights' (2012) 6 *Law and Financial Markets Rev.* 387; D. Ferreira et al., 'Shareholder Empowerment and Bank Bailouts', ECGI Finance Working Paper no. 345/2013 (2013), at <http://ssrn.com/abstract=2170392>.

72

JOURNAL OF LAW AND SOCIETY
VOLUME 41, NUMBER 1, MARCH 2014
ISSN: 0263-323X, pp. 73–94

Post-crisis Corporate Governance and Labour Relations in the EU (and Beyond)

CHARLOTTE VILLIERS*

This article attempts to explain how corporate governance and macroeconomic policies have impacted on the role of workers and their representatives in the corporate environment and to consider how this has affected their capacity to protect themselves in the context of the financial crisis. It also considers the strategies they might adopt to strengthen their position in the future. It argues for the need to reposition labour law in the legal hierarchy as a first condition but also, and more importantly, that for democratic reasons, trade unions need to work collectively with other civil society and protest movements to hold corporations, national governments, and European institutions to account and, internally, to develop the class consciousness of old and new members.

INTRODUCTION

In country after country, workers are on the back foot, facing austerity measures imposed by governments that have racked up massive public debt in response to the crisis of private debt just a short time earlier.

Despite the self evident failure of neoliberalism, 'the right wing narrative has dominated'. And unions are finding it hard to be heard, as social dialogue is under pressure, while non-governmental organisations are heard in European forums, sometimes ahead of the unions.[1]

This gloomy picture presented by Le Queux and Peetz indicates bleak prospects for labour relations in the post-crisis corporate governance trajectory. My objective in this article is to explain how corporate governance and

* University of Bristol Law School, Wills Memorial Building, Queens Road, Bristol BS8 1RJ, England
C.Villiers@bristol.ac.uk

---

1 S. Le Queux and D. Peetz, 'Between "Too Big to Fail" and "Too Small to Matter": The Borderless Financial Crisis and Unions' (2013) 34 *International J. of Manpower* 198.

macro-economic policies have impacted on the role of workers and their representatives in the corporate environment and to consider how this has affected their capacity to protect themselves in the context of the financial crisis. Strategies they might adopt to strengthen their position in the future are also considered. In part 1, I observe the problems in the corporate governance system and their part in the financial crisis. Part 2 shows how these problems, together with macro-economic policies, have impacted on working conditions and worker involvement, and how the crisis itself has further affected workers and their representatives across the EU. Part 3 explains the political and economic relevance of large corporations and seeks to show why worker involvement is therefore also politically necessary. In part 4, I outline the current obstacles to worker participation. Part 5 argues for the need to reposition labour law in the legal hierarchy as a first condition but also, and more importantly, that for democratic reasons, trade unions need to work collectively with other civil society and protest movements to hold corporations, national governments, and European institutions to account and, internally, to develop the class consciousness of old and new members. The crisis, according to Froud et al., opened 'a window of opportunity for increased democratic control over markets'.[2] At this point, in the aftermath of the crisis, such democracy in the market place has not been achieved. Trade unions must not admit defeat. With other movements, they have the capacity to democratize working-class organizations and to achieve a more egalitarian society.[3]

PROBLEMS IN THE CORPORATE GOVERNANCE SYSTEM

The global and the Eurozone financial crises had many causal factors.[4] Corporate governance cannot be blamed wholly for the crisis, but it has played a part. There remain significant structural differences between the Anglo-American model and some continental European models, not least that between the co-determination boardroom structure found in Germany which contrasts with the single-tier structure found in countries within the Anglo-American model. Despite these continuing variations, a general trend has emerged which demonstrates the increasing significance of the shareholders. This trend has led to claims that the Anglo-American and

2 J. Froud et al., 'Wasting a Crisis? Democracy and Markets in Britain after 2007' (2010) *Political Q.* 25, at 25.
3 S. Ross, 'Social Unionism and Membership participation: What Role for Union Democracy?' (2008) 81 *Studies in Political Economy* 129, at 153.
4 See, for example, J. Bellamy Foster and F. Magdoff, *The Great Financial Crisis: Causes and Consequences* (2009); J. Crotty, 'Structural causes of the global financial crisis: a critical assessment of the "new financial architecture" ' (2009) 33 *Cambridge J. of Economics* 563; G. Kirkpatrick, *The Corporate Governance Lessons from the Financial Crisis* (2009).

74

European models of corporate governance are converging, with the outcome that shareholders have become more powerful in companies on both sides of the Atlantic.[5] As is observed by Vitols, 'the clear primary responsibility of managers hired to run the firm is to the shareholders, and to the mandate of increasing the value of the firm',[6] and this corporate governance model is 'now the hegemonic model'.[7] This development has partly resulted from the influence of the law and economics theories of the firm, with agency theory being especially prevalent.[8] That influence has been widespread and has travelled from the United States to Europe and elsewhere. Agency theory gives prominence to shareholder interests as 'best suited to make decisions about corporate strategy'.[9] Corporate governance has thus evolved, in the United States and in Europe, to focus on the relationship between shareholders and managers. Shareholders are regarded as the only actor bearing risks and are therefore the most representative of a company's interests. This requires a company's management, as agent, to seek to satisfy the interests of the shareholders as principal. This leads to structures and corporate governance regulation based on disclosure to shareholders, who are given voting rights, and to alignment of management and shareholder interests through appointment of independent directors and construction of remuneration packages and incentives connected to share price.

An alternative theory that has been developed in the literature is the stakeholder approach which holds that the company's management should take into account the interests of those 'who can affect or are affected by the achievement of the organization's objectives'.[10] The corporate governance arrangements should accommodate the interests of other internal and external actors such as employees, suppliers, customers, local community or

---

5 H. Hansmann and R. Kraakman. 'The End of History for Corporate Law' (2000–2001) 89 *Georgetown Law J.* 439. Compare P.A. Hall and D.W. Soskice (eds.), *Varieties of capitalism: The institutional foundations of comparative advantage* (2001).

6 S. Vitols, 'The evolving European system of corporate governance: implications for worker involvement' (2008) 14 *Transfer: European Rev. of Labour and Research* 27, at 29.

7 id.

8 The seminal works here are M.C. Jensen and W.H. Meckling, 'Theory of the Firm: Managerial Behavior, Agency Costs and Ownership Structure' (1976) 3 *J. of Financial Economics* 305; M.C. Jensen, *A Theory of the Firm: Governance, Residual Claims and Organizational Forms* (2000); E.F. Fama and M.C. Jensen, 'Separation of Ownership and Control' (1983) 26 *J. of Law and Economics* 301.

9 L. Horn, 'Corporate Governance in Crisis? The Politics of EU Corporate Governance Regulation' (2012) 18 *European Law J.* 83, at 86.

10 See, for example, R.E. Freeman, *Strategic Management: A Stakeholder Approach* (1984); W.M. Evan and R.E. Freeman, 'A Stakeholder Theory of the Modern Corporation: Kantian Capitalism' in *Ethical Theory and Business*, eds. T. Beauchamp and N. Bowie (1988) 75; T. Donaldson and L.E. Preston, 'The Stakeholder Theory of the Corporation: Concepts, Evidence, and Implications' (1995) 20 *Academy of Management Rev.* 65.

75

society at large.[11] The development of corporate social responsibility has accompanied the corporate governance agenda and has made some room for the stakeholder view to be acknowledged but this has also coincided with a pursuit of market liberalization which has weakened the other stakeholders rather than strengthened their position.[12] Horn remarks on the fact that at European level, developments in company law and corporate governance reveal a shift from industrial democracy to shareholder democracy and a shift from harmonization to marketization. Crucially, corporate governance has been incorporated into a framework for financial market integration and capital market liberalization, and is seen in a narrower sense, understood as a principal-agent relationship 'with the share price as prime mechanism to align shareholder and manager interests'.[13]

Consequently, at European level, it is possible to observe an increasing focus on the rights and interests of shareholders,[14] and a lighter-touch regulatory approach that responds to the demands of liberalized capital markets.[15] Thus, corporate governance codes have widely adopted the comply-or-explain approach developed in the United Kingdom corporate governance system, and they emphasize the manager-shareholder relationship, shareholder democracy, and performance-based pay with performance measured by share value.[16] According to Galanis:

> the 'financialization' of the economy, as a structural development that emphasizes the interests of the financial sector, has increased shareholder power so that profitability problems cannot be accommodated by flexibility in financial claims.[17]

Europe appears to 'remain firmly on track of a marketization of corporate control'.[18]

Yet it is this shareholder-oriented model of corporate governance that has been implicated in the financial crisis, not surprisingly, given its role in the implementation of neoliberalism, efficient capital market theories, financialization, and shareholder profit maximization. The de Larosière

---

11 A. Conchon, 'Employee representation in corporate governance: part of the economic or the social sphere?', ETUI Working Paper 2011.08 (2011) 13.

12 See fn. 42 below and surrounding text on p. 79, and further at p. 86.

13 Horn, op. cit, n. 9, pp. 92–7.

14 See, for example, European Commission, 'Modernising Company Law and Enhancing Corporate Governance in the European Union – A Plan to Move Forward' (COM(2003) 284, May 2003).

15 See, for example, European Corporate Governance Forum Annual Report 2011, at <http://ec.europa.eu/internal_market/company/docs/ecgforum/ecgf-annual-report-2011_en.pdf>.

16 For access to corporate governance codes around the world, see European Corporate Governance Institute, Index of Codes, available at <http://www.ecgi.org/codes/all_codes.php>.

17 M. Galanis, 'The Impact of EMU on Corporate Governance: Bargaining in Austerity' (2013) 33 Oxford J. of Legal Studies 475, at 494.

18 Horn, op. cit., n. 9, p. 107.

76

Report of 2009 said that corporate governance was one of the most important failures behind the present financial crisis[19] and the OECD Report in the same year stated that the financial crisis 'can be to an important extent attributed to failures and weaknesses in corporate governance arrangements.'[20] The OECD observed financial sector remuneration that seemed little related to company performance, risk management systems that did not consider the firm as a whole and the risk inherent in compensation schemes, and boards that were in a number of cases unaware of the peril faced by their company until too late. Moreover, shareholders as a whole appeared to be subject to similar short-term incentives as traders and managers (that is, their interests were temporarily aligned) and were therefore not effective in the oversight of boards.[21] Further problems included board failure on strategy and oversight; misaligned or perverse incentives; empire building; conflicts of interest; weaknesses in internal controls; incompetence and fraud.[22]

Jaap Winter identified problems and failures for each of the three key players in corporate governance: the executives, non-executives, and shareholders.[23] For executives the problems appear to have been twofold. First, risk management of financial institutions failed dramatically, partly because financial institutions relied too heavily on quantitative risk models, which typically use historical data, ignoring the actual behaviour of market players.[24] Individual institutions might not have been sensitive to the systemic risk caused by the multitude of players in highly interwoven markets.[25] The second problem relating to executives is how they are paid. Performance-based pay and the system of target setting and measuring gives way to cheating in order to ensure, first, that targets are relatively easy to meet and, second, that targets are indeed met, even if the ultimate cost to the company is huge, or are seen to be met while they are not.[26] Winter remarks that substantial performance-based pay brings out the worst in us. More than anywhere, this has happened in the financial industry, with a singular focus on immediate personal financial gain, regardless of the risks to the institution, let alone to customers, other outsiders, and society at large.[27]

19 J. de Larosière (chair), *Report of the High-level Group on Financial Supervision in the EU* (2009) (de Larosière Report) 10.
20 OECD, *Corporate Governance and the Financial Crisis: Key Findings and Main Messages* (2009) 2.
21 id., p. 12.
22 M. Becht, 'Corporate Governance and the Credit Crisis' in *Macroeconomic Stability and Financial Regulation: Key Issues for the G20*, eds. M. Dewatripont, X. Freixas, and R. Portes (2009) 165.
23 J. Winter, 'The Financial Crisis: Does Good Corporate Governance Matter and How to Achieve It?' (2011) DSF Policy Paper no. 14, 5–8, at <http://ssrn.com/abstract=1972057>.
24 id., p. 5.
25 id.
26 id.
27 id., p. 6.

With regard to independent directors, Winter suggests that they had no significant and meaningful contribution to the core business strategy, and risk appetite and management of the banks. Not only do they frequently lack expertise but also they often resort to box ticking without really being involved or understanding the true nature of the company's business, its prospects and challenges.[28]

Shareholders are criticized for being too focused on short-term proceeds, and for having been insufficiently engaged in the governance of financial institutions to contribute to the disciplining of management.[29]

THE IMPACT ON WORKERS AND THEIR REPRESENTATIVES

During the earlier period of company law development at European level there were fierce debates about the role of workers in corporate structures. I have discussed elsewhere the history of European company law and the place of those debates in the shaping of the company law system we now have.[30] I argued that the issue of workers' participation in company board-rooms represented a perceived challenge to the power structures then in place, though it has since been argued that industrial democracy did not entail a fundamental change of control within the corporation, but would, rather, be a way of alleviating the antagonism between capital and labour by steadily integrating labour into the social relations of production organized and constituted by capital.[31] In order for progress to be made and for the company law programme to move forward, compromises became necessary, with worker involvement issues having to be relegated as matters of social legislation and policy.[32] The narrowing of the perception of corporate governance, in which the principal-agent relationship came to dominate the agenda, and the objective of regulation coming to focus on support for efficient capital markets, had the effect of workers' rights being 'consigned to social policies'[33] and the increasing integration of capital markets became 'concomitant to an increasing fragmentation of workers' rights at the European level.'[34] Since workers do not have a direct stake in capital market laws they are not recognized as directly relevant for regulatory debates.[35] Thus workers and their representatives were kept outside the crucial

---

28 id., pp. 6–7. A problem long-recognized in the United Kingdom: see, for example, D. Higgs, *Review of the role and effectiveness of non-executive directors* (2003).
29 Winter, op. cit., n. 23, pp. 7–8; and de Larosière Report, op. cit., n. 19.
30 C. Villiers, *European Company Law – Towards Democracy?* (2008).
31 Horn, op. cit., n. 9, p. 99.
32 Villiers, op. cit., n. 30.
33 Horn, op. cit., n. 9, p. 94.
34 id., p. 101.
35 id., p. 92.

corporate strategic decision-making arena.[36] Boardroom participation eventually became a matter for national political decision and remains so, having more or less been dropped from the corporate law or governance debates.[37] The Reflection Group on the Future of EU Company Law treated boardroom worker participation in this way in its 2011 Report, stating that 'codetermination on the board level is basically an issue of a consciously taken *political choice* which must be respected',[38] and asserts that:

> the appropriate attitude for the EU legislator is therefore (a) not to ask Member States which have not considered such a system or have deliberately decided against it to introduce it; (b) not to ask Member States to restrict or cut down on the extent or form of the codetermination chosen by them.[39]

Another commentator, Professor Dr Martin Henssler, adopted a similar approach at the conference held in Brussels in May 2011, following the Report's publication. Henssler stated that 'the European Union should not concentrate its efforts on reaching this unattainable goal. Legislation on workers' participation should instead remain the domain of the member states.'[40] Nevertheless, the existence of European legislation such as the European Works Councils Directive[41] perhaps will go some way to maintaining a place on the policy agenda for workers' participation in Europe.

The fact that worker involvement appears to have dropped off the corporate governance agenda does not mean that workers are irrelevant, nor that corporate governance is not important for workers. Indeed, as corporate governance succumbed to the neoliberal agenda and became financialized and globalized, this had a dramatic impact on labour. This globalization:

> allowed maximum freedom in the flow of capital goods, but imposed restrictions on the ability of civil society, particularly labour, to respond effectively and constrain the consequences of these renewed freedoms of capital.[42]

---

36 Conchon, op. cit., n. 11.
37 The European Commission, *Report of the Reflection Group On the Future of EU Company Law* (2011) (Reflection Group Report) devotes just over one page in an 80-page document. No mention is made of the subject in the paper published by the International Finance Corporation, *The EU Approach to Corporate Governance – Essentials and Recent Developments* (2008).
38 Reflection Group Report, id., p. 53.
39 id.
40 M. Henssler, 'Workers' Participation', paper for panel discussion at conference on 'European Company Law: the Way Forward' (2011) 2, at <http://ec.europa.eu/internal_market/company/docs/modern/conference201105/henssler_en.pdf>.
41 European Works Councils Directive (94/45/EC) and recast Directive 2009/38/EC: Directive 2009/38/EC of the European Parliament and of the Council of 6 May 2009 on the establishment of a European Works Council or a procedure in Community-scale undertakings and Community-scale groups of undertakings for the purposes of informing and consulting employees (Recast) [2009] OJ L122/ 28.
42 Le Queux and Peetz, op. cit., n. 1.

Thomas Kochan noted in 2008 that with the expansion of capital markets, shareholder concerns drive executive decision making and compensation arrangements, as fluctuating stock markets have become a source of public anxiety as are financial scandals.[43] Galanis observes that the rising power of the financial sector brought with it changes in management incentives and an alliance between managers and investors, with the consequence of neutralizing the role of the corporation as a bargaining party and imposing financial interests upon corporate governance as a whole.[44] Financialization has brought with it rising income inequality, greater employment risk, and a shift from employers to employees of responsibility for occupational pensions. Integration into global markets has led to intensified competition, and firms cutting labour costs which also impose downward pressure on wages and working conditions. This is reinforced by macroeconomic policy arrangements concerned with keeping low inflation[45] and competitive corporatism, that affects the power balance between the parties involved in the bargaining game.[46] Such policies 'affect unemployment levels and thus determine the power balance between labour and the corporation as an employer'.[47] Competitive corporatism leads to a 'downward spiral in wage setting' and corporate governance becomes a 'channel for a redistribution of income from labour to the financial sector.'[48] Emphasis on shareholder wealth has resulted in dispersed organizational structures that outsource and have intellectual property at the centre, requiring fewer employees and sending production overseas.[49] In addition, new technologies increased capital mobility, and more flexible work processes have given to employers more options on where and how to organize work and therefore gives them greater bargaining power.[50]

These conditions have resulted in strategies that include low wages and high unemployment rates,[51] downsizing, outsourcing, off-shoring, and close-ended contracts with limited protections. Downsizing is often a first, rather than a last, resort. Work becomes fragmented, dispersed over a variety of places and territories with a variety of working conditions.[52] Coordinated

---

43 T. Kochan, 'Finance and Labor: Perspectives on Risk, Inequality, and Democracy' (2008–9) 30 *Comparative Labor Law and Policy* 17.
44 Galanis, op. cit., n. 17, p. 495.
45 J. Madrick, 'The Deliberate Low-Wage, High-Insecurity Economic Model' (2012) 39 *Work and Occupations* 321, especially at 325–6.
46 Galanis, op. cit., n. 17, p. 499.
47 id.
48 id.
49 See G.F. Davis and J A. Cobb, 'Corporations and economic inequality around the world: The paradox of hierarchy' (2010) 30 *Research in Organizational Behaviour* 35.
50 S. Hayter et al., 'Review Essay: Collective Bargaining for the 21st Century' (2011) 53 *J. of Industrial Relations* 225, at 226.
51 Madrick, op. cit., n. 45.
52 M. Pedaci, 'The Flexibility Trap: Temporary Jobs and Precarity as a Disciplinary Mechanism' (2010) 13 *Working USA: J. of Labour and Society* 245.

market economies have experienced reduced working hours, while liberal market economies have experienced wage restraint,[53] and Mediterranean economies have more precarious employment and high levels of unemployment.[54] The young and low-skilled workers have suffered most and temporary workers and fixed-term contract workers have been most severely affected by redundancies in countries such as the United Kingdom and Spain.[55] Redundancy procedures and requirements have been simplified in many countries.

Such job insecurity can provide a form of 'disciplinary training'.[56] The result is a more compliant workforce that is more adaptable, willing to accept declining terms and conditions, work disproportionate hours, meeting targets, complying with reorganization, and playing down participation in trade union organizations and collective actions. These working conditions have been 'accompanied by the deregulation of labour markets and a rollback in policy support for collective bargaining institutions.'[57] Not least, this trend has been given impetus in the infamous quartet of ECJ judgments relating to the application of the Posted Workers Directive.[58] The Viking/ Laval/Rüffert/Luxembourg cases[59] have arguably confirmed that market freedoms come before fundamental rights to collective bargaining and action in the hierarchy of norms within the EU legal framework, the collective bargaining and action rights being regarded as potential restrictions on the economic freedoms.

The crisis itself has had serious repercussions for society and employees and welfare systems. The Eurozone has become deeply unstable and uncertain. Severe austerity plans have been put in place across Europe.[60] The response of the European Commission to the crisis has been to extend further its flexibility agenda. In 2010 the Commission stated in a Communication:

---

53 Note, for example, Institute of Fiscal Studies research highlighting wage freezes and cuts: P. Johnson, 'This Time Is Different: The Macroeconomic Consequences of the Great Recession' (2013) 34 *Fiscal Studies* 139.

54 See M. Lallement, 'Europe and the economic crisis: forms of labour market adjustment and varieties of capitalism' (2011) 25 *Work Employment and Society* 627.

55 J. Gennard, 'The Financial Crisis and Employee Relations' (2009) 31 *Employee Relations* 451.

56 Pedaci, op. cit., n. 52, referring to the work of Michel Foucault, especially, *Surveiller et punir* (1975).

57 Hayter et al., op. cit., n. 50, p. 226.

58 Directive 96/71/EC of the European Parliament and of the Council of 16 December 1996 concerning the posting of workers in the framework of the provision of services, [1997] OJ L18/1.

59 See C-438/05 *The International Transport Workers' Federation and The Finnish Seamen's Union* [2007] ECR I-10779; C-341/05 *Laval un Partneri* [2007] ECR I-11767; C-346/06 *Rüffert* [2008] ECR I-1989; C-319/06 *Commission vs Luxembourg* [2008] ECR I-4323.

60 Galanis, op. cit., n. 17.

81

flexicurity policies are the best instrument to modernise labour markets: they must be revisited and adapted to the post-crisis context, in order to accelerate the pace of reform, reduce labour market segmentation, support gender equality and make transitions pay.[61]

Even recognizing the different experiences arising as a result of the varieties of capitalism, overall the position of workers and their representatives has been weakened. In reality the labour reforms implemented by many member states generally have loosened minimum standards and emphasized the use of soft law rather than hard law resulting in a large-scale deregulation of labour law across Europe. The ETUI points to the 'lack of democratic foundations underlying the reforms and their negative impact on fundamental social rights and workers' protection.'[62] The general result is that the reforms, including measures affecting social dialogue and collective bargaining, 'undermine the protective role of both individual and collective labour law, thus putting workers in a more precarious and unprotected situation both in general and in the workplace.'[63] With regard to industrial relations and collective bargaining systems, the main trend has been to decentralize,[64] shifting from national and sector levels to company level and there is evidence of allowing lower-level bargaining outcomes to deviate from and undermine the protection provided by legislation or higher-level collective agreements.[65] Some member states have introduced possibilities for non-trade-union representatives to step into the roles of the trade unions, and alternative dispute resolution mechanisms have been introduced with reduction of access to tribunals.

THE CONTINUED POLITICAL IMPORTANCE OF COMPANIES AND THE DEMOCRATIC RELEVANCE OF WORKERS AND THEIR REPRESENTATIVES

The above narrative supports the view that capital has been resilient in the global financial crisis. Consequently, 'the most powerful elements of financial capital maintained and strengthened their position, and the concentration of ownership of [US] corporations in the hands of a small number of financiers has increased.'[66] Despite being implicated in the financial crisis, companies are still very important. They are a mainstay of the economy and

---

61 European Commission, Communication on 'An Agenda for new skills and jobs: A European contribution towards full employment' (COM(2010) 682 final) 2.

62 S. Clauwaert and I. Schomann, 'The crisis and national labour law reforms: a mapping exercise', ETUI Working Paper 2012.04 (2012) 7.

63 id., p. 8.

64 See, also, V. Glassner et al., 'Collective bargaining in a time of crisis: developments in the private sector in Europe' (2011) 17 *Transfer* 303.

65 See, also, Gennard, op. cit., n. 55.

66 Le Queux and Peetz, op. cit., n. 1.

82

employment. As Crouch has outlined, large companies are key actors in maintaining overall stability. Their significance has been increased as a result of neoliberal policies that have led to greater involvement of corporations in public sector activities and through privatization and marketization.[67]

Indeed, the response to the financial crisis across Europe has been a massive austerity programme. This has been presented as an economic necessity focused not on the high-risk strategies of banks, but on the 'unwieldy and expensive welfare state and public sector'.[68] The austerity programme has been an ideological work designed 'to further entrench neoliberal capitalism'[69] and it has given rise to the 'triumph of a new neoliberal settlement'.[70] The class-based focus of this agenda is clear to see. As O'Connell observes:

> the costs of the economic crisis induced by neoliberal capitalism, are now being paid for predominantly by ordinary working people, with the net effect being the increased and systematic undermining of the entire gamut of socio-economic rights, from the right to housing, healthcare, education, social welfare through to the right to work and to organize in trade unions.[71]

In this context, business actors are major political players, from providing funding for election and party campaigns, to lobbying powerfully nationally and in Europe and internationally. Through globalization they have also come to act as equals rather than as subordinates to international and transnational agencies, and many business firms have assumed social and political responsibilities that fill the regulatory vacuum in global governance.[72] Companies are also politically powerful in this context because governments have adopted policies that have effectively propped up business so that they become too big and too necessary to fail. Corporations are politically relevant because of their contribution to public activity. Thus, externally, their political significance is clear. Internally, they are also politically relevant because their structures demonstrate power and represent the class struggle between capital and labour. Through corporations social distributions are made – income distribution, and risk distribution. Thus, the remuneration of executives before and after the economic crisis has come to be regarded as a signal of who is really expected to pay for the crisis. As

---

67 C. Crouch, *The Strange Non-Death of Neoliberalism* (2011) 118.
68 J. Clarke and J. Newman, 'The alchemy of austerity' (2012) 32 *Critical Social Policy* 299, at 300.
69 P. O'Connell, 'Let them Eat Cake: Socio-Economic Rights in An Age of Austerity' in *Human Rights and Public Finance*, eds. A. Nolan, R. O'Connell, and C. Harvey (2013) 59.
70 Clarke and Newman, op. cit., n. 68, p. 300.
71 O'Connell, op. cit., n. 69, p. 66.
72 A.G. Scherer and G. Palazzo, 'The New Political Role of Business in a Globalized World: A Review of a New Perspective on CSR and its Implications for the Firm, Governance and Democracy' (2011) 48 *J. of Management Studies* 899.

O'Connell has shown us, whilst governments crack down on those on benefits, including workers receiving poverty wages, executives and top-level finance workers have continued to receive massive levels of pay with the effect of dramatically increased levels of wealth and income inequality.[73] In addition, 'corporate governance policies have increasingly oriented management remuneration to the stock market, thereby unhitching management pay from the norms applicable to the rest of the workforce.'[74] Setting managers apart in this way also exacerbates their structural power within the company. Furthermore, their level of wealth gives to them significantly greater economic and political power. Evidence suggests that this income inequality can lead to 'mean management' which exploits and objectifies workers lower down the corporate hierarchy.[75]

The fact that collective bargaining has been damaged by labour law reforms introduced as responses to the crisis signifies an attack on democratic and participatory foundations. The ETUI point to the fact that the reforms, which have a negative impact on fundamental social rights and workers' protection, also lack democratic foundations, 'many such reforms being introduced without recourse to democratic and participatory (legislative) procedures, but rather through using emergency procedures, bypassing parliaments or the social partners.'[76] Similarly, bank bail-outs have occurred through bending democratic procedures and use of emergency procedures, thereby shielding such deals largely from parliamentary and popular scrutiny.[77] One response to this undermining of democracy is to demand a balance of power between the countervailing social interests, notably between the organizations of capital and labour.[78] Trade unions are a key source of democracy both in the political arena and in the workplace. Whether policies and reforms continue to be carried out by democratic state institutions, or as Crouch suggests, by large corporations who will shape economic policy, trade unions will have a role to play in promoting democratic rights.[79] Collective bargaining is regarded as 'a cornerstone institution for democracy, a mechanism for increasing workers' incomes, improving working conditions and reducing inequality, a means for ensuring fair employment relations and a source of workplace innovation.'[80]

73 O'Connell, op. cit., n. 69, p. 65.
74 K. Vandaele, 'Do Unions and Worker Representation Bodies Make for More or Less Inequality?' (2012), at <http://works.bepress.com/kurt_vandaele/103>.
75 S.D. Desai et al., 'Meaner Managers: A Consequence of Income Inequality' in *Social Decision Making – Social Dilemmas, Social Values and Ethical Judgments*, eds. R.M. Kramer et al. (2010) ch. 13, 315.
76 Clauwaert and Schomann, op. cit., n. 62, pp. 7–8.
77 R. Erne, 'European Unions After the Crisis', DEI Working Paper 11-1 (2011), at <http://www.ucd.ie/t4cms/WP%2011-1%20Roland%20Erne.pdf> .
78 id.
79 id.
80 Hayter et al., op. cit., n. 50, p. 225.

Trade unions and worker representation are said to lead to a more equal and fair society. Vandaele, for example, highlights the fact that trade unions foster high collective bargaining coverage and redistribution policies, thereby contributing to more equal societies by tackling diverging pay levels and status. At the company level, worker participation and union action, such as involvement at board level, contribute to narrowing the wage gap between rank-and-file workers and the top 1 per cent of the population.[81] Of course, that does not prevent the existence of deep inequalities across the broader workforce, particularly between unionized and non-unionized labour. Indeed, the evidence shows the lowest paid and most precarious jobs are more likely to be non-unionized. But rather than necessitating a decline in union membership, this evidence gives rise to the argument that trade unions are necessary more broadly for improving the protection of workers from exploitation and that there is a need to organize the unorganized as a preliminary step to tackling inequality.

CURRENT OBSTACLES TO ACHIEVING WORKER DEMOCRACY

Having noted that there is a strong argument in favour of worker participation, both for the sake of better corporate governance and for democracy, it is necessary to point out that there are currently numerous obstacles to worker involvement. These are found in the existing corporate structures and objectives as well as in the state of workers and their trade unions in the post-crisis context.

Inside companies several barriers obstruct the path to effective worker involvement. First, the national differences across Europe mean not only that it depends on which country one finds oneself located as to the possibility of boardroom participation but also that the differences can lead to inequality and discrimination against workers located in different parts of a trans-national company.[82] A second barrier is the narrow vision of corporate governance that has come to prevail in the EU. The shareholder focus narrows the goals to financial performance though workers are not given a share in the resulting profits. The inevitable short-term focus tends to operate against workers' interests rather than support their need for job security. In the United Kingdom, the fundamental review of company law that took place in the first decade of the twenty-first century, and led to the Companies Act 2006 missed an opportunity to redress the imbalance. Much has been written on the enlightened shareholder-value approach adopted and mani-

---

81 Vandaele, op. cit., n. 74, pp.104, 111.
82 See C. Villiers, 'The Rover Case (1) The Sale of Rover Cars by BMW – The Role of the Works Council' (2000) 29 *Industrial Law J.* 386.

fested especially in section 172 of that Act.[83] From the workers' perspective, that section has arguably worsened their position rather than improved it as now they have to compete with other stakeholders to get their voice heard.[84] In a similar vein, the rise of corporate social responsibility has not delivered on its promises. It is no coincidence that business leaders have committed themselves to corporate social responsibility at the same time as power shifted away from unions to employers.[85] Whilst corporate social responsibility may have had a limited ameliorative effect it has also 'complemented liberalization and the ascendant neo-liberal institutional regime.'[86]

Against this backdrop, the interests of workers in a company are unlikely to gain much salience with the managers. In reality, the current structures are not conducive to genuine power sharing. Even boardroom participation might be regarded as no more than a token gesture towards participation in this context.[87] Moreover, the remuneration of managers aligns managers and shareholders' interests and can have the effect of distancing the managers further from their workforce. This can, in turn, generate a culture of defensive silence through which the workforce, rather than use voice to express ideas, information, and opinions about work-related improvements, remains silent. During periods of economic stress there is reduced employee participation, less organizational learning, less innovation, and less receptiveness to change.[88] During the push towards financialization and globalization, the emphasis has turned towards human resources rather than human rights. Labour has become a market resource and those humans who provide that resource are market actors.[89]

Collective bargaining has resulted in concession bargaining and trade-offs.[90] This is confirmed by Glassner et al. who have observed concession bargaining in which workers make concessions in exchange for some form

---

83 For example, A. Keay, *The Enlightened Shareholder Value Principle and Corporate Governance* (2012).
84 C. Wynn-Evans, 'The Companies Act 2006 and the Interests of Employees' (2007) 36 *Industrial Law J.* 188, at 191.
85 D. Kinderman, ' "Free us up so we can be responsible!" The co-evolution of Corporate Social Responsibility and neo-liberalism in the UK, 1977–2010' (2012) 10 *Socio-Economic Rev.* 29, at 29. For an account of the United States experience, see R. Marens, 'Generous in victory? American managerial autonomy, labour relations and the invention of Corporate Social Responsibility' (2012) 10 *Socio-Economic Rev.* 59.
86 Kinderman, id., p. 50.
87 L. Talbot, *Progressive Corporate Governance for the 21st Century* (2013).
88 F. Schlosser and R. Zolin, 'Hearing voice and silence during stressful economic times' (2012) 34 *Employee Relations* 555.
89 C. Crouch, 'The governance of labour market uncertainty: towards a new research agenda' (2008) 2, at <http://www2.warwick.ac.uk/fac/soc/wepn/esrc/pe/seminar1/colin_crouch_paper.pdf>.
90 C. Crouch, 'Flexibility and security in the labour market: An analysis of the governance of inequality' (2010) 43 *Zeitschrift für ArbeitsmarktForschung* 17.

86

of employment guarantee such as promises to avoid compulsory redundancies should job loss occur. The key themes of collective agreements in this context have focused on short-time work schemes, prevention or mitigation of job loss, support for redundant workers, wage moderation, and greater flexibility in and/or decentralization of wage setting.[91] The emerging picture is of trade-offs between employment and income aspects of uncertainty, employee concessions and widespread unilateral employer responses.[92] The result is 'a weakening of the bargaining positions of workers and to their bearing the increased burden of uncertainty.'[93] Moreover, indirect forms of employee involvement have been most susceptible to cutbacks and outsourcing, whilst direct and informal employee involvement and participation are deemed by employers to be more crucial than ever, especially if the workers involved have plenty of responsibility for assuring product quality or providing high levels of customer service.[94] The increasingly predominant model of participation is, according to Cressey, 'functional, voluntary and unitarist in outlook.'[95]

A further barrier is the decline of trade union membership during the last few decades with the effect of limiting the potential scope of collective agreements. The evidence of declining union density across the world is compelling. In the OECD area, for example, trade union density has declined from 33.6 per cent of employees in 1960 to 18.1 per cent of employees in 2010.[96] Steen Scheuer suggests, similarly, that since 2000 the decline has been universal across Europe.[97] Blanchflower has also documented a steady decline in the United Kingdom in union density since the end of the 1970s in both the public and private sectors. In particular, he notes that for Great Britain the union density rate fell from 32.2 per cent in 1992 to 26.4 per cent in 2003 and that there was an absolute decline of more than 700,000 in the total number of members (7,857,000 members between 1992 to 7,136,000 and 2003). During the period between 1900 and 2000, the density rate peaked in 1920 at 38.7 per cent but then fell to a low of 23.0 per cent in 1933 and thereafter the density rate rose steadily until 1978, reaching its 'high

---

91 Glassner et al., op. cit., n. 64.

92 V. Glassner, M. Keune, and P. Marginson, 'Collective bargaining in a time of crisis: developments in the private sector in Europe' (2011) 17 *Transfer: European Rev. of Labour and Research* 303.

93 Glassner et al., op. cit., n. 64, p. 318.

94 M. Marchington and A. Knighou, 'The dynamics of employee involvement and participation during turbulent times' (2012) 23 *International J. of Human Resource Management* 3336, at 3350.

95 P. Cressey, 'Employee Participation' in *Employment Policy in the European Union: Origins, Themes and Prospects*, ed. M. Gold (2009) 139.

96 See OECD, 'Trade Union density in OECD countries 1960–2010', long abstract, at <http://www.oecd.org/LongAbstract/0,3425,en_2649_33927_39891562_1_1_1_1,00.html>.

97 S. Sheuer, 'Union membership variation in Europe: A ten-country comparative analysis' (2011) 17 *European J. of Industrial Relations* 57, at 57.

watermark' of 52.4 per cent in 1978. Union density in the United Kingdom has been in a downward spiral since that time: according to the Department for Business Innovation and Skills, the most recent figures, for the last quarter of 2010, show density rates of 26.6 per cent.[98] Although density rates have remained strong in countries whose governments are somewhat sympathetic to unions such as Belgium, Finland, and Sweden, Bryson, Ebbinghauser, and Visser note that between 2000 and 2008 union membership in the EU dropped generally from 46 to 43 million whilst, at the same time, waged employment increased from 120 to 140 million employees, showing a density drop from 27.8 to 23.4 per cent. In fact, over three decades, union density halved.[99]

Such density decline is certain to impact upon collective bargaining since union membership itself may be a vital prerequisite for a union's 'capability to sign and implement collective agreements for the represented employees and pressure government policy.'[100] Notably, it is observed that union membership decline co-evolves with other long-term changes in labour relations and institutions such as collective bargaining, employment protection, and social insurance.[101] Thus Scheuer suggests that the consequences of declining union membership include the loss of support for employees that they could previously obtain from their union, leaving them more vulnerable to their employer.[102] Moreover, diminished collective bargaining can itself further reduce union density levels. As Scheuer suggests, 'perceived presence of a collective agreement actually triples the likelihood of union membership.'[103]

RESOLVING THE WORKER PARTICIPATION DILEMMA

The impact of corporate governance policies and the crisis on labour as well as the obstacles identified for their involvement are also reasons for finding more progressive, transformative, and sustainable forms of worker involvement. The ETUC suggests that:

> The key lesson drawn from the crisis is on the need for a strengthening of worker resilience through better and stronger information, consultation and participation, a worker-focused skills agenda and strong public industrial policies supporting active labour market policies at all levels.[104]

98 Department for Business Innovation and Skills (BIS), *Trade Union Membership in 2010* (2011).
99 A. Bryson et al., 'Introduction: Causes, consequences and cures of union decline' (2011) 17 *European J. of Industrial Relations* 97.
100 id., p. 98.
101 id., p. 99.
102 Scheuer, op. cit., n. 97, p. 57.
103 id., p. 68.
104 ETUC, 'Resolution: Anticipating change and restructuring, ETUC calls for EU action', adopted at the Executive Committee on 6–7 March 2012, 14.

More could be made of legislative provisions such as the European Works Councils Directive, which has been shown to give rise to more positive management responses to worker representation.[105] Yet, in reality, what has been evident is that current employment and labour laws, nationally and at EU level, appear to be too weak to stand up to changes in the corporate environment. Restructuring has been shown to weaken the position of labour. Moreover, in times of economic crisis, legal processes are bypassed and replaced with 'emergency' requirements. Sometimes legal provisions are blatantly ignored. In the United Kingdom, for example, there is evidence of employers paying below the legal minimum wage[106] and of youth working for free.[107] Sometimes legal provisions are amended or repealed. In the United Kingdom again, recent changes include extension of time before an unfair dismissal claim can be made[108] and more restricted access to employment tribunals.[109] Overall, the strength of employment protections, as measured by the OECD's Employment Protection Legislation index, has been weakened in many countries during the past 30 years.[110] It appears that workers cannot rely on employment legislation or corporate governance as a guarantee of protection. Moreover, it is necessary to recognize the processes of neoliberalism and financialization as a form of labour discipline; financialization leads to new competitive pressures on capital to perform in which labour is also treated as a form of capital, a risk to be decomposed, priced, hedged, and managed.[111] As Heyes et al. suggest, neoliberalism involves state policies 'designed to weaken the position of labour and deliver a decisive shift in the balance of social forces in favour of the capitalist class.'[112] In line with such policies, 'flexible labour markets, minimal welfare states and individualised wages are entirely consistent with the optimising logic of unfettered financial capital seeking out its most profitable activities.'[113]

What is evident is a two-dimensional class conflict: the first dimension consists of distributional aspects of crisis management in the scope, focus,

---

105 See J. Mohrenweiser et al., 'What triggers the establishment of a works council?' (2012) 33 *Economic and Industrial Democracy* 295.
106 See, for example, Low Pay Commission, *National Minimum Wage Report 2013* (2013; Cm. 8565) 122.
107 See the Court of Appeal ruling in *Reilly and Anor, R (on the application of)* v. *Secretary of State for Work and Pensions* [2013] EWCS Civ 66.
108 The Unfair Dismissal and Statement of Reasons for Dismissal (Variation of Qualifying Period) Order 2012 No. 989.
109 Enterprise and Regulatory Reform Act 2013, Part 2 (Employment).
110 J. Heyes, 'Flexicurity, Employment Protection and the Jobs Crisis' (2011) 25 *Work, Employment and Society* 642.
111 R. Martin et al., 'Financialization, Risk and Labour' (2008) 12 *Competition and Change* 120, at 121.
112 J. Heyes et al., 'Varieties of Capitalism, Neoliberalism and the economic crisis of 2008–?' (2012) 43 *Industrial Relations J.* 222, at 224.
113 id., p. 226.

and composition of austerity packages or the numerous efforts to improve national competitiveness through cost-cutting labour market and social reforms. The second dimension is the top-down, often non-democratic, character of the political process and the pivotal role of financial market actors therein. Thus we see a twofold political legitimacy crisis in the European stabilization measures: on the one hand, issues of social distribution and reproduction and on the other, issues of democratic participation and control.[114] Kochan argues that:

> there is nascent conflict because the median worker owns but a pittance in equities and because many executives – encouraged by stock options – have cast their lot with owners. Perhaps the most prevalent game today is the 'war of all against all': executives exploit owners and workers; owners try to do the same to executives and workers. The vast majority of workers, however, are powerless; the result is income inequality and stagnation.[115]

This class dimension becomes the basis of a progressive, transformational politics that focuses not just on growing financial fragility in capital markets.[116] Indeed, this class dimension points us towards possible solutions to the huge dilemma faced by unions and workers in the austerity period. Once we accept that the current institutional arrangements for corporate government represent a political construct, we should also see the relevance of this to democracy. It is clear that neoliberalism has tremendous staying power[117] and with that the continuing political force of large corporations. It is crucial for trade unions, workers, and others therefore to challenge and hold governments, European and international institutions, and corporations to account. As Erne suggests, invoking Polanyi's notion of counter-movements restoring the primacy of society over the economic system, 'the time now seems set for one of increasing conflict.'[118] How might unions go about these challenges successfully, given their lower density levels and their general struggle against the powerful economic and political elites? Their reduced power does not necessarily reduce their relevance to the labour markets landscape. Indeed, industrial relations scholars show that 'notwithstanding the continuing decline in the diffusion of the "traditional" union-based model of workplace representation, union presence is still a prerequisite for effective representation.'[119] Trade unions have traditionally provided organizational cohesion and strength to representation systems.[120] Thus, what is necessary is to identify the most effective strategies for unions in this post-crisis context.

114 H.J. Bieling, 'EU facing the crisis: social and employment policies in times of tight budgets' (2012) 18 *Transfer: European Rev. of Labour and Research* 255, at 268.
115 Kochan, op. cit., n. 43, p. 34.
116 Martin et al., op. cit., n. 111.
117 Crouch, op. cit., n. 67.
118 Erne, op. cit., n. 77, p. 19.
119 A. Charlwood and M. Terry, '21st-century models of employee representation: structures, processes and outcomes' (2007) 38 *Industrial Relations J.* 320, at 320.
120 id., p. 335.

The economic and political landscape has changed significantly and the need for modernization thus also applies to trade unions themselves. Trade union structures and procedures are widely regarded as ossified. Thus, neither a servicing model of unionism, in which members do little more than pay their dues in return for union services delivered by stewards and higher-level union representatives,[121] nor a top-down organizing model of unionism[122] is adequate for dealing with the changed external environment. As Upchurch and Mathers suggest, 'the changing relationship of trade unions to the state is a central matter to consider' and 'the political dimension is at the heart of an analysis of how union identities are changing in relation to neoliberal globalization.'[123] They warn that 'the end of the "compact" between union and the state or employers increases the risk of repression',[124] and this brings about the need for greater mobilization and 'innovative forms of action to sustain opposition'.[125]

An increasingly significant strategy for trade unions is to use the possibility of their associational power and to shift towards a social movement footing.[126] They might therefore seek alliances with other organizations. Indeed, arguably, through financialization, labour is already being forced into new forms of associations.[127] As suggested by Estanque and Costa:

> Labour relations of our time are crossed by precariousness and by a new and growing precariat which also gives rise to new social movements and new forms of activism and protest. Thus labour relations and social movements have been pushed toward new ways and new discourses. In fact the new socio-labour movements are movements of society, of a younger generation legitimately protesting against the lack of career opportunities, against the lack of jobs, against the irrationalities of nowadays economic austerity policies.[128]

Gajewska talks in terms of social and institutional networks for collective action and articulating oppositional ideology.[129] Already trade unions have recognized the need to generate solidarity with groups such as migrant

121 B. Nissen and P. Jarley, 'Unions as Social Capital: Renewal through a Return to the Logic of Mutual Aid?' (2005) 29 *Labor Studies J.* 1.
122 id.
123 M. Upchurch and A. Mathers, 'Neoliberal Globalization and Trade Unionism: Toward Radical Political Unionism?' (202) 38 *Critical Sociology* 265, at 276.
124 id., p. 276.
125 id., p. 277.
126 R. Sullivan, 'Labour market or labour movement? The union density bias as barrier to labour renewal' (2010) 24 *Work, Employment and Society* 145, at 147 and 152.
127 Martin et al., op. cit., n. 111, p. 130.
128 E. Estanque and H. Augusto Costa, 'Labour Relations and Social Movements in the 21st Century' in *Sociological Landscape – Theories, Realities and Trends*, ed. D. Erasga (2012) 257, at 257–8.
129 K. Gajewska, 'The Emergence of a European Labour Protest Movement?' (2008) 14 *European J. of Industrial Relations* 104.

workers.[130] They are also joining other global social justice movements and beginning to broaden their agenda to take up issues such as housing and healthcare as well as pay and working conditions.[131]

The current financial crisis brings into question the legitimacy of global free-market capitalism and in such a context, 'we should expect a rise of protective counter-movements that aim to subordinate the economy to society.'[132] These counter-movements are growing and they signify the fact that consent to austerity measures being imposed across Europe is not assured but, rather, that European citizens are disaffected and angry about the blatant wealth and health inequalities, and feel let down by their political systems. This anger is being manifested currently in a variety of responses, ranging from riots among the dispossessed, resentments against migrants, outrage about bankers' bonuses and MPs' expenses, and in demonstrations and protests against austerity as well as in the rise of populist anti-political parties and movements, outside of the political mainstream.[133] The Occupy Wall Street movement recently quickly spread and attracted support from trade unions. With slogans like 'We are the 99 per cent' highlighting that 1 per cent take most of the wealth, it is clear that the Occupy resistance movement saw itself as having a potentially broad and diverse membership joining workers and non-workers in a bid for global social justice and democracy.[134] Yet, at the same time, the movement was ambivalent about building alliances with established groups or politicians that could have helped articulate a programme and mobilize the public. The movement preferred to keep the unions at a distance. Thus, despite the initial flurry of publicity and the optimism surrounding the Occupy movement, its efforts did not achieve very much, partly because its disruptive tactics were swiftly and strictly contained but also arguably because the movement itself appeared to lack structure and discipline and the ability to articulate a clear alternative to the existing economic and political structures.[135] A potential mistake might therefore be for labour, by joining up with other protest and social movements, effectively to depoliticize and de-class its own campaign, and thereby 'to be relegated to being one actor among many within a wider milieu of social movementism.'[136] The role for the trade unions, then, is to emphasize

---

130 R.P. Munck, 'Globalization and the Labour Movement: Challenges and Responses' (2010) 1 *Global Labour J.* 218, at 228.
131 id.
132 Erne, op. cit., n. 77, p. 2.
133 J. Clarke and J. Newman, 'The alchemy of austerity' (2012) 32 *Critical Social Policy* 299, at 308.
134 See, further, Occupy Wall Street at <http://www.OccupyWallSt.org>.
135 See, for example, A. Roberts, 'Why the Occupy Movement Failed' (2012) 72 *Public Administration Rev.* 754; S. Tarrow, 'Why Occupy Wall Street is Not the Tea Party of the Left' *Foreign Affairs*, 10 October 2011.
136 Upchurch and Mathers, op. cit., n. 123, p. 276.

their relevance and to reinforce the class aspect of the struggle for social and economic justice.[137]

Internally, unions need to democratize themselves by developing workers' skills and knowledge and enabling their members to be active rather than passive.[138] Indeed, this calls for a social-movement unionism orientation rather than an economistic or business unionism approach that defines workers' interests more narrowly and frequently leads to compromises with capital.[139] A social-movement unionism approach is more concerned with achieving an equitable society and advancing the interests of both union and non-union members.[140] This requires the unions to emphasize not so much their servicing function as their organizing and educating functions that prioritize building up the capacities of workers inside and outside their workplaces, assisting local and community participation, and developing workers' understanding of the relationships and structures in which they participate.[141]

CONCLUSION

Workers' participation in corporate governance has never been very strong. Even in those jurisdictions traditionally connected to the European social model, workers and trade unions have not been given full parity with managers or investors. The expansion of neoliberalism across Anglo-American and European political economies has served to push trade unions further away from the centre of decision making, and workers are increasingly treated as disposable commodities, forced into more precarious working conditions. The economic crisis has brought with it a crisis for democracy in the workplace and in mainstream politics. Whilst an urgent measure is for trade unions to campaign for a prioritization of basic social rights over economic freedoms, and to fight against the precarization of jobs,[142] much more radical measures need to be taken over the longer term.

Trade unions are at a critical point in their history. A positive and important point to observe is that 'unions are part of class relations and class struggle, and thus are not going to go away.'[143] Unions have begun to recognize that a way forward is when workers, unionized and non-unionized,

137 id.
138 M. Upchurch et al., 'Political Congruence and Trade Union Renewal' (2012) 26 *Work, Employment and Society* 857, at 862.
139 L. Panitch, 'Reflections on Strategy for Labour' in *Socialist Register 2001: Working Classes, Global Realities*, eds. L. Panitch and C. Leys (2001) 367, at 377.
140 Ross, op. cit., n. 3.
141 Panitch, op. cit., n. 139; Ross, id.
142 Bieling, op. cit., n. 114, p. 269.
143 P. Fairbrother, 'Social Movement Unionism or Trade Unions as Social Movements' (2008) 20 *Employment Responsibility and Rights J.* 213, at 214.

'are conscious of the linkage between workplace, civil society, the state and global forces and develop a strategy to resist the damaging pressures of globalization through creating a movement linking these spheres.'[144] In this era of austerity amid globalization and continued neoliberalism, such a reinvention of solidarity[145] is crucial. Without it, labour's continuing decline is inevitable and the prospects for worker participation in corporate governance remain dismal. If, however, a genuine solidarity is achieved, that may bring about a more democratic control of the processes of production in which companies may be truly owned by the workers and be part of a 'different system capable of delivering superior social, economic and ecological outcomes.'[146]

144 R. Lambert, 'Globalization: can unions resist?' (1988) 22 *South African Labour Bull.* 72, at 73 (cited by Fairbrother, id., p. 215).
145 Panitch, op. cit., n. 139, p. 389.
146 See, further, J. Guinan, 'Social democracy in the age of austerity and resistance: the radical potential of democratising capital' (2013) 20(4) *Renewal* 9, at 16.

JOURNAL OF LAW AND SOCIETY
VOLUME 41, NUMBER 1, MARCH 2014
ISSN: 0263-323X, pp. 95–120

Harmonization Process for Effective Corporate Governance in the European Union: From a Historical Perspective to Future Prospects

Veronique Magnier*

In 2011, the European Commission launched a public consultation on 'the European Corporate Governance framework', reflecting the EU's increasing concern about corporate governance issues, and the changes and reforms needed in the aftermath of the financial crisis. The question raised is twofold: first, should new objectives be established, and secondly, which of the various regulatory mechanisms, the traditional unification/coordination tools or the more recent comply-or-explain rule, would best fulfill these objectives? The article discusses how the financial crisis has made the harmonization of corporate governance more imperative, why the objectives of corporate governance rules must be enlarged to preserve the interests of companies as a whole, and which mechanism would best achieve these changes. More specifically, it tackles the comply-or-explain rule already widespread in Europe, discussing its major advantages and flaws, as well as the efficiency of its control by national and European market authorities.

INTRODUCTION

The financial crisis has affected corporate governance in such a way that changes and reforms must be seriously considered at both European and national levels. Corporate governance has long been kept in the 'soft law' area. So far, there has been very partial regulation or no regulation at all. At the EU level, the Commission adopted a very cautious position and decided not to regulate corporate governance. This is quite understandable as corporate governance is a matter of conduct, of human behaviour, and it

* Institute for Law, Ethics, Patrimony, Paris Sud University, 54 Bd. Desgranges, 92330 SCEAUX, Paris-Sud, France
veronique.magnier@u-psud.fr

95

would not be pertinent to impose unified rules all over the EU, to regulate such conduct. This explains why the Commission has only drafted recommendations, so far.

But the global financial crisis may have changed our way of thinking. Corporate governance, like most legal regimes, is a cultural phenomenon. At the national level, we witness a proliferation of codes of good conduct or good practice which, so far, remain a tool of self-regulation, drafted by the very persons that must comply with it. In such a context, the Commission has a duty to reflect upon the effectiveness of the existing corporate governance framework for EU companies. It is for this reason that, in June 2010, the Commission first launched a public consultation on its Green Paper, 'Corporate governance in financial institutions and remuneration policies',[1] followed by the Green Paper, 'The EU corporate governance framework',[2] which is the subject of the present public consultation. Regardless of the outcome, it reflects, at least, an increasing concern by the European Union on corporate governance issues in the aftermath of the financial crisis, possibly heralding a European regulation on corporate governance, leading to some kind of harmonization in the near future. What can we expect the new pattern to be?

The article will discuss how soft-law developments in member states will shift European corporate governance and argue why it is pertinent that new objectives be assigned to corporate governance at the European level. Of the various mechanisms available to regulate corporate governance inside Europe, namely, the traditional unification/coordination tools and more recent ones such as the 'comply-or-explain' rule, what would be the most efficient in order to comply with these objectives?

Part one briefly details why the crisis has affected corporate governance regulation in such ways that reforms are needed in the national and transnational European contexts, a crucial factor that will undoubtedly go further to specify European corporate legal culture and help set up a new European corporate governance framework. At this stage, soft law, through the proliferation of codes of corporate governance, seems to be the answer to the crisis, more so than hard law and in spite of its lack of *normative value*. Part two explores the theoretical basis for the legitimacy of new legal objectives to corporate governance in Europe, that is, a stakeholder-oriented objective, alongside its total absence from the traditional lexicon of corporate governance theory. It examines how corporate governance history completes this portrait of stakeholder-oriented public and private regimes and of an extensive history of public participation in private corporate

1 European Commission Green Paper, 'Corporate governance in financial institutions and remuneration policies' (COM(2010) 284 final).
2 European Commission Green Paper, 'The EU corporate governance framework' (COM(2011) 164 final), at <www.ec.europa.eu/internal_market/company/docs/modern/com2011-164_en.pdf>.

governance. Part three explores the traditional tools of unification, harmonization, and coordination as well as the more recent comply-or-explain rule. Part Four argues that the latter is European corporate governance's most adapted tool, in spite of present pitfalls. Adapting the 'comply or explain' mechanism and making it the tool for corporate governance would thus help harmonize corporate governance rules and practice.

In conclusion, it is argued that the comply-or-explain rule, if adapted, may serve to heighten the harmonization effort to adopt best practice of governance, and may thus foster a greater coherence in European corporate culture.

I. NEED FOR A EUROPEAN FRAMEWORK

1. *Proliferation of recommendatory codes in the EU member states*

Numerous official reports sprang up after the financial crisis,[3] which revealed large gaps in corporate governance best practice, specifically in financial institutions. The same reports showed that, more widely, certain private companies had not always adopted good corporate governance practices (an insufficient level of involvement of boards of directors, high risk taking, excessive bonuses, and so on).

On a national level, the majority of European countries, including France, have legislated little – in contrast to the United States – on corporate governance matters, even in the aftermath of the financial crisis. Those measures that do exist essentially concern obligations of financial disclosure and the reinforcement of transparency, notably in relation to the salaries of company officers, for listed companies. This relatively limited legislative intervention may be explained by the fact that corporate governance is more a question of conduct and human relations than of rules and procedures.

But law does not consist only of statutes, nor only of formal sources. The emergence of corporate governance codes in most European countries, of which the recommendations display a certain level of convergence between countries,[4] effectively illustrates the necessity, in postmodern societies, of admitting the coexistence of hard and soft law, and of considering that these codes constitute soft law.

The United Kingdom was a precursor in the formulation of corporate governance recommendations but it also was the first one to initiate the implementation of a monitoring system of compliance with these recommendations through the 'comply-or-explain' rule. An initial report, the

---

3 See, for example, OECD, *The Corporate Governance Lessons from the Financial Crisis* (2009).

4 K. Hopt, 'Comparative Corporate Governance: The State of the Art and International Regulation' (2011) 59 *Am. J. of Comparative Law* 1.

Cadbury report of 1992,[5] was supplemented by several successive reports, which were then consolidated to make the Combined Code. This code, which was reviewed and commented upon by the London Stock Exchange (LSE), also established the 'comply-or-explain' rule. In France, the stages in the process of formulating flexible corporate law are well known: first there was the CNPF-AFEP report of July 1995 on the boards of directors of listed companies,[6] then the December 1998 report on corporate governance,[7] and the AFEP-MEDEF report of October 2003 on the corporate governance of listed companies,[8] all of which were consolidated, at the instigation of Parliament, into a 'Code of corporate governance for listed companies' as from December 2008. Strictly speaking, the code falls under the heading of soft law, in so far as companies may choose whether or not to adopt it. The 'comply-or-explain' rule requires only that companies choosing the latter option should explain their reasons for not adopting the rules of good corporate governance proposed in the code.[9] All other member states, like Germany, Belgium, Sweden, and so on, have now implemented a code of corporate governance as well.

One core objection to corporate governance codes is that they may weaken the governance structure overall as they do not belong to hard-law regulation. The objection that codes contain nothing but recommendations stripped of any binding force must be refuted, because a rule that has a weak normative *value*, which is simply 'recommendatory', may have an extremely strong normative *effect*, in so far as it is seen as binding by those it targets.[10]

It is this effect that should be reinforced in corporate governance, in so far as these codes present numerous advantages over legislation and represent

---

5 Sir A. Cadbury (chair), *Report of the Committee on the Financial Aspects of Corporate Governance* (1992). In this report pride of place is given to the composition and functioning of boards of directors, the naming of independent directors, the question of the remuneration of directors and, finally, the monitoring functions exercised by non-executive directors.

6 CNPF-AFEP, *The Boards of Directors of Listed Companies in France* (1995) (Viénot I report).

7 AFEP-MEDEF, *Recommendations of the Committee on corporate governance* (1998) (Viénot II report).

8 AFEP-MEDEF, *Promoting Better Corporate Governance in Listed Companies* (2002) (Bouton report),

9 As regards this rule, see the references in V. Magnier, 'La règle de conformité ou l'illustration d'une acculturation méthodologique complexe' in *La gouvernance des sociétés cotées face à la crise. Pour une meilleure protection de l'intérêt social*, ed. V. Magnier (2010) 249.

10 See the important work of C. Thibierge et al., *La force normative, naissance d'un concept* (2009). Thibierge defines normative effect as 'an aspect of normative force related to the effects of the rule' ('Synthèse', p. 785), the other aspect of normative force being normative *value*, which is connected to the formal source of the rule; see, also, C. Chatelin-Ertur and S. Onnée, 'Des forces normatives des codes de gouvernance des entreprises à la puissance normative du paradigme en économie organisationnelle', id., p. 649.

the most suitable normative level for codes of conduct, even though their normative force is still often contested, whether rightly or wrongly. Of all the advantages of codes, the following are the most evident:

- the drafting process of recommendations is quick and straightforward;[11]
- they are more responsive to the economic situation;
- they are flexible in scope and can be modified according to the size, legal status, and shareholding of a given company;
- they 'responsibilize' actors more effectively;
- they may be accompanied by a test of efficacy, through the 'comply-or-explain' rule, thus endowing them with real normative effects.

We should also mention the grading systems published by specialized organizations,[12] which make adherence to code recommendations a factor in investment decisions.

Experts question the effectiveness of these codes, however, and the wisdom of self-regulation is the subject of some debate. The present system of corporate governance in the EU remains essentially founded on self-regulation through codes, on the basis of 'comply or explain', often complemented by self-monitoring.[13] The creation of rules by the very individuals bound by them now seems inadequate. Is it legitimate to continue to claim that by formulating their own rules, company directors will be able to disregard the conflict of interest in which they find themselves, to limit their appetites, and impose reasonable rules of governance on themselves?[14]

2. *Recent evolutions in the EU*

In such a context, the Commission has a duty to reflect upon the effectiveness of the existing corporate governance framework for EU companies. By tradition, according to the principle of subsidiarity, the EU may only act where the action of individual countries is insufficient. The principle was established in 1992, after the Treaty of Maastricht, justifying the fact that the Commission, in matters of corporate governance, has so far operated only by way of making recommendations.[15]

11 The code has not been officially published in France. It is only available online, which signals, in the absence of indications to the contrary, its entry into force.

12 For example, Governance Metrics International, ISS-Corporate Governance Quotient, Standard & Poors, the Corporate Library or Deutsche Bank.

13 In France, AFEP and MEDEF have decided to publish annual reports on the development of and adherence to the recommendations contained in the code.

14 Y. Paclot, 'La juridicité du code AFEP/MEDEF de gouvernement d'entreprise des sociétés cotées' (2011) *Revue des sociétés* 395.

15 European Commission, 'Commission Recommendation complementing Recommendations 2004/913/EC and 2005/162/EC as regards the regime for the remuneration of directors of listed companies and Commission Recommendation on remuneration policies in the financial services' (2009), at <http://ec.europa.eu/internal_market/company/docs/directors-remun/COM(2009)_211_EN.pdf>.

Today, however, the Commission can no longer stand aside from this debate which is why it launched its public consultation on the two Green Papers.[16] Regardless of the outcome of this consultation, it reflects at least an increasing concern by the EU with corporate governance issues in the aftermath of the financial crisis, and may decide European regulation on corporate governance in the future. The question is twofold: first, is it pertinent to assign new objectives to corporate governance at the European level, and secondly, what method would be the most efficient in order to comply with these objectives?

II. NEW CORPORATE GOVERNANCE OBJECTIVES

The merits of shareholder and stakeholder primacy have been debated for a decade. Shareholder primacy places the responsibility for and purpose of a corporation in the hands of shareholders. This system, in place for decades, has reached its apogee in the United States, as regulators and companies adopt provisions to give shareholders a say on everything from corporate policy to executive compensation. One obvious, somewhat contested, element of a shareholder orientation is an attendant focus on short-term profitability. In contrast, stakeholder governance recognizes that shareholders, as solely the owners of a corporation's residual interests, are but one of many communities the corporation exists to serve. From a contractual standpoint, bondholders and other creditors come before shareholders, but stakeholder governance goes beyond that to encompass a range of people affected by the corporation's decisions, including workers, customers, communities, and governments. Stakeholder governance reflects the multifaceted central role corporations play in contemporary society.

1. *The traditional theory of shareholder primacy*

The thinking that produced the idea of 'corporate governance' can be traced back to the United States, to the aftermath of the 1929 financial crisis. The starting point of Berle and Mean's founding text, *The Modern Corporation and Private Property*,[17] was the observation that the increasing liquidity of American financial markets had brought about a separation between capital ownership and management, the origin of an excessive concentration of power in the hands of managers. This precipitated the idea of rebalancing power in favour of shareholders and of placing greater limits on managers to force them to prioritize the interests of the corporation over their own selfish

---

16 European Commission, op. cit., n. 1; European Commission, op. cit., n. 2.
17 A.A. Berle and G.C. Means, *The Modern Corporation and Private Property* (1932/ 1968, revised edn.).

interests.[18] These premises are based on the economic model of agency theory, which was developed from the work of Jensen and Meckling,[19] and led to the affirmation of the superiority of the power of shareholders.

Hence, shareholders' interests – and, with that, the supremacy of 'shareholder value' – became the priority, to the point of confusing this interest with that of the business, the company's interest. And in order to protect the interests of shareholders, only an active and competitive market could achieve an optimal processing of information, destined to be integrated in the fairest manner into the value of the share, to the detriment of any regulation.

It is interesting that the stakeholder-shareholder debate relies on a clear and central geographic divide. Although corporate governance in the United States rests on shareholder primacy, stakeholder governance is much more commonplace in Europe – it is even part of the regulatory scheme in many countries.[20] Even if this American analysis were to be followed in Europe, and in spite of the fact that widespread corporate governance codes in Europe still reflect this conception, the crisis may change the European conception of corporate governance.

2. Changes in the aims of the governance of EU businesses

Today, several factors, both economic and more general, have prompted the European Commission to question the state of practice in corporate governance on both a micro- and macro-economic level, in order to restore confidence in the single market, for shareholders and also all the other stakeholders in wider society.[21]

The global financial crisis at the end of the 2000s was the first to reveal the limits of the present system of governance of financial institutions. The economic crisis that followed this financial crisis weakened every economy, in all sectors. Without bringing the fundamentals of the governance of private law companies into question, in this post-crisis period we should concern ourselves with the development of corporate governance, which, by nature, is not static.

Whereas economists always asserted,[22] on the grounds that price reflects the scarcity of resources, that management should aim at maximizing shareholder wealth, a widespread view in politics and public opinion in Europe is that corporations should serve a larger social purpose and be 'responsible,' that is,

---

18 A. Rebérioux, 'Gouvernement d'Entreprise et Contrôle des Dirigeants: 1932–2008, d'Une Crise à l'Autre' in Magnier (ed.), op. cit., n. 9, p. 3.

19 M. Jensen and W. Meckling, 'Theory of the Firm: Managerial Behaviour, Agency, Costs and Ownership Structure' (1976) 3 *J. of Financial Economics* 305.

20 F. Allen et al., 'Stakeholder Capitalism, Corporate Governance and Firm Value', ECGI Working Paper no. 190 (2009).

21 European Commission, 'Towards a Single Market Act For a Highly Competitive Social Market Economy' (COM(2010) 608 final) 2.

22 J. Tirol, *The Theory of Corporate Finance* (2005).

they should reach out to other stakeholders and not only to shareholders. Their decisions impact upon various groups, such as employees, communities, and creditors. The effect of these decisions should compel corporations to maintain ethical considerations and duties towards these groups.

Before discussing the implementation of stakeholder-oriented corporate governance on a theoretical basis, it is necessary to address two issues. We should, first, be aware that, paradoxically, the theory of stakeholder-oriented governance is more elaborated in the United States than it has ever been in Europe, whereas its practice is far more widespread in Europe.[23] Secondly, we must address the issue of what exactly the concept refers to. As a matter of fact, stakeholder-oriented corporate governance may be twofold.[24] On the one hand, the stakeholder concept may refer to a 'broad mission of the management'.[25] According to this view, management should aim at maximizing the sum of the various stakeholders' surpluses. On the other hand, stakeholder-oriented corporate governance may refer to the sharing of control by stakeholders,[26] like co-determination in Germany. Presumably, the two notions are related[27] – for instance, it would be hard for a manager to sacrifice profit to benefit some stakeholder – and what follows takes the view that stakeholder-oriented corporate governance means both a broad managerial mission and divided control.

This wide definition has a double impact on the implementation of stakeholder-oriented corporate governance. First, it gives priority to long-term strategy. As a matter of fact, according to the 'broad mission of the management' device, managers have to pay attention not only to share-holders' interest, but also to the interests of employees, creditors, and, as regards ethical issues, the public interest itself. These new managerial missions naturally imply that the corporation is durable, profitable, and even prosperous in the long run. The managerial vision becomes more long-term than short-term.[28]

Secondly, it compels one to re-examine the notion of 'corporate interest'. The argument can be challenged to the extent that the notion of 'profit' can clearly be distinguished from the notion of 'value.' Corporate governance recommendations today, at least in EU countries, seek to provide economic

---

23 See V. Magnier and D. Rosenblum, 'Quotas and the Transatlantic Divergence of the Corporate Governance Culture' (2014) 34 *J. of International Law & Business* (forthcoming).
24 Tirol, op. cit., n. 22, p. 56, fn. 93.
25 id.
26 id.
27 id.
28 This priority strengthens the firm establishment of stable shareholding in the capital of large companies, a little like the 'hard cores' of the 1980s. For a redefinition of this notion, see Y. Paclot, 'Le gouvernement d'entreprise, pour quoi faire? Quelques reflexions en relisant le code de gouvernement d'entreprise des societies cotées' in Magnier (ed.), op. cit., n. 9, p. 279.

102

operators with the means to create value. This is nothing new, given that it was already the underlying idea of agency theory, that is, the idea that good governance practices should help a corporation to perform better and thus create more value (which is more global than mere profit). The analysis differs today in that it reverts to a more respectful notion of the corporation, regarded as a legal person independent of its associates, who are not the 'owners' of the corporation itself. Corporations indeed appear to have a broader objective than merely creating shareholder value, which results in distinguishing between the corporation's interest and the common interest of the shareholders. 'Creating value' would thus suppose that the corporation itself, and not solely its shareholders, grow richer.[29]

In this respect, the corporation's interest does not boil down to the selfish interest of the shareholders, but implies taking account of all the interests that companies must guarantee. In fact, recognition of a corporation's broader interest, and the aims of governance as they have just been set out, tally perfectly: corporate bodies must fulfill their mission of protecting the corporation's interest, in other words, create value for the benefit of all the stakeholders. The resurgence of the corporation's interest,[30] of which corporate officers are the guardians, is at the centre of new theories seeking to restore the real dimension of companies: to create value, not solely for shareholders, but in the interests of all, that is, the 'stakeholders'. In the light of this notion, the role of executives can be redefined and corporation management integrated into a long-term scheme.[31]

One core objection to stakeholder governance is that it may weaken the governance structure overall. One issue with the sharing of control between investors and natural stakeholders is that it focuses less on income generation than would occur with investor control.[32] But there are two arguments against that objection. First and foremost, it is noticeable that when priority

---

29 It is interesting to note than even United Kingdom legislation seems to have shifted toward a more stakeholder-oriented concept. The enactment of section 172 of the Companies Act 2006 codified the duty to act in the interest of the company. Now directors of a British company must act in the way they consider, in good faith, would be most likely to promote the success of the company, 'for the benefit of its members as a whole and in doing so must have regard to the interests of employees, the environment, the local community, suppliers and customers.'

30 For a redefinition of this notion, see Paclot, op. cit., n. 28.

31 See F.-G. Trebulle, 'Stakeholder theory et droit des sociétés'(2006–2007) Bull. Joly Sociétés 1337. M.E. Porter and M.R. Kramer, 'Creating Shared Value: How to Reinvent Capitalism – and Unleash a Wave of Innovation and Growth' (2011) 89 Harvard Business Rev.; see, also, M.E. Porter and M.R. Kramer, 'Strategy and Society: The Link Between Competitive Advantage and Corporate Social Responsibility' (2006) 84 Harvard Business Rev. 78, at 78–92, 163; R.J. Fisman, G. Heal, and V.B. Nair, 'Corporate Social Responsibility: Doing Well by Doing Good?' Wharton School Working Paper (2005); P. Escande, 'Michael Porter plaide pour la shared value' Les Echos, 14 March 2011.

32 Tirol, op. cit., n. 22, pp. 59–60.

is given to a long-term strategy, it strengthens the firm establishment of stable shareholding in the capital of large companies. Historically, France experimented with this in the 80s, with the so-called 'hard core'.[33] Today, the concern is also shared by ethical investment funds in which good governance practices, such as sustainable development and ethical commitments, are key factors in assessment by market players.[34] Here, we must recall how Socially Responsible Investment (SRI) has become an important financing tool for listed corporations, and how well it resisted the financial crisis.[35]

A second issue with the concept of stakeholder-oriented corporate governance is managerial accountability. Unlike a manager who has a well-defined mission when he or she is instructed to maximize shareholder value – which is quite an objective task – the socially-oriented manager faces a wide range of missions, most of which are by nature not quite measurable.[36] Concretely, the concern is that the management's invocation of multiple and hard-to-measure missions be an excuse for 'self-serving behaviour,' making managers less accountable. This argument has been taken into account by new managerial theories suggesting that the competency criterion should be restored.[37]

---

33 What was called the '*noyaux durs*' in the 1980s in France, or 'hard core', meant that the new privatized corporation still had a concentrated ownership, but this was too small to have the majority on important decisions as takeover or big strategic changes.

34 It is interesting to note that the crisis does not appear to have weakened the trend in favour of socially responsible investing; C. Malecki, 'L'investissement socialement responsable: quelques remarques sur une valeur montante de la gouvernance d'entreprise "verte"' in Magnier (ed.), op. cit., n. 9, p. 263.

35 With 37 per cent growth in a time of crisis, SRI confirms its status as a 'safe investment' and provides the advantage, today, of insisting upon the 'green' economy. In a nutshell, SRI is a collective or individual investment based on social, ethical, environmental or corporate governance criteria. And if its variety is a source of complexity, it nonetheless offers an important new way of investing. The doctrine, primarily in English-speaking countries, took a very early interest in this type of investment. This can involve socially responsible funds or so-called sustainable development funds that focus on the adherence of companies to sustainable development criteria (the Scandinavian countries and Germany are developing more of the 'green funds' technique), or of exclusion funds (more faithful to the initial concept of such funds that were born in the United States with the philanthropist Quaker movement, that prohibited its members from investing in companies operating in the weapons, tobacco, or even alcohol industries). Despite these differences, a special feature of SRI is that, unlike most common funds, it represents an investment in the future. It is open to *long-term* institutional investors who are aware that, far from being a 'marketing' concern, these funds make it possible to consider, within long-term strategies, questions related to climate change, to threats to fundamental human rights, and to matters surrounding corporate governance. Therefore, SRI is at the heart of stakeholder-oriented governance and spreads stakeholder values into labour and environmental laws; M. Flam, *L'Economie verte* (2010).

36 Tirol, op. cit., n. 22, p. 60.

37 See, most recently, G. Charreaux, 'Droit et gouvernance: l'apport du courant comportemental' in Magnier (ed.), op. cit., n. 9, p. 223.

Rather than aiming to give power back to shareholders – power they never really had in a large number of European countries[38] – the aim of good corporate governance is to create value for the benefit of all (the shareholders and stakeholders in the business), which implies that all the interests guaranteed by the business should be taken into account. The authors of the Green Paper on the European corporate governance framework do not express themselves any differently when they adopt the OECD principles of corporate governance on their own behalf.[39] The OECD effectively defines corporate governance as 'the system by which companies are directed and controlled' and as 'a set of relationships between a company's management, its board, its shareholders and its other stakeholders.'[40]

The emergence of a broadly-defined company interest, as stakeholder theory understands it, now reinforces the anchorage of stable shareholdings in the capital of large companies and invites directors to adopt a more long-term strategy. These new developments also tackle the traditional 'one size does fit all' principle, meaning that every company, regardless of sector and size, has to implement uniform rules. On the other hand, more flexible and adapted ruling is needed, questioning the best tools for harmonization in the EU.

III. TRADITIONAL VERSUS NEW MECHANISMS OF HARMONIZATION

Once the conceptual framework had been fixed, the next question was the tools with which to implement it. The EU has traditionally had various tools at its disposal to implement its goals. Harmonization is, of course, one of the most common and well-known of these, although it can be embedded through many methods such as coordination, rapprochement or even unification.[41] Nevertheless, traditional tools do not seem adapted to corporate governance issues, which have more to do with conduct than prescriptions. Hence, a less common and more subtle tool devised in the United Kingdom, the 'comply-or-explain' rule, enforced by a directive and transposed to all member states, seems much more suited to the issue.

38 P.-Y. Gomez, 'Propos conclusifs' in Magnier (ed.), id., p. 290.
39 European Commission, op. cit., n. 2, p. 2; see, also, OECD, *OECD Principles of Corporate Governance* (2004) at <http://www.oecd.org/dataoecd/32/18/31557724.pdf>.
40 OECD, id., p. 11.
41 See my thesis, V. Magnier, *Rapprochement des droits dans l'Union européenne et viabilité d'un droit commun des sociétés* (1999), which argues that unification and even hard harmonization is not adapted to corporate law in Europe, and that harmonization of such laws would be more efficient if the EU let the member states draft rules out of a *jus commune* set of principles, that would apply soft law to corporations.

105

1. Harmonization of corporate law in the EU

The harmonization of corporate law started about 50 years ago, on the basis of the Treaty of Rome. According to article 280 of the Treaty on the functioning of the European Union:

> In order to exercise the Union's competences, the institutions can adopt either regulations, or directives, decisions, recommendations and opinions.
> A regulation shall have general application. It shall be binding in its entirety and directly applicable in all Member States.
> A directive shall be binding, as to the result to be achieved, upon each Member State to which it is addressed, but shall leave to the national authorities the choice of form and methods.
> A decision shall be binding in its entirety. A decision which specifies those to whom it is addressed shall be binding only on them.
> Recommendations and opinions shall have no binding force.

Both directives and regulations are binding. The former is binding in its entirety and directly applicable in all member states. As such, a EU regulation is, without doubt, hard law. Regarding directives, their binding effect is not direct: only the results to be achieved are binding, which leaves member states room for adjustment. Still, all directives must be transposed by the national authorities and, once transposed, they become regulations, regardless of form.

The harmonization of corporate law had a precise aim in the construction of Europe, namely, allowing commerce freedom of establishment, which was one of the most challenging priorities of European institutions at this time. In order to attain this freedom, and according to Article 50 of the Treaty on the functioning of the European Union, 'the European Parliament and the Council, acting in accordance with the ordinary legislative procedure and after consulting the Economic and Social Committee, shall act by means of directives.' Article 50.2 of the Treaty gives more details:

> The European Parliament, the Council and the Commission shall carry out the duties devolving upon them under the preceding provisions, in particular ...
> (g) by coordinating to the necessary extent the safeguards which, for the protection of the interests of members and others, are required by Member States of companies or firms ... with a view to making such safeguards equivalent throughout the Union.

'Firms' is defined within the meaning of the second paragraph of Article 54, according to which:

> Companies or firms formed in accordance with the law of a Member State and having their registered office, central administration or principal place of business within the Union shall, for the purposes of this Chapter, be treated in the same way as natural persons who are nationals of Member States.
> 'Companies or firms' means companies or firms constituted under civil or commercial law, including cooperative societies, and other legal persons governed by public or private law, save for those which are non-profit-making.

106

Article 54.2(g) became the basis for the work of harmonizing corporate law undertaken by the European institutions from the sixties onwards. No less than 12 directives emerged from this work. Almost all fields were covered and thus harmonized: corporate registration, corporate capital, corporate accounts and auditors, mergers, subsidiaries, and so on. Nonetheless, among those projects which never evolved into a harmonized text was the project of the Fifth Directive which aimed at first unifying, then harmonizing – according to the project's numerous amendments and options – the internal structure of a corporation. In a way, this draft would have been the first to have harmonized corporate governance issues at European Union level, but it never emerged. This comprehensive failure meant that new harmonization tools, more flexible and better adapted to the issue of corporate governance, were required.

In my work on the harmonization of corporate law in the European Union,[42] I demonstrated that European harmonization of corporate law was a semi-success, the main flaws being the fact that establishing detailed substantial rules applying uniformly to all member states, if not theoretically impossible, was impracticable. Of course, setting uniform or quasi-uniform EU rules is always possible (and expected) as long as it complies with the EU subsidiarity principle. Indeed, some directives set out very detailed rules. Nonetheless, in order to gain the agreement of all member states, many directives have to contain more flexibility than expected. Hence, many options or exceptions are introduced in EU directives that allow member states to derogate from the EU rules. And these exceptions are quite substantial. Even though many examples of this assertion are meaningful,[43] directive 2004/25/CE on takeover bids offers one of the most convincing pattern for such derogations,[44] aiming to create favourable regulatory conditions for takeovers and to boost corporate restructuring within the EU. However, the directive's main provisions, which would restrict companies' options for defending themselves against bidders – for example, by subjecting 'poison pills' to shareholder approval or by making share transfer restrictions unenforceable against the bidder – are not mandatory (articles 9 and 11). Furthermore, the directive allows member states to exempt their companies from applying these provisions if the bidder is not subject to the same obligations (article 12). The Commission closely monitored the way in which the directive works in practice, and published a report on member states' implementation of it into national law on takeover bids.[45] This showed that, in many cases, a large number of member states had used these

---

42 id.

43 id.

44 See H. Le Nabasque, 'Les mesures de défenses anti-OPA depuis la loi du 31 mars 2006' (2006) No. 2 Revue des sociétés 256.

45 'Report on the implementation on the Directive on Takeovers Bids', Commission Staff Working Document SEC(2007) 268, at <http://ec.europa.eu/internal_market/company/docs/takeoverbids/2007-02-report_en.pdf>.

options and exemptions, and some had even strengthened the role of management with regard to using takeover defences against a bidder. The report concludes that this could create new barriers in the EU takeover market, rather than eliminate existing ones.[46]

Of course, corporate governance issues differ from takeover bids ones in that the topic is less technical and more based on human relations. On a national level, and unlike what happened with takeover bids, European countries have legislated little on corporate governance. But, as noted above,[47] this relatively limited legislative intervention may be explained by the fact that corporate governance deals more with human conduct and relations than rules and procedures. Consequently, soft rules present numerous advantages over legislation. They indeed represent the most suitable normative level for codes of conduct and have many advantages.

In view of these remarks, I suggest that the development of a flexible means of intervention in corporate governance matters should be preferred, privileging codes of best practice over a European (or national) law establishing detailed substantial rules applying uniformly to all member states (or all companies), at the risk of impracticability. At the same time, the code method has to be efficient. The comply-or-explain rule is the best way to make these codes efficient, as long as the rule is well implemented, and improve their implementation as well as their scope.

2. The comply-or-explain rule and its implementation in the member states

Unlike the means of harmonization previously discussed, the 'comply-or-explain' principle is a soft-law harmonization tool perfectly adapted to corporate governance that has, until now, relied in part on self-regulation. It finds its source in recommendations, formulated in reports, which have, over time, crystallized or become 'consolidated' in corporate governance codes. The financial crisis demonstrated the limits of such self-regulation and led people to seek the considerable reinforcement of the normative value or effect of these codes.

The United Kingdom was a precursor in the formulation of corporate governance recommendations as well as in the implementation of a monitoring system of compliance with these recommendations through the

---

46 Presenting this report, Internal Market and Services Commissioner Charlie McGreevy said:

Too many Member States are reluctant to lift existing barriers, and some are even giving companies yet more power to thwart bids. The protectionist attitude of a few seems to have had a knock-on effect on others. If this trend continues, then there is a real risk that companies launching a takeover bid will face more barriers, not fewer. That goes completely against the whole idea of the Directive.

47 See above, p. 99.

108

comply-or-explain rule. Directive 2006/46/EC[48] introduced the rule at EU level and its transposition made it binding on all member state jurisdictions. A company has the choice either to comply with a code of corporate governance, or explain why it has decided not to comply and what rules replace those in the code.

Theoretically, many advantages are expected from the comply-or-explain rule, both for the company itself and for the market.[49] For companies, this principle advocates a more flexible approach that allows them to adapt faster in a competitive environment. It is believed to improve corporations' competitiveness, because the cost of compliance with a corporate governance code is lower than the cost of compliance with regulation, such as the Sarbanes-Oxley Act.[50] It also favours adapted practice as it is based on the idea that there is not a 'ready-to-wear' approach in corporate governance. As for the market, it aims at ensuring transparency by inducing listed companies either to sign up to a corporate governance code, or to explain why it does not apply such a code, or why it derogates from the provisions of this code; it favours good practice with the aim of improving the dialogue between companies and investors. Doing so, it reinforces the standards of good corporate governance in listed companies ('comply'), adding to legal requirements and provides at the same time a flexible framework that takes into account each listed company's particularities ('explain').

In spite of its simplicity and flexibility, this rule has demonstrated some flaws when put into practice either at national or EU level. At the EU level, these flaws come from different conceptions of 'codes of reference' throughout the member states, some being more stringent than others. Other discrepancies and disparities in the implementation of the rule at national level[51] are

48 Directive 2006/46/EC of the European Parliament and of the Council of 14 June 2006 amending Council Directives 78/660/EEC on the annual accounts of certain types of companies, 83/349/EEC on consolidated accounts, 86/635/EEC on the annual accounts and consolidated accounts of banks and other financial institutions and 91/674/EEC on the annual accounts and consolidated accounts of insurance undertakings

49 A. Couret, 'The comply-or-explain principle: from a simple financial market to a wide method of regulation' (2010) 4 *Rev. Trimestrielle de Droit Financier* 4, and the references cited.

50 The Sarbanes-Oxley Act 2002 is a United States federal law that set new or enhanced standards for all public company boards, management, and public accounting firms.

51 For the United Kingdom, see S. Arcot, V. Bruno, A. Faure-Grimaud, 'Corporate governance in the UK: Is the comply or explain approach working?' (2010) 30 *International Rev. of Law and Economics* 193; S.R. Arcot and V.G. Bruno, 'One Size Does Not Fit All, After All : Evidence From Corporate Governance' (2007), at <http://ssrn.com/abstract_id=887947>; for France, see B. Fasterling and J.-C. Duhamel, 'Le comply or explain: la transparence conformiste en droit des sociétés' (2009) XXIII *Rev. Internationale de Droit Économique* 129.

attributable to differing degrees of normativity within one code or from one code to another.[52]

(a) Different conceptions of 'codes of reference'[53]

As already mentioned, the United Kingdom led the way in formulating corporate governance recommendations and was also the first to implement a monitoring system of compliance with these recommendations through the comply-or-explain rule. An initial report, the Cadbury report,[54] was supplemented by several successive reports, which were then consolidated in the Combined Code. This code, which was reviewed and commented upon by the London Stock Exchange (LSE), also established the comply-or-explain rule: it contains recommendations that listed companies must comply with, or otherwise explain their reasons for derogating from them. The Combined Code, which is the object of declarations by listed companies, has five sections and includes two different sorts of provision for each section: first, general principles, further elaborated upon by 'supporting' principles, namely, the technical provisions of the Combined Code.

This dichotomy between general principles and technical provisions is reflected in the very structure of the declaration that British listed companies must make. It is the United Kingdom Listing Authority (UKLA), which regulates the LSE, under the auspices of the Financial Services Authority (FSA), which requires that companies listed on the main market be subject to the Combined Code. The LSE is therefore the only binding source of the obligation to declare in the United Kingdom. The Financial Reporting Council (FRC) is an independent regulatory authority which promotes good corporate governance standards through the Combined Code. This authority is not, however, in charge of monitoring or implementing the code. Meanwhile, very serious studies have shown that the comply-or-explain rule started off being well implemented in the United Kingdom, even though improvements can be made.[55] The German Code, for its part, originates from a commission named by the government (*Regierungskommission Deutscher Corporate Governance Kodex*) and is the only code of reference for applying the comply-or-explain rule that is legally binding.[56]

---

52 The following sections are extracted from the Trans Europe Experts (TEE), 'The European Corporate Governance Framework: Response to the European Commission public consultation paper' ed. V. Magnier (2012).
53 For changes in the 2013 version of the AFEP-MEDEF corporate governance code for listed companies, and an updated comparison with the German and British codes, see M. Germain, V. Magnier, and M.-A. Noury, 'Corporate governance in listed companies' *La Semaine Juridique*, 21 November 2013, 17–72.
54 Cadbury, op. cit., n. 5.
55 Arcot et al., op. cit., n. 51; Arcot and Bruno, op. cit., n. 51.
56 German Corporate Governance Code, Government Commission, as amended on 15 May 2012, s. 161.

110

Hence, the United Kingdom and Germany have one single corporate governance code for listed companies serving as an obligatory and exclusive reference for the application of the comply-or-explain rule. In contrast to this is the situation in France. Even before the transposition of Directive 2006/46/EC, French law was familiar with the comply-or-explain principle. This principle was never formally expressed in relation to share-issuing companies however, in contrast to asset-management companies which were subject to the rule under the law of 1 August 2003. But the transposition of the comply-or-explain principle in France had the effect of weakening the functioning of the principle, originally conceived of in England, to oblige issuers to provide detailed information on their governance practices in relation to every standard contained in a code of reference.

France chose the least demanding transposition possible. The French system effectively exploited the simultaneously alternative and cumulative character of the options opened by the European law.[57] As a result, the situation in French law is this: optional reference to an optional corporate governance code. First, companies may choose whether or not to apply a governance frame of reference. If they decide not to apply one, they must explain the reasons why. If a company does choose to apply a frame of reference, it must comply with it or specify the provisions derogated from and justify this position. Secondly, the legislature does not impose any code of reference. Several codes or recommendations thus flourished at the end of the 2000s. Today, however, practice respects the AFEP/MEDEF code.[58] In

---

57 Articles L. 225-37 of the Commercial Code provide that:
    when a company voluntarily refers to a corporate governance code formulated by organisations representing companies, the report must specify the provisions it has derogated from and the reasons why it has done so. The company specifies where this code may be consulted. If a company does not refer to such a code, the report must indicate the rules the company has imposed upon itself in addition to legal requirements and, where applicable, must explain why the company has decided not to apply any of the code's provisions.
    See B. Fasterling and J.-C. Duhamel, 'Bilan de l'application du comply or explain par les sociétés françaises du SBF 120' (2009) 6 *Bull. Joly Bourse* 524; V. Magnier, 'Le principe "se conformer ou s'expliquer", une consécration en trompe l'oeil?' *La Semaine Juridique*, 5 juin 2008, 3; Couret, op. cit., n. 49.
58 In October 2008, when the AFEP and the MEDEF published the new version of their recommendations on the remuneration of company directors, the government immediately made it known that unless 'the boards of directors of the businesses concerned adhere formally to these recommendations before the end of 2008, and to ensure their rigorous application, they will be taken up by a bill by 2009'. Listed companies adhered to the AFEP/MEDEF Code from then on. This code became, in effect, the code of reference for listed companies. This code, now a de facto frame of reference, is entirely self-regulated. It originated in effect with a private initiative and was written, originally, uniquely for the grand patrons of the CAC 40. Furthermore, it has never been legitimated by any authority, apart from implicitly by the French Prime Minister in December 2008.

111

France, in practice, there are now two codes of reference: the AFEP-MEDEF code and the MiddleNext code for smaller values.[59]

(b) Differing degrees of normativity within one code or from one code to another

A second series of flaws in the implementation of the comply-or-explain rule arises from differing degrees of normativity within one code or from one code to another. This flaw is certainly linked to a variety of code sources.

It may be observed that, in the beginning, the drafters of codes varied from one country to another, and different steps were taken to promote corporate governance codes as well as the comply-or-explain rule. According to a large-scale study carried out by RiskMetrics, four categories of code sources can be distinguished:[60]

- The obligation to refer to the provisions of the corporate governance code and to implement it through the comply-or-explain principle results from the rules governing the listing of companies (United Kingdom, Denmark, Ireland, Romania)
- The corporate governance code itself determines how it functions (Luxemburg, Finland, Sweden, Estonia)
- The rules governing the listing of companies requires reference to the code and the law imposes recourse to the comply-or-explain rule (Austria, Italy, Poland)
- The law not only establishes the principle of referring to a code but also recourse to the comply-or-explain rule (the Netherlands, Germany, Hungary, Portugal, Spain, and France, with the differences described below).

Along with this variety in sources, we notice differing degrees of normativity within one code or from one code to another. In their structure, as well as their content, the level of details contained in corporate governance codes within each member state differs noticeably from one country to another. As for the structure of the codes, some contain standards corresponding to different levels of obligation. Thus, general mandatory principles

---

59 The MiddleNext code was written by a French independent professional association that exclusively represents mid-cap listed companies. This code contains 'points to watch' and recommendations for these companies. The points to watch enumerate the main questions that the board of directors must ask itself on corporate governance. They do not, strictly speaking, constitute recommendations requiring explanation in case of non-compliance that must feature in the president's report. Companies that chose to apply the MiddleNext code must, however, indicate in this report that the board of directors is aware of the points to watch.
60 RiskMetrics, *Study on Monitoring and Enforcement Practices in Corporate Governance in the Member States* (2009), at <http://ec.europa.eu/internal_market/company/ecgforum/studies_en.htm>.

may be elaborated upon by recommendations that must be implemented through the comply-or-explain rule. These recommendations may be supplemented by explanatory suggestions to which the comply-or-explain rule does not apply.[61] Some corporate governance codes also provide for a variable application of their recommendations according to company size.[62] Differences in the structure and content of corporate governance codes must be seen in perspective with the legal systems of each member state. Effectively, the level of detail in a code cannot be understood except from the point of view of the place left to soft law by imperative regulations.

Despite these differences, according to the RiskMetrics study, cases of 'codex shopping', in which companies choose to submit themselves to the recommendations that suit them the best, are rare. Moreover, with a view to resolving this issue, the European Corporate Governance Forum has already made some proposals in its declaration of 23 March 2009.[63]

IV. ADAPTING THE COMPLY-OR-EXPLAIN RULE FOR GREATER COHERENCE IN EUROPEAN CORPORATE CULTURE

In order to adapt the comply-or-explain rule to create greater coherence in European corporate culture, two ways of improvement are suggested: the first regarding the code itself, the second on the implementation of the comply-or-explain rule.

1. *Improvements in the code itself*

Some recommendations can be suggested, requiring compulsory reference to a single code at national level, without it being thought useful to adopt a code at European level. Companies issuing shares admitted to trading on a regulated market must be able to conform their practices to a single corporate governance code, to which the representatives of different market actors have contributed.

First, the lack of a single code prevents the comply-or-explain rule from fulfiling its role. Corporate governance standards must in effect be homogenous in order to usefully inform shareholders of their implementation. The readability of declarations and their comparison with other companies are indispensable to a disclosure which, without these preconditions, would be purely formal. Thus, the choice of a single code of governance (as opposed

---

61 See the examples in J.-B. Poulle, *Réflexions sur le droit souple et le gouvernement d'entreprise. Le principe 'se conformer ou expliquer' en droit boursier* (2011) 163.
62 id.
63 EUCGF, 'Statement of the European Corporate Governance Forum on Director Remuneration', 23 March 2009, at <http://ec.europa.eu/internal_market/company/docs/ecgforum/ecgf-remuneration_en.pdf>.

to the possibility of referring to several codes as in France, at least legally) is a precondition for an in-depth study, including comparisons, of the information provided by companies.

Second, the elaboration of a code of reference assumes that, at a given moment, it will be accorded true normative legitimacy. One of the aims of good corporate governance is to satisfy the company interest, that is to say, the creation of value for the benefit of all (the shareholders and stakeholders in the company), which requires that all the interests guaranteed by the company be taken into account. The code must then reflect the interest of all *stakeholders*. In Germany and the United Kingdom, the formulation of corporate governance codes has been the work of companies and the financial, legal, and academic sectors, whereas in France, codes issue only from the directors of CAC40 listed companies.

It is recommended, for this reason, that such a code be formulated, in all European countries, following a large-scale consultation with all market actors and not only with a professional organization which, by its nature, cannot represent the various interests present.[64] The participation of all market actors in the drafting of the code should give it greater legitimacy. Then, an official procedure should establish it definitively. The German example, where the code was established by a specialist commission composed of representatives of market actors concerned with corporate governance which must propose annual amendments where necessary, would be a good one to follow in countries with a civil law tradition.

On a national level, if a new code of reference is to be recommended, its provisions may nonetheless still be adapted to company size (for example, certain provisions will not apply to companies with low market capitalization) and/or industry type (certain provisions could concern only investment companies, insurance companies, and credit institutions).

Conversely, it is not recommended that a code be implemented on a European level. First, the dynamism and diversity of private actors or economic operators must continue to be prioritized in the drafting and updating of corporate governance codes. The rules they establish are essentially codes of conduct and should therefore continue to be non-binding on state or European level. It is preferable to retain the diversity of codes, thus promoting innovation and best practice, factors in good performance (the 'race to the top').[65]

Secondly, as highlighted above, only a limited number of cases of codex shopping have been observed, according to the RiskMetrics study. Although codex shopping, which is likely to favour competition between codes, could, in theory, allow a model code to emerge (seen to be 'the best' by issuers of

64 See the Preamble of the French Code of Corporate Governance, June 2013, 1.
65 A. Landier, D. Sraer, and D. Thesmar, 'Bottom Up Corporate Governance' (2013) 17 *Rev. of Finance* 161.

114

shares), in practice, it seems that codex shopping would (currently) come up against the variety of national laws and serious difficulties of articulation between national imperative rules and the non-imperative rules contained in the code.

Finally, the elaboration of such a code risks being ineffective, or even counter-productive. Such an approach would effectively require the elaboration of excessively strict rules, through precise and detailed regulations. Corporate governance rules, as we recall, are codes of conduct, flexible by nature and applied case-by-case. European intervention would, on the contrary, imply that 'one size fits all'. Conversely, it seems much more effective to require economic actors to better account for their good governance practices with regard to objectives, recommendations, and standards of reference. The impetus for these elements of reference must come from the European Union. The comply-or-explain rule would then make perfect sense.

The application of and adherence to corporate governance codes on a national level is a key element for allowing investors, and the public in general, to obtain pertinent and reliable information on the governance practices of the companies they invest in. The European-level study, however,[66] reveals gaps, in the implementation of the comply-or-explain rule. Its findings have been corroborated by more local studies. These gaps call for improvements in the implementation and monitoring of company declarations.

2. *Improvement in monitoring the comply-or-explain principle*

Recent progress has been made, meaning that the rule needs time in order to ensure better implementation. The RiskMetrics study[67] demonstrates that the listed companies of member states not only respect their duty to declare but also, in the vast majority of cases, the recommendations of corporate governance codes. Thus, out of the 270 companies in 18 different member states studied, 242 said they refer to their national corporate governance code, nine refer to the code of another member state, five refer to the OECD Code and just 55 refer to another document relating to corporate governance. The comply-or-explain rule therefore appears to be well respected in a large number of European countries (for example, Belgium, the Netherlands, Germany, and France).

As for France, recent progress has been made following the transposition of the 2006/46 Directive in 2008, which introduced the comply-or-explain rule. Whereas the Autorité des Marchés Financiers (AMF) found that one third of the companies concerned did not comply with their duty to declare in

---

66 RiskMetrics, op. cit., n. 60.
67 id.

2008, it indicated in its 2009 report on corporate governance[68] that 81 per cent of listed companies did make declarations and stated that they referred to the AFEP/MEDEF code; 67 per cent declared that they did not comply with at least one provision in the code. The AFEP/MEDEF also furnished information in its report on the application of its code by SBF120 companies.[69] There as well, the vast majority of SBF120 companies had chosen the AFEP/MEDEF code.

A very instructive academic study[70] allows us to conclude that, first, the vast majority of French share issuers comply with most of the recommendations in the code, or at least declare that they do so, and, second, provide precise explanations (36 per cent) in cases of non-compliance. The study demonstrates, however, that companies seem to have adopted a cautious approach, prohibiting them from breaking away from the AFEP/MEDEF code's recommendations. Furthermore, the study does not give any indication of the exactness of the declarations, that is, how accurately they reflect reality. It should be noted that a certain number of the recommendations of the AFEP/MEDEF code are not structural in nature but subjective, and are therefore difficult to measure.[71]

In addition, it should also be noted that many disparities exist between countries.[72] Furthermore, on deeper analysis, the results show themselves to be more worrying in their details. Notably, the information provided by companies appears to fall below the necessary standard. First, the quality of the information furnished by issuers of shares, in relation to their governance practices, depends on the type of subject concerned and certain explanations are too short and imprecise. Second, and more worryingly, it appears that the conduct of some companies differs from their declarations.

Studies undertaken in member states[73] further confirm what has been revealed on a European level, namely, that the comply-or-explain rule is not effective enough within the European Union and that companies most often content themselves with a 'box-ticking approach'. These studies also prompt one to wonder at the lack of interest investors have in these declarations. They suggest that the latter are not curious enough about the information given and that it is important for them to be able to seek and understand what, in detail, justifies derogations from the codes.[74] This requirement demands, as a prerequisite, greater precision in the declarations of companies subject to the comply-or-explain rule.

---

68 AMF, *AMF 2009 Report On Corporate Governance and Internal Control* (2009).
69 AFEP/MEDEF *Reports on Corporate Governance* (2009 and 2010).
70 Fasterling and Duhamel, op. cit., n. 57.
71 For example, the remuneration of directors must be 'measured, balanced and fair ...'.
72 P. Sanderson, D. Seidl, J. Roberts, and B. Krieger, 'Flexible or not? The Comply-or-Explain Principle in UK and German Corporate Governance', CBR Working Paper no. 407 (2010), at <http://www.cbr.cam.ac.uk/pdf/WP407.pdf>.
73 In the United Kingdom, see Arcot and Bruno, op. cit., n. 51.
74 Arcot et al., op. cit., n. 51.

The Belgian experience presents an exception, which must be highlighted, in that it offers shareholders a greater role in the monitoring of corporate governance declarations. Belgian law effectively allows shareholders to demand explanations from the company by adding an item to the agenda of the general meeting, in order to question the directors on this subject during the meeting, or even to demand management expertise. In addition, the Enterprise Chamber of the Amsterdam Court of Appeal can hold that a company has been badly managed and revoke the mandates of the executive directors or the supervisory board, and even demand the dissolution of the company.[75] Without going to this extreme, greater shareholder involvement may be recommended in a general meeting in which a declaration is presented in compliance with the comply-or-explain rule.

SOME CONCLUDING RECOMMENDATIONS

1. *Informal external monitoring*

A first approach aims to put in place an external monitoring system. This may however prove to be unsuitable in practice if it involves the creation of a binding soft-law rule. The 'comply-or-explain' rule was intended to sub-stitute for the coercive power of the state and, notably, the coercion of the market, which justified until then an approach free from any administrative or other kind of intervention. Furthermore, the market authority is not there to 'monitor' companies but to ensure the proper functioning of the market. Even though, in France, the AMF has a duty to publish an annual report on the governance practices of listed companies,[76] it does not actively monitor the content of declarations.

Nevertheless, market authorities can play an effective role through more informal methods of intervention. In the United Kingdom, the Financial Services Authority (FSA) closely monitors governance practices. Market authorities could also be encouraged to regularly undertake substantial inspections (to investigate flagrant factual inaccuracies in corporate govern-ance declarations, for example, to verify whether a company that announces it has (x) number of independent directors is telling the truth) on a randomized basis (for example, two randomly selected companies per year), to publish the results of these inspections and, where required, impose sanctions in cases of dishonest information (such as a declaration of full compliance despite the fact that the company manifestly does not comply with certain provisions in the code of reference).

---

75 E. Schieman, 'Le dirigeants de Naamloze Vennoostchap aux Pays-Bas' in *La direction des sociétés anonymes en Europe: vers des pratiques harmonisées de gouvernance?*, eds. Y. Chaput and A. Lévi (2008) 337.
76 Article L. 621 of the Monetary and Financial Code.

Another method could consist of tasking auditors with a duty to investigate incoherencies or flagrant factual inaccuracies in corporate governance declarations. A report would then be given to the issuer concerned. If the company concerned failed to take appropriate measures to correct its declaration, the auditors would then report this to the market authority.

Finally, the carrying out of inspections and their costs could be assumed by professional associations or by the commission charged with formulating a corporate governance code.

2. *Greater involvement of investors*

Shareholders, and the wider public, are the addressees of the information contained in corporate governance declarations. Earlier we highlighted the relative passivity of shareholders regarding these declarations. In order for the comply-or-explain rule to really be effective, at a minimum, declarations must be readable and contain sufficiently relevant elements of comparison to allow them to be effectively evaluated. In addition, shareholders must be able, where necessary, to question directors and demand clarifications of the declarations.

(a) Evaluating respect for the duty to justify non-conformity

It seems useful to demand *a certain degree of harmonized explanations* in company declarations, which would, first, enhance the readability of the declarations and their 'comparability', and would, second, have the practical advantage of reducing the costs involved in inspecting them. Thus, a certain degree of formalism in corporate governance declarations could be envisaged on a European level.

This formalism could aim to highlight the salient points of the declaration, without neglecting the details, and distinguish two parts in its presentation. In the first part, issuers would be responsible for drawing the attention of investors to the important points in their declaration, in a free format, particularly in relation to the company's main derogations from the code of reference, the explanations justifying them, and the practices chosen to replace them. In the second part, issuers should be required to state, provision by provision, according to *a standard format* (to facilitate reading and comparison) whether they comply with every provision in the code and, if not, explain the reasons for non-compliance as well as the practices chosen to replace them.

For the rest, the response should nevertheless remain free, but under the responsibility of each issuer (to be able to justify its response).

(b) Favouring dialogue between directors and shareholders

The practices of companies in different European countries have led to the establishment of an often informal dialogue with the reference shareholders of the companies concerned. These practices are highly developed, even though they may constitute a breach of the principle of equality in the right to information of different shareholders.[77] It is not certain, however, that the subject of the declaration is always broached on this occasion.

In order to formalize the involvement and the interest of shareholders in such a declaration, it would be interesting to take inspiration from the Belgian model. Without adopting the Belgian law in its entirety, it would be useful in effect to give shareholders the option of demanding explanations from the company, by requiring that an item be added to the agenda of the general meeting, to enable them to question the directors on this subject at the meeting. This recommendation presents several advantages: it requires directors to take care in drafting the declaration for which the shareholders may hold them liable and involves the shareholders more in the company's information processes. This last element in addition conforms with Directive 2007/36 on the protection of certain shareholders' rights. It should nevertheless be noted that, as it consists of adding an item and not a resolution to the agenda, this question shall only be subject to a debate and not a vote at general meeting.

3. *Retaining a flexible law with a certain normative effect*

Interestingly, the RiskMetrics[78] study reveals that not all markets have the same degree of 'maturity', but that the comply-or-explain rule functions a little better every year. The implementation of the code by issuers and the information they provide in case of non-compliance constitutes an open-air laboratory of governance practices, allowing the legislature to identify those provisions which are not followed (or are not systematically followed) and to threaten to intervene, or to actually intervene by introducing a coercive law. Issuers also demonstrate that they are gradually learning to self-monitor in matters of governance and to better inform the market every year. It seems at first that those issuers who provide insufficient or unconvincing information are not really punished by the market itself (by a fall in their share value) nor by investors (voting with their feet).

Conversely, the notably civil liability of issuers but, above all, of their directors appears to be well-adapted to the task of making the principle more effective (inaccuracies or omissions in information given to the market). Another sanction that may be envisaged, complementary to liability, consists of publishing the names of those companies that do not comply with the duty to disclose on the website of the market authority (to 'name and shame' in order to increase the power of transparency).

In conclusion, what could be the recommended level of intervention? As codes of conduct, corporate governance principles participate in soft law, the

---

77 A. Sotiropoulou, *Les obligations d'information des sociétés cotées en droit de l'Union européenne* (2012).
78 RiskMetrics, op. cit., n. 60.

119

particular *normative effect* of which has been highlighted, even in the absence of *normative value*. Adopting an excessively strict approach, through regulations or directives, seems here to be counterproductive, in so far as flexibility, responsiveness, and adaptability are the key assets of corporate governance codes. It is just as essential to prevent these codes from becoming *dead letters*, which is a real risk in the absence of effective monitoring, either in their application or through avoidance. Economic actors must thus be compelled to account for their compliance with corporate governance rules, and the implementation of the comply-or-explain rule, still poorly understood, must be improved.

If economic actors must justify rule avoidance, this should be in relation to a common goal, a general policy of governance. It seems essential, henceforth, that legal texts such as Commission communications establishing general EU policies, directions, and standards of conduct be implemented. This type of framework, very common in European competition law and well-integrated by the Court of Justice in terms of normative value, may usefully be called upon.[79] Such instruments, applied to private codes of a behavioural nature, such as corporate governance codes, could offer a useful general analytical framework and, in time, contribute to the establishment of a veritable culture of governance among European economic actors – not to mention that these instruments form part of the new regulation policy, which the European Commission has been following for around fifteen years.[80] Hence, a soft European intervention with the help of coordinating legal texts is definitively advocated, in order to create a harmonized culture of governance in Europe, so that corporate governance private codes acquire an incontestable normative *effect*, without having a real normative *value*. Even so, the level of auto-regulation by the private actors is still the best way so far, in order to set good practice in corporate governance by means of codes and the comply-or-explain rule.

79 L. Idot, 'A propos de l'internationalisation du droit, Réflexions sur la *soft law*' in *Mélanges en l'honneur d'Hélène Gaudemet-Tallon* (2007); see, also, L. Boisson de Chazournes, 'Policy Guidance and Compliance: The World Bank Operational Standards' in *Commitment and Compliance: The Role of Non-binding Norms in the International Legal System*, ed. D. Shelton (2003) 281; E. Bernard, *La spécificité du standard juridique en droit communautaire* (2010). Conversely, it is noted in different branches of law, the fastidious approach of regulations or directives produces complexity, which can obscure the aims pursued; see, also, S. Rials, 'Les standards, notions critiques du droit' in *Les notions à contenu variable en droit*, eds. C. Perelman and R. Vander Elst (1984) 39.
80 L. Senden, 'Soft Law, Self-regulation and Co-regulation in European Law: Where Do They Meet?' (2005) 9(1) *Electronic J. of Comparative Law*, at <http://www.ejcl.org/91/issue91.html>.

JOURNAL OF LAW AND SOCIETY
VOLUME 41, NUMBER 1, MARCH 2014
ISSN: 0263-323X, pp. 121–51

Understanding the Board of Directors after the Financial Crisis: Some Lessons for Europe

JOSEPH A. MCCAHERY* AND ERIK P.M. VERMEULEN*

There are numerous studies on the effectiveness of boards that primarily focus on legal formalities, including gender diversity, board size, remuneration, board evaluation, and the role of the chairman of the board. While attempting to design a one-size-fits-all framework, scholars approaching board independence from an agency-cost perspective have been less concerned with analysing board structures that contribute to strategic decision making and corporate performance. We examine the factors and board strategies that are associated with value creation and innovation by analysing the composition of high-performance and high-growth companies. The article shows that venture capitalists, with their specific expertise and experience, continue to play an important role as independent board members in the post-IPO period. We specifically investigate the importance of diversity, showing that there are significant differences between the companies in terms of age, gender diversity, and business expertise (which is dependent on the stage in the company life cycle).

INTRODUCTION

There is a general feeling that we need better corporate governance.[1] This is not surprising if we realize that the corporate governance frameworks that were developed by policymakers, regulators, academics, and practitioners in the 2000s had little or no significant impact on the performance of listed

* Department of Business Law, Tilburg Law School, Tilburg University, Warandelaan 2, Tilburg, The Netherlands
j.a.mccahery@tilburguniversity.edu
e.p.m.vermeulen@tilburguniversity.edu

1 See, for instance, M. Barnier, 'Making Europe an Attractive Place To Do Business' (2010), at <http://europa.eu/rapid/press-release_SPEECH-10-54_en.htm>.

companies during the crisis.[2] The last decade has seen attempts to answer some key questions including: what is the role of the board of directors? What is the most effective mix of directors? What are their responsibilities in terms of good governance?

The existing literature has mainly focused on the principal agent relationships between the shareholders, board of directors, and senior and executive management in listed companies.[3] Scholars have emphasized that the monitoring and oversight role of the independent outside directors is crucial to prevent managerial misbehaviour and misconduct and maximize shareholder wealth.[4] In countries with controlling shareholders, a common structural arrangement in Europe, a second element has been added to the debate about the role of the board of directors: board members should protect the interests of minority investors and other stakeholders in the company.[5] This is necessary because controlling shareholders may employ several strategies to extract resources and assets from companies they control.[6] The heterogeneity of large shareholders across firms and board structures may imply differences in the level of oversight and monitoring.

Following the financial crisis, however, recent studies have suggested that a predominantly independent board is essential to serve as the necessary and dynamic wedge between the company and its insiders, on the one hand, and the capital market and the short-term investors on the other,[7] thereby reducing the three-way agency problems between the executive managers and the varying types of investors and stakeholders.[8] There is a general

---

2 See K. Gupta, C. Krishnamurti, and A. Tourani-Rad, 'Is Corporate Governance relevant During the Financial Crisis?' (2013) 23 *J. of International Financial Markets, Institutions & Money* 85; M. Humphery-Jenner, F. Lopez de Silanes, and J.A. McCahery, 'Managerial Entrenchment, Credit Ratings, Covenants and Fees' (2012).

3 See J. Dahya, O. Dimitrov, and J. McConnell, 'Dominant shareholders, corporate boards and corporate value: A cross-country analysis' (2008) 87 *J. of Financial Economics* 73.

4 See J.N. Gordon, 'The Rise of Independent Directors in the United States, 1950–2005: Of Shareholder Value and Stock Market Prices' (2007) 59 *Stanford Law Rev.* 1465. See L. Bebchuk and J. Fried, 'Executive Compensation as an Agency Problem' (2003) 17(3) *J. of Economic Perspectives* 71; R.W. Masulis and S. Mobbs, 'Are All Inside Directors the Same? Do They Entrench CEOs or Enhance Board Decision-Making?' (2011) 66 *J. of Finance* 812.

5 See W.-G. Ringe, 'Independent Directors: After the Crisis' (2013) 14 *European Business Organization Law Rev.* 401.

6 See M. Gutiérrez Urtiaga and M. Saez, 'Deconstructing Independent Directors' (2013) 13 *J. of Corporate Legal Studies* 63. See, also, C. Malberti and E. Sironi, 'The Mandatory Representation of Minority Shareholders on the Board of Directors of Italian Listed Corporations: An Empirical Analysis', Bocconi Legal Studies Research Paper No. 18 (2007), at <http://ssrn.com/abstract=965398>.

7 See, for example, Gordon, op. cit., n. 4.

8 See W.W. Bratton and M.L. Wachter, 'The Case Against Shareholder Empowerment' (2010) 158 *University of Pennsylvania Law Rev.* 653.

impression that the board of directors should be insulated from shareholder influence and interventions as long as institutional shareholders fail to engage properly with executive management and the board of directors.[9] Board independence and insulation are necessary to offer resistance to the short-term mentality that currently prevails in the investor community and capital markets.[10] Additionally, policymakers and regulators seek to understand better the factors that impact the effectiveness of boards. So far, the discussion focuses on a number of legal formalities and requirements, including gender diversity, optimal board size, remuneration, board evaluation processes, and the role of the chair of the board. This is clearly the approach of the European Commission as detailed in its Green Paper of 2011 where it identifies the most relevant issues for good governance.[11]

This article argues that the attempt to design a one-size-fits-all framework is based on a general misconception and misunderstanding about corporate boards, which often leads to counterproductive behaviour.[12] The preoccupation with reducing agency cost and building long-termism in listed companies limits our understanding of boards. In this context, this leads to introducing a third dimension to corporate governance, which is usually

9 See, for a different view, L.A. Bebchuk and A. Cohen, 'The costs of entrenched boards' (2005) 78 *J. of Financial Economics* 409; L.A. Bebchuk, 'The Myth That Insulating Boards Serves Long-Term Value' (2013) 113 *Columbia Law Rev.* 1637; J.A. McCahery, E.P.M. Vermeulen, and M. Hisatake, 'The Present and Future of Corporate Governance: Re-Examining the Role of the Board of Directors and Investor Relations in Listed Companies' (2013) 10 *European Company and Financial Law Rev.*117.

10 The short-term mentality is explained by M. Isaksson and S. Celik, 'Who Cares? Corporate Governance in Today's Equity Markets' (2013), at <www.oecd-ilibrary.org/governance/who-cares-corporate-governance-in-today-s-equity-markets_5k47zw5kdnmp-en>. The importance of board insulation is described by S.M. Bainbridge, 'Response to Increasing Shareholder Power: Director Primacy and Shareholder Disempowerment' (2006) 119 *Harvard Law Rev.* 1735. See, for a different view, M.J. Roe, 'Corporate Short-Termism – In the Boardroom and in the Courtroom' (2013) 68 *Business Lawyer* 977.

11 European Commission, Green Paper, 'The EU corporate governance framework' (COM(2011) 164 final). See M. Belcredi and G. Ferrarini, 'The European Corporate Governance Framework: Issues and Perspectives', ECGI Law Working Paper No. 214/2013 (2013), at <http://ssrn.com/abstract=2264990>. See, also, Heidrick & Struggles, *European Corporate Governance Report 201: Challenging Board Performance* (2011), at <http://www.heidrick.com/PublicationsReports/PublicationsReports/HS_EuropeanCorpGovRpt2011.pdf >.

12 See, also, W. Drobetz, F. Von Meyerinck, D. Oesch, and M.M. Schmid, 'Is Director Industry Experience a Corporate Governance Mechanism?' (2013), at <http://ssrn.com/abstract=2256477>; O. Faleye, R. Hoitash, and U. Hoitash, 'The Costs of Intense Board Monitoring' (2011) 101 *J. of Financial Economics* 160; D. Gilshan and C. Jackson, 'A Call on U.S. Independent Directors to develop Shareholder Engagement Strategies' (2013), at <http://blogs.law.harvard.edu/corpgov/2013/04/24/a-call-on-u-s-independent-directors-to-develop-shareholder-engagement-strategies/>.

associated with innovation and value creation and reflected to some extent by the strategies adopted by growth-oriented companies.[13] We construct this third dimension to allow us to identify the characteristics of independent directors associated with the expertise, skills, capabilities, and affinities that can help give rise to a market-leading company (which generally outperforms the stock market index and offers a better resistance against stock market volatility).

The articles makes three distinct contributions to the research on boards. First, it highlights the importance of board dynamics as a source of change in a firm's corporate policy (which is often initiated by a disappointing stock price performance). Consider Apple, for example. The company's late CEO, Steve Jobs, understood early on the important role of the board of directors for Apple's growth and innovation needs, but also to build relationships with its suppliers and customers. In order for the board of directors to become a competitive advantage and help carry Apple forward, its members needed to have a thorough understanding of the computer industry and the firm's products.

Second, it confirms that the role of the board of directors is broader than constraining managerial misbehaviour and maximizing shareholder value.[14] We look at how innovative and high-growth companies like Apple differ from less successful ones in terms of the structure and the composition of the board of directors. In general, a major difference is that innovative and high-growth firms focus on valued industry expertise and firm knowledge more than independence and appropriate risk-oversight qualities. Our central aim is to show that board structure and organization also come to play an important role in stimulating the focus on strategic advice and overall board effectiveness.

Third, we investigate the characteristics common to directors appointed to boards of growth-oriented companies.[15] What can we learn from these

---

13 This view is not new. To be sure, in general, the corporate governance debate offers a single-minded analysis and overemphasizes the importance of risk management and remuneration policies, the engagement of shareholders, and the independence of directors. Interestingly, however, the Organisation for Economic Co-operation and Development (OECD)'s *Principles of Corporate Governance* (2004) explicitly states in its preamble that '[t]o remain competitive in a changing world, corporations must innovate and adapt their corporate governance practices so that they can meet new demands and grasp new opportunities.' Still, policymakers generally seem to struggle with the implementation of entrepreneurial boards (see Barnier, op. cit., n. 1). It is therefore not surprising that in the aftermath of the financial crisis, the OECD launched an initiative to refocus the corporate governance discussion on value creation and growth. See OECD, *Corporate Governance, Value Creation and Growth, The Bridge between Finance and Enterprise* (2012).
14 See Faleye et al., op. cit., n. 12.
15 See, also, A.J. Epstein, *The Perfect Corporate Board, A Handbook for Mastering the Unique Challenges of Small-Cap Companies* (2013).

124

companies?[16] In order to give an answer, we make use of two new hand-collected data sets that consist of (i) seventy venture capital backed companies that were involved in initial public offerings (IPOs) on United States stock markets between 2011 and the first half of 2012 (VC-70), and (ii) the top forty of the world's largest companies in the Financial Times Global 500 2012 List (including corporations from the United States, Europe, and Asia) (FT-40).[17] The data allow us to obtain a clear understanding of the composition and dynamics within these boards. The evidence in the data holds important lessons for academics and other researchers, but also for policymakers, investors, and company boards. Unsurprisingly, these lessons go beyond, and even contradict, the traditional and current thinking about the role of the board of directors in listed companies.

The article is structured as follows. In the next section, we suggest that a new approach to corporate governance, which we have labeled the three-dimensional model, can be effective in understanding a firm's growth and innovation strategy.[18] To illustrate the dynamics of the model, we start with a succinct description of the Apple board to show how the composition and operations of the boards can contribute to the introduction of successful and innovative products and improved firm performance. The Apple case confirms that issues about board structure, composition, and practices should be discussed against the background of a company's growth and value creation potential (and not only against the background of agency problems and long-termism). Having examined the Apple case, we provide an analysis of the empirical results. We examine the board practices and strategies that enhance firms' competitive advantage in their efforts to develop innovative products and services. It follows from our data that the structure and organization of boards cannot be captured in a one-size-fits-all framework. This article argues that the traditional principal-agent based approach to corporate governance takes insufficient account of growth-oriented companies. The next section addresses which legal system is likely to enhance board performance. We focus on the differences between one-tier and two-tier boards. The latter are common in civil law countries in Europe, and arguably put more emphasis on the monitoring and oversight function of the board. While there have been numerous theoretical and empirical studies on the beneficial effects of two-tier boards, we observe a formal convergence in Europe towards the Anglo-American one-tier board system. The article

16 It is argued that the structure, organization, and management of boards can be significantly improved by learning from peers with high-impact boards: see C. Bhagat, M. Hirt, and C. Kehoe, 'Improving Board Governance: McKinsey Global Survey Results' (2013), at <http://www.mckinsey.com/insights/strategy/improving_board_governance_mckinsey_global_survey_results>. In this article we follow a similar approach by focusing on high-growth companies.
17 We have excluded energy, oil and gas producers, and financial institutions from the data set.
18 See McCahery et al., op. cit. n. 9.

concludes that, from the three-dimensional perspective, this trend should be welcomed, since it arguably contributes to the success of growth-oriented companies in Europe.

'CONFLICTING' ROLES OF THE BOARD OF DIRECTORS

In this section, we begin with a very brief account of the crucial role played by the board of directors in Apple's history. Although the Apple case seems to suggest that there are two conflicting theories of the board of directors, it should be noted that most legal systems around the world recognize that boards not only have a vital role to play in the area of monitoring and risk oversight, but also in giving 'informal' advice and strategy support to management. Nevertheless, there is a gap between theory and practice. Because the legal corporate governance framework emphasizes the importance of oversight, supervision, and risk management, there is usually simply not enough time for boards to perform their advisory function adequately. It is therefore timely to introduce a new wave of corporate governance research that redirects the role of a company's board to enhancing management decision making and future growth and value creation.

1. The Apple case study

Corporate governance experts often struggle with the question: how is it possible that Apple is one of the world's most admired companies,[19] one of the world's most valuable companies,[20] and one of the world's most innovative companies?[21] Indeed, the question is particularly pertinent when one realizes that corporate governance experts often believe that Apple's culture of secrecy has severely weakened its corporate governance structure.[22] There are many things to say about Apple's governance structure. Our focus is on the distinctive features of the board of directors which has played a crucial, but allegedly increasingly obedient, role in Apple's history of success.

---

19 Apple ranks number one in the World's Most Admired Companies' ranking assembled by CNNMoney in 2008, 2009, 2010, 2011, 2012 and 2013, at <http://money.cnn.com/magazines/fortune/most-admired/2013/snapshots/670.html>.
20 See S. Russolillo, 'Apple Loses Throne as World's Biggest Company' *Wall Street J.*, 17 April 2013.
21 See H. Shaughnessy, 'Apple and Google, #1 and #2 Of World's Most Innovative Companies. Why?' *Forbes*, 15 January 2013, at <http://www.forbes.com/sites/haydnshaughnessy/2013/01/15/apple-and-google-1-and-2-of-worlds-most-innovative-companies-why/>.
22 See J. Nocera, 'Apple's Culture of Secrecy' *New York Times*, 26 July 2008. See, also, B. Stone and A. Vance, 'Apple's Obsession With Secrecy Grows Stronger' *New York Times*, 22 June 2009.

126

Recall that it was the board that removed Steve Jobs as Head of the Macintosh division in 1985. Following his return in 1997, Jobs, who was initially employed in an advisory role (along with being the CEO and Chairman of a computer animation company, called Pixar), quickly regained more control over the company's affairs.[23] This became clear in the keynote address during the Macworld Expo in Boston on 6 August 1997,[24] where he explicitly avoided the announcement of new and innovative products, but revealed the appointment of four new, hand-picked, board members.[25] Jobs was convinced that changing the composition of the board of directors was a necessary first step to bring back focus, relevance, and interaction (with the outside world) to the company in its journey to introduce disruptive innovations and creative products to its potential customers.[26]

What is most interesting, in light of this article, is that Jobs knew that in order for the board of directors to become a competitive advantage and help carry Apple forward, its members needed to have experience in the computer industry and be passionate Apple users. Perhaps this is primarily the reason why Mr. Woolard, Chairman and former CEO of Dupont, and Mr. Chang, a senior executive at Hughes Electronics, were 'allowed' to stay, for their leadership skills and knowledge of the Asian market respectively. Mr. Ellison (software expertise and co-founder of Oracle), Mr. York (Former CFO with experience with reorganizations at both Chrysler and IBM), Mr. Campbell (CEO of Intuit and former Vice-president of Sales and Marketing at Apple) were added to the board of directors. As expected, Jobs was also asked to join the board.

The above indicates that Jobs designed, modelled, and moulded the board of directors to Apple's growth and innovation needs, but also to his personal tastes.[27] The latter, of course, spurred the debate among conventional corporate governance experts about the quality and performance of the Apple board (particularly after the corporate failures and corporate govern-ance reforms of 2001–2002). From a traditional corporate governance standpoint, it is difficult to understand that Jobs valued industry expertise, passion, and loyalty more than independence and appropriate risk-oversight qualities. The preference for outside directors with firm specific and industry knowledge became again clear when Mr. Gore Jr. joined the Apple Board in 2003. Jobs was excited about his election when he stated that:

---

23 See D. Kawamoto, 'Jobs Rejects Apple Chairman Post' *CNET News* 31 July 1997, at <http://news.cnet.com/Jobs-rejects-Apple-chairman-post/2100-1001_3-201978.html>.

24 See J. Davis, 'Jobs To Keynote Macworld Expo' *CNET*, 29 July 1997, at <http://news.cnet.com/Jobs-to-keynote-Macworld-Expo/2100-1001_3-201931.html>.

25 See M. Costello, 'Apple Gets New Corps', *CNNMoney*, 6 August 1997, at <http://money.cnn.com/1997/08/06/technology/apple/>.

26 See <http://www.youtube.com/watch?v=PEHNrqPkefI>.

27 See W. Isaacson, *Steve Jobs* (2011).

Al [Gore] brings an incredible wealth of knowledge and wisdom to Apple from having helped run the largest organization in the world – the United States government – as a Congressman, Senator and our 45th Vice President. Al [Gore] is also an avid Mac user and does his own video editing in Final Cut Pro.[28]

Do these remarks suggest marked differences from the role of directors advocated by traditional corporate governance experts? Indeed, when assessing the nomination, most expert commentators were critical of Gore's monitoring and oversight value, effectively ignoring the fact that he was instrumental in launching public/private partnership efforts to bring technology to educational institutions in the United States.[29]

The above rationales offered against the Gore nomination suggest that the experts had a 'different type of governance model' used to evaluate appointments to boards. First, it is noteworthy that the experts argued that a politician without any business experience would add no value to the company. Second, they were of the opinion that Apple's board contained too many 'friends of Steve'. That is, board members were (too) loyal to Jobs, which allegedly undermined the CEO's accountability to investors and other stakeholders. Interestingly, the institutional investors as well as the employees and the customers continued to show confidence in Jobs and 'his' board of directors. Consider the stock price performance of the company during the relevant period: between 6 August 1997 (the day of the keynote address in Boston) and 23 August 2011 (Jobs's last day as CEO of Apple), the stock price soared from $25.25 to $360.30, increasing 1,327 per cent. An important question remained as to what would happen to the composition of the board after Jobs passed away in 2011. Corporate governance experts knew the answer.[30] The disappearance of a dominant CEO coincided with the demand for members of the board of directors to re-engage themselves by demanding more transparency, accountability, and oversight. This created the opportunity to appoint a new outside chairman to the board of directors to assess the current members of the board.

Unsurprisingly, however, the composition and orientation of the board of directors has so far not undergone the expected major transformation, again challenging the traditional way of thinking about corporate governance. That is not to say that there were no changes to the composition of Apple's board. Think of boards of directors as 'fluid' in composition: they must evolve with the organizational and business needs of the company at any given time. This, in turn, explains why Genentech's chairman, Mr. Levinson, who had

28 'Former Vice President Al Gore Joins Apple's Board of Directors' Apple press release, 19 March 2003, at <www.apple.com/pr/library/2003/03/19Former-Vice-President-Al-Gore-Joins-Apples-Board-of-Directors.html>.
29 See D. Sellers, 'BusinessWeek: Gore Appointment to Apple Board A Mistake' Macworld, 27 March 2003, at <http://www.macworld.com/article/1016691/byte.html>.
30 See J.S. Lublin, 'Apple Board Faces Scrutiny' Wall Street J., 7 October 2011.

© 2014 The Author. Journal of Law and Society © 2014 Cardiff University Law School

already served as a member of Apple's board since 2000, replaced Jobs as the chairman in November 2011. What is more striking is that by adding Mr. Iger, President and CEO of the Walt Disney Company and Jobs's friend and business partner, to the board of directors, Apple (as well as its investors and other stakeholders) continued to value industry expertise and firm-specific knowledge more than independence and risk-management skills. Consider the strong commercial ties between the Walt Disney Company and Apple, which arguably raise questions about Mr. Iger's independent oversight qualities,[31] but at the same time can explain why he could make a valuable contribution to Apple's further move into the media industry.[32] It is encouraging to see how investors and other stakeholders attributed more importance to Mr. Iger's purchase of approximately $1 million worth of Apple shares in both November 2011 and November 2012, giving him more 'skin in the game', than to his alleged relationship with Apple's executive managers.[33]

It follows from the Apple case study that we can roughly distinguish between two approaches to the theory and practice of the role of the boards of directors. Note, first, that under the traditional corporate governance model, the boards of directors have generally evolved to perform an oversight function independently of the CEO and other executive managers. This contradicts Jobs's view, outlined in his keynote presentation in Boston in 1997, that the board serves as an extension of management, providing outside expertise and experience where and when needed. Presuming that board members are dedicated and visionary, they can challenge management decision making, identify opportunities, and network with governments, society, investors, and other stakeholders.[34]

2. The three-dimensional model of corporate governance

The Apple case seems to suggest that policymakers, academics, and corporate governance experts often ignore what really matters to the players in the corporate governance arena (such as short-term investors, long-term investors, customers, and employees of a firm): value creation through sustainable growth and innovation. Our approach is to emphasize the three-dimensional corporate governance model, with a focus on the dynamics in

31 See I. King and P. Burrows, 'Apple Names Levinson Chairman, Disney's Bob Iger to Board' *Bloomberg*, 17 November 2011, at <http://www.bloomberg.com/news/2011-11-15/apple-names-levinson-chairman-adds-iger-to-board-following-death-of-jobs.html>.
32 See J.E. Vascellaro, 'Apple Adds Disney's Iger to Board, Names Levinson Chairman' *Wall Street J.*, 16 November 2011.
33 See O. Thomas, 'Disney's CEO Is Selling His Company's Stock And Buying Apple' *Business Insider*, 20 November 2012.
34 See D. Cossin, 'Corporate Boardrooms are in Need of Education' *Financial Times*, 9 January 2012.

129

the practice of corporate governance. In the one-dimensional model, which prioritizes shareholder wealth maximization, enhanced regulatory intervention is needed to resolve the principal-agent problems between the investors, the corporate insiders, and other stakeholders. The responsibility for upholding corporate governance standards is shifted to policy makers and regulators. Although it is acknowledged that the rules and regulations that were introduced in the wake of the scandals at the beginning of the twenty-first century have created minimum standards and guidelines of corporate governance that actually improved the functioning of listed companies, it is far from clear whether more stringent and detailed rules for the companies would have a similar effect. A new two-dimensional corporate governance model, which accentuates the importance of long-termism, has confirmed this view. The proponents of the two-dimensional model suggest that, in order to build long-termism into the corporation, it is essential to change the behaviour of the investors and insulate the board from the short-term nature of the capital markets.[35]

In an earlier paper,[36] we proposed a three-dimensional model that focuses primarily on future growth and value creation. This model is important for a number of reasons. First, the benefit is that it has the potential to resolve the corporate governance dilemma resulting from the imbalance between short-term investment strategies and a long-term outlook. Evidence suggests that shareholder (and stakeholder) value and long-term commitments are very much interrelated with a firm's growth and innovation prospects. Second, the importance of a growth-oriented model is that companies (and their executive managers and executive and non-executive directors) are in the first instance responsible for the implementation of governance arrangements that produce better firm and stock market performance.

Again, the three-dimensional model is already reflected in most of the legal frameworks. Irrespective of the legal structure, boards have an important responsibility in the area of risk oversight, compliance, and the setting of remuneration packages. But, in line with the three-dimensional model, the legal corporate law frameworks generally also envision a role in improving corporate performance by approving strategy directions and giving advice to the executive managers.[37] In practice, however, because the oversight and risk-management tasks involve increasingly complex

---

35 See C. Mayer, *Firm Commitment, Why the Corporation is Failing Us and How to Restore Trust in It* (2013).
36 See McCahery et al., op. cit. n. 9.
37 See R. Adams, B.E. Hermalin and M.S. Weisbach, 'The Role of Boards of Directors in Corporate Governance: A Conceptual Framework & Survey' (2010) 48 *J. of Economic Literature* 58; R. Adams, 'The Dual Role of Corporate Boards as Advisors and Monitors of Management: Theory and Evidence' (2002), at <www.cepr.org.uk/meets/wkcn/5/567/papers/adams.pdf>. See, also, L.A. Bebchuk and M.S. Weisbach, 'The State of Corporate Research' (2010) 23 *Rev. of Financial Studies* 939.

challenges, the latter role receives less and less attention. Moreover, as this observation suggests, the traditional corporate governance discussions have framed corporate boards as nothing more than excessively formal control mechanisms on executive managers, particularly the CEO. For instance, most weight is put on procedures that ensure independence and long-termism, such as board composition requirements, age requirements, maximum-term requirements, gender diversity,[38] and splitting the roles of chairman and CEO.[39] This view is confirmed by recent empirical studies.

The current (and often overregulated) legal corporate governance framework tends to overemphasize the importance of oversight, supervision, and risk management (which makes sense in light of the one-dimensional corporate governance model). There are four different factors that support this view. First, there is simply not enough time to discuss strategy development and value creation due to the increasingly formal responsibilities of board members. Second, increasingly lawyers, governance experts, and financial specialists, who are generally viewed as best qualified to engage in the supervisory and oversight role (but are not in the best position to contribute to strategy discussions), are appointed. Third, researchers have identified the link between excessive independent director oversight and the reduction in the quality of information, making it harder for boards to monitor effectively.[40] Fourth, the fear of inadvertently 'shirking' the risk-oversight responsibilities (which could result in reputational damage and imprisonment) has resulted in a short-term, check-the-box, mentality.

Given these considerations,[41] we propose an alternative approach that is in line with the three-dimensional model of corporate governance.[42] In order

---

38 Countries increasingly promulgate legislation that mandates the appointment of a certain number (quota) of women on the board of directors of listed companies. For instance, quota legislation can be found in Austria, Belgium, France, Iceland, Italy, Norway, and Spain. Other countries, like Australia, Finland, Germany, Greece, Poland, Slovenia, Sweden, and the United Kingdom follow a softer approach by including gender diversity principles in their corporate governance codes. See L. Linnainmaa and A. Horttanainen, 'The Glass Ceiling is Cracking, Self-regulation Beats Quotas' *FinnCham*, 15 November 2012.

39 See P. Whitehead, 'Non-Executive Director: A Task for Which No One is Qualified' *Financial Times*, 10 April 2013.

40 See R.B. Adams, 'Asking Directors About Their Dual Roles' (2009), at <http://apps.olin.wustl.edu/FIRS/PDF/2010/1635.pdf>.

41 A common solution to the 'weaknesses' in the functioning of the board is to separate the oversight role from the strategy-oriented role. In this view, there will be two boards with different responsibilities: one board focuses on compliance issues and another – a strategic advisory board – deals with business challenges; see P. Whitehead, 'Think-tank Searches for Good Governance' *Financial Times*, 5 June 2013. There may be something to this idea. Still, the separation is likely to dilute and fragment leadership and professional responsibilities. Moreover, since the board of directors is more embedded in the 'legal' structure of the corporation, a well-composed, balanced, and knowledgeable board of directors is sure to create more value.

42 See W.G. Bowen, *The Board Book, An Insider's Guide for Directors and Trustees* (2011).

to have well-balanced boards, it is important to move beyond the usual selection criteria, such as independence, integrity, competence, reliability, good judgement and, preferably, a financial background. According to such logic, boards need outside directors who are product- and market-oriented and able to ask the right, often technical, questions.[43] Arguably, a well-balanced board with a mix of compliance- and growth/innovation-focused members was essential in making Apple the successful high-growth company that has generated significant returns for its investors and other stakeholders.[44] To capture this insight with more precision, we present the results of our empirical findings in the section below.

THE BOARD OF DIRECTORS: EMPIRICAL EVIDENCE

In this section, we examine 110 listed companies that have either more than average growth potential or show a more than average interest in product and market innovation. We report that corporate governance mechanisms that contribute to value creation are difficult to capture in a one-size-fits-all and pre-defined rulebook. We do not attempt, however, to explain all the variance in corporate governance in firms. We utilize our database to investigate the influence of the third dimension in the composition and workings of the board. We attempt to show that there are some general points of good practice, which could provide companies with a competitive advantage. In this section, we will proceed as follows. First, we will describe the data. Second, we will discuss the board dynamics and composition of boards in the companies in our data set.

1. The data

This sub-section briefly describes our data and methodology. Two hand-collected data sets were used to study 'best-practices' in growth-oriented listed companies. Our sample consists of seventy venture-capital backed companies that conducted an IPO on United States stock exchanges between 2011 and the first half of 2012 (VC-70) (see Appendix A). In order to avoid selection bias, we include all the venture-backed companies that went public between 2011 and mid-2012. We extracted information for the companies listed in 2011 from the complete database directory of DowJones VentureSource. For 2012, the data on the complete set of companies that

---

43 Experienced board members agree with this view. See D. Medland, 'Non-Executives Must "Delve Into All Areas"' *Financial Times*, 7 March 2013.
44 Arguably, the board of directors also contributed significantly to making Steve Jobs the best performing CEO in the world in terms of creating shareholder returns. See M. Hansen, H. Ibarra and U. Peyer, '100 – The Best-Performings CEOs in the World' *Harvard Business Rev.*, January–February 2013.

132

floated their shares was obtained from the Preqin Venture Deals Analyst database. To examine the board characteristics, particularly the information regarding the composition of the board of directors, and the experience and expertise of members of the board of directors at the time of their appointment, we were able to collect the relevant documents by analysing the companies' websites.

Financial information regarding IPO performances was gathered from the Nasdaq's market activity website. We use the same sources to gather similar information for our second hand-collected database, which consists of the top-40 companies that appeared in the FT Global 500 2012 list (FT-40). Note that in order to make the comparison with the 'young' listed companies more relevant, we exclude companies that operate in the oil and gas industry and the financial industry. The forty companies in the sample are also listed in Appendix A.

The VC-70 and FT-40 companies have two important things in common. First, both the VC-70 and the FT-40 companies can be considered important 'job creators'. At the end of 2012, the VC-70 companies employed 90,482 persons. The FT-40 companies have created 599,671 new jobs between 2009 and 2012. Second, both the VC-70 and the FT-40 companies are growth-oriented firms. Firms in such a context have either aspirations to become world leaders in specific technologies (the venture-capital-backed companies) or are already considered to be world-class companies (the Top-40 of the FT Global 500). Both the VC-70 and FT-40 companies have a strong strategic focus on innovation. This is obvious for the VC-70 companies that are still backed by venture capital. But, also, the FT-40 companies seem driven by innovation. This is evidenced by the fact that 80 per cent are considered to belong to the list of most influential units in the area of corporate venturing and corporate venture capital.[45]

2. Board dynamics and composition

Our goal in this section is to underscore the importance of board dynamics and composition (particularly the role of board members with business experience and expertise, academics, and venture capitalists) as key governance mechanisms that are often ignored in the corporate governance debate. While policymakers and regulators around the world have emphasized the need to increase the role of boards in the area of risk-management and managerial oversight, our assessment of the data indicates that boards of directors can play a much bigger role in the creation of growth and business value than initially thought.

Consider the VC-70 companies. These companies tend to follow a predetermined life cycle. In order to survive the 'valley of death' (which can be

45 See <www.globalcorporateventuring.com>.

defined as the period between the initial capital contribution and the time the company starts generating a steady stream of revenue), the start-up firm will attempt to attract investments from angel investors and venture capital funds (which will become shareholders in the respective companies). This brings us to the first observation: the important role of venture capitalists (or other private investors) on the board of listed companies.

(a) Venture capitalists on the board of directors

Typically, venture capitalists prefer to have board seats on their portfolio companies to protect the funds' interests. However, venture capitalist board members are not only supposed to control and monitor the CEO's and other executive managers' actions, but arguably provide value-added services that help bring the company and its entrepreneurs to the next stage of their development. For example, venture capitalists as board members in start-up companies can be quite beneficial. It is likely that they have expertise in the general areas of governance and financing, but may also have experience and knowledge about product development, sales strategy, and talent searches.[46] Importantly, entrepreneurs appreciate the contributions of venture capitalist board members. As for the facilitation of business, they recognize the necessity to have an engaged board that is interactive, candid, and passionate.[47] Furthermore, in order to be engaged, board members need to be strategically (not operationally) involved and understand the fundamental dynamics and drivers of the business.[48] Theoretically, the presence of venture capitalists continues until after the moment that private investors exit the company by floating it on the stock exchange (or selling it to another company).[49]

Prior studies have established that there is usually no lack of growth-oriented spirit on the boards of companies that just completed their IPOs. Lock-up periods, which prevent venture capitalists from exiting the company upon or immediately after the IPO, partly explain the position of venture capitalists on boards of newly listed companies (see Table 1). However, prior research also underscores the importance of having venture capitalists (with

---

46 See E. Mendell and M. Jeffers, '"A Seat at the Table" – A Study of Venture-Backed Company Boards', DowJones and NVCA presentation (2005).
47 See M. Blumberg, 'The Good, The Board, and The Ugly' *Only Once*, 25 July 2004.
48 See M. Blumberg, 'The Board of Directors: Guest Post From Matt Blumberg' *AVC Musings of a VC in NYC*, 23 April 2012.
49 Please note that most high potential companies do not follow the traditional life cycle. Trade sales (acquisitions by financial or strategic investors) are currently the most important and even preferred exit for private investors. The going-public decision, under the life-cycle theory, is typically triggered by the insider owner's loss of information advantage over outside owners in making accurate valuations of their firm. See E. Maug, 'Ownership Structure and the Life-Cycle Theory of the Firm: A Decision to Go Public' (2001) 5 *European Financial Rev.* 167.

Table 1. Board composition and diversity in VC-70 companies (independent directors only) on 31 December 2012

Diversity Indicators	Average	Median	Max.	Min.
Number of Directors (total)	8	8	12	5
Number of Independent Directors	6	6	10	3
Age (years)	54.2	54	85	27
Time on the Board (years)	4.8	4.7	21	0
Women on the Board	< 1 (0 (49%) / 1 (47%) / 2 (4%))	1	2	0
General Expertise	< 1 (0 (51%) / 1 (33%) / 2–3 (16%))	0	3	0
Financial Expertise	< 1 (0 (49%) / 1 (43%) / 2 (8%))	1	2	0
Business Expertise	< 2 (0 (13%) / 1 (43%) / 2–4 (44%))	1	4	0
'Former' VCs	< 3 (0 (7%) / 1 (13%) / 2–5 (80%))	2	5	0
'Independent' Investors	< 1 (0 (61%) / 1 (25%) / 2 (14%))	0	3	0

their specific expertise and experience) on the boards of these young listed companies and how they have a positive effect on their IPO performance.[50] To be sure, there could be circumstances where it might be advisable to replace some venture capitalists for more independent financial experts on the boards of such companies.[51]

Yet the role of venture capitalists remains important. It is common knowledge that companies often start losing their entrepreneurial spirit beyond the IPO. They may become less responsive to disruptive innovations and see talented employees leave for hotter start-up companies.[52] In this

---

50 See S. Chahine and M. Goergen, 'VC Board Representation and IPO Performance' (2011) 38 *J. of Business Finance & Accounting* 413.

51 See A.J. Epstein, 'Are Venture-Backed Companies Keeping Pace?' *NACD Directorship*, 5 March 2013. The accounting issues that Groupon experienced in their post-IPO era are great examples of this. See D. Aubin, 'Analysis: Groupon Accounting Problems Put Spotlight On Board' *Reuters*, 12 April 2012. This also explains the renewed discussion about Apple's board of directors when director York passed away in 2010. He was viewed as an independent director who had to be replaced in order to maintain a balanced board. See Y.I. Kane and J.S. Lublin, 'On Apple's Board, Fewer Independent Voices' *Wall Street J.*, 24 March 2010.

52 See C. Cain Miller, 'Trying to Recapture Start-Up's Feel, Google's Chief Fights Hard Against What He Sees As Its Worst Enemy: Itself' *Herald Tribune*, 10 November 2011.

135

Table 2. Board composition and diversity of FT-40 companies (independent directors only) on 31 December 2012

Diversity Indicators	Average	Median	Max.	Min.
Number of Directors (total)	13	12	20[a]	7
Number of Independent Directors	9	10	16	0
Age (years)	61	61	92	35
Time on the Board (years)	7.7	7.5	43	0
Women on the Board	3	3	5	0
General Expertise	4	4	9	0
Financial Expertise	2	2	4	0
Business Expertise	2	2	7	0
Investors/VCs	1	1	4	0
CEO = Chairman		35%		
Chairman = Insider		42.5%		
Chairman = Outsider		22.5%		

[a] Due to co-determination requirements, the German companies in our data set have relatively large boards of directors.

context, the recruitment of experienced venture capitalists to the board could provide a partial solution.[53] Moreover, they could assist a mature company's executive management with initiating open innovation strategies through which the company partners with (or acquires) smaller start-ups.[54] Certainly, these open innovation strategies, which are increasingly viewed as a successful 'healthy ageing' model in the life cycle of listed companies,[55] provide a possible explanation for the relatively high number of private investors and venture capitalists that were appointed to the boards of directors of the FT-40 companies (see Table 2). In this respect, it is interesting to mention iFund, a US$200 million investment initiative created by Kleiner Perkins Caufeld Beyers (a renowned venture capital fund) in partnership with Apple. The investment collaboration targets the development of applications, services, and components for Apple's iPhone, iPod Touch, and iPad. Thus, it is not surprising that Al Gore is a senior partner at Kleiner Perkins Caufeld Beyers. From the perspective of the increasing importance of corporate venturing activities (as well as the three-dimensional corporate governance model), the awareness of their value-

53 See Bowen, op. cit. n. 42.
54 See U. Celikyurt, M. Sevilir, and A. Shivdasani, 'Venture Capitalists on Boards of Mature Public Firms' (2014) 27 *Rev. of Financial Studies* (forthcoming).
55 See S. Murray, 'Corporate R&D: Big Groups Struggle to Bring Ideas to Fruition' *Financial Times*, 28 October 2011.

136

added contributions is beyond any doubt. It is only to be expected that this number will increase in the near future.[56]

(b) Board diversity: age, gender, and business expertise

An analysis of the FT-40 companies as well as the VC-70 companies clearly shows the importance of board diversity. Tables 1 and 2 present evidence on board diversity in terms of age, gender, and expertise. The results indicate that there are significant differences between the VC-70 companies and the FT-40 companies. For instance, Tables 1 and 2 show that the average age of directors in the FT-40 companies is significantly higher than their average age in the VC-70 companies. The reasons for this are straightforward. First, the directors of the FT-40 companies (compared to the directors of the VC-70 companies) have, as expected, served for a longer period on the board. Second, board members are usually recruited from the networks of the existing board members, which often consist of people of the same gender and age group.[57]

There are also differences in gender diversity. The FT-40 companies tend to take gender diversity more seriously than the VC-70 companies. The average percentage of women on the board of the FT-40 companies (20 per cent) is much higher than the average percentage in the VC-70 companies (7 per cent). One rationale for the increasing number of women directors is that the more mature FT-40 companies are more sensitive to the policy and media attention regarding gender diversity than the companies that have just completed their IPOs. This is confirmed by the fact that more than 75 per cent of the female independent board members were appointed in the period 2005–2012 (when gender diversity gradually became a key corporate governance issue). The increased media and investor attention can also explain why most (85 per cent) of the relatively few women on the boards of the VC-70 companies were generally appointed during the IPO preparation process (67 per cent) or shortly after they floated their first shares on the stock market (23 per cent) in either 2011 or 2012 (see the bar charts in Figure 1).

An obvious question that arises is whether companies with women on their boards are likely to outperform companies that do not take gender diversity seriously. Note that there is considerable debate about the role of women on boards and firm performance. A recent study suggests that

---

56 Arguably, venture capitalist board members can play a crucial role in assisting executive managers to create a corporate culture in which the established (or to be established) corporate venturing unit can thrive. See J. Von Heimburg, 'Driving Innovation by Corporate Venturing: How to Master Governance and Culture Challenges' *Innovation Management*, 7 January 2013.

57 Strong support for this view is provided by the FT-40 data set. It is striking to observe that board members usually hold the same additional positions in other profit and non-profit organizations.

gender-diverse boards enhance financial and stock-market performance.[58] Furthermore, gender diversity positively affects corporate social responsibility ratings which, in turn, improves the reputation of a company.[59] Some authors have argued, however, that board diversity in general may restrict the ability of firms to adapt to changing business circumstances.[60] This view is supported by the results of another study that appears to show that gender diversity may reduce the appetite of companies for engaging in risk-taking activities. A possible explanation may be found in the empirical research that shows that there is a correlation between female management and risk aversion.[61] Interestingly, our findings are consistent with the latter study in the sense that only 5 per cent of the FT-40 companies do not have gender-diverse boards. This percentage is much higher (49 per cent) in the more risky VC-70 companies.

It follows from this discussion that it is difficult (and often impossible) to provide clear-cut answers to questions of whether and, more importantly, why gender diversity has a positive, neutral or negative impact on firm performance. Moreover, it may be difficult to predict the most efficient level of board diversity. This becomes clear when we compare the percentage of women on the board to the stock price performance of the FT-40 companies in 2012. We find that the percentage of women on the board of the best performing companies (with a 2012 stock price performance in excess of 20 per cent) varied from 0 per cent to 25 per cent. The percentage of women on the board of companies that showed a 2012 stock price performance lower than 15 per cent was between 12 per cent and 45 per cent. Yet, our results may provide a plausible explanation why gender-diverse boards could potentially outperform other boards.[62] Figure 1 shows that the appointment of women to the board often increases the diversity in expertise and experience.[63] The pie charts graphically illustrate that 41 per cent of the women on the boards of the FT-40 companies bring academic, business, and marketing expertise and skills to the company. Figure 1 reveals also that 52

---

58 See A. Chanavat and K. Ramsden, 'Mining the Metrics of Board Diversity' *Thomson Reuters*, June 2013.

59 See S. Bear, N. Rahman, and C. Post, 'The Impact of Board Diversity and Gender Composition on Corporate Social Responsibility and Firm Reputation (2010) 97 *J. of Business Ethics* 207.

60 See J. Goodstein, K. Gautam, and W. Boeker, 'The Effects of Board Size and Diversity on Strategic Change' (1994) 15 *Strategic Management J.* 241.

61 See Credit Suisse Research Institute, 'Gender Diversity and Corporate Performance' (2012).

62 It is usually not clear why gender-diverse boards work better in practice: see K.D. Krawiec, J.M. Conley, and L.L. Broome, 'The Danger of Difference: Tensions in Directors' Views of Corporate Board Diversity' (2013) *University of Illinois Law Rev.* 919.

63 This is confirmed by B. Groom, 'Females Add Diversity to Boards' *Financial Times*, 3 Mach 2013. An identical argument can be made for the diversity in age: see 'Boardroom Age: Only a Number?' *Financial Times*, 6 September 2013.

Figure 1. Gender diversity in the board of directors of the VC-70 and FT-40 companies (the bar charts show when the women were appointed as independent directors; the specific expertise and skills of the women is reflected in the pie charts)

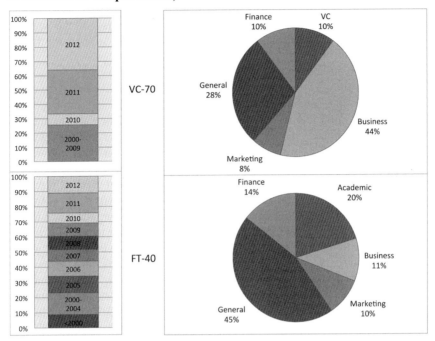

per cent of the women that are introduced to the board of directors of the VC-70 companies shortly before or after the IPO add specific business or marketing value.

Consistent with these observations, most companies in our sample have boards that consist of members not only with general business expertise (which is usually met by the presence of other CEOs, former CEOs or business consultants), but also include financially literate people (account-ants, CFOs or former CFOs). Our results also show substantial support for the view that the companies appear to take diversity seriously. What is more important is that boards of growth-oriented companies increasingly select a number of individuals with substantive knowledge of particular industries, sectors and/or markets.[64] Consider Toyota Motors' recent decision to appoint three real independent directors (which was approved by the shareholders in June 2013). Ikuo Uno, an adviser to Nippon Life Insurance

---

64 This number is higher in the VC-70 companies. However, we observe that the more mature companies increasingly understand the importance of experience and expertise diversity in boards of directors.

Co., Haruhiko Kato, president and chief executive officer of Japan Securities Depository Center Inc., and Mark Hogan, a former group vice-president at General Motors, were recently added to Toyota's board of directors. Historically, Toyota's seven 'auditor directors' focused mainly on financial oversight and internal control issues. The three additional independent directors, on the other hand, contribute general expertise in the area of transparency, but also business expertise that is likely to support the firm's global expansion plans.

As highlighted above, Figure 1 shows that 20 per cent of the women on the boards of the FT-40 companies are academics. It should therefore come as no surprise that, if we look at the total data set, a significant number of the independent board members hold academic positions, particularly in the area of biotech, medicine, and engineering. This is of course a rather general observation in VC-70 companies that are typically spun out from universities and research centres. Similarly, a comparison of the FT-40 companies further supports our view and shows that 35 per cent of the directors appointed include one or more academics. This is consistent with our intuitions that their presence can be invaluable in identifying technical issues and opportunities.[65] More importantly, they are also able to add vision and passion to the board of directors.[66] The evidence indicates that most scientist are appointed to the boards of directors of companies that operate in uncertain or fast-moving and highly competitive markets, such as pharmaceuticals, biotech, and internet (where specialized product and/or markets knowledge is necessary to identify the fast-changing market movements). This is also reflected in Figure 2, which confirms that the composition of the board of directors is sector-specific for the VC-70 companies. In addition, a more than average number of board members with specific business expertise can be found in companies that operate in volatile and unpredictable sectors, such as cleantech, internet, and biotech (which are generally also characterized by lower IPO performances). For instance, the average 6-month IPO performance of the IT companies in our sample was 51 per cent, whereas the average 6-month IPO performance of the cleantech companies was −31 per cent.

(c) Board dynamics and the alleged insulation from the capital markets

Our results in the previous section are reinforced by the Apple case: there is no one-size-fits-all blueprint for the composition of the board of directors in the three-dimensional model. Board requirements are firm-specific and vary across life-cycle stages, sectors, and cultures. And there is more. The unique governance issues that result from including growth in the corporate

65 See Bowen, op. cit. n. 42.
66 See P. Whitehead, 'Better Boards: Company Secretaries Give Their Views on Non-Executive Roles' *Financial Times*, 19 June 2013.

140

Figure 2. Board composition of the VC-70 companies per sector

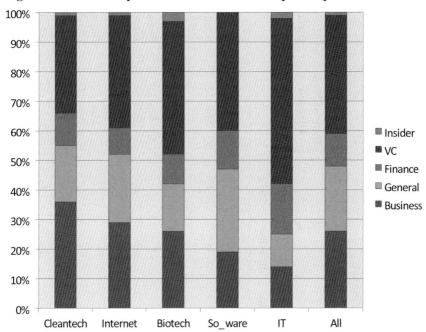

governance discussion are part of a complex, three-dimensional continuum, wherein each of the dimensions (managerial control, long-term commitments, and growth) are intertwined and constantly evolving. For instance, it is only to be expected that if a company seeks to expand to emerging markets, it might require international experience on the board.[67] Consider a company that has board members with a wealth of international know-how but, at the same time, should also have other directors with more technical risk-management and accounting skills.

Corporate governance is thus dynamic in nature.[68] We predict that the many innovative and successful firms will tend to address board composition issues when the going gets tough.[69] This claim is confirmed by our analysis of the VC-70 companies. It turns out that Jobs's approach to make changes to the composition to the board of directors as a necessary first step to deal with business or accounting challenges is also followed by companies that have only recently completed the IPO process. These results confirm the

---

67 See J.H. Daum and J.C. Norris, 'Adding International Expertise: Opening The Board's Window On The World' (2007), at <http://content.spencerstuart.com/sswebsite/pdf/lib/Cornerstone_Opening_the_boards_window_on_the_world.pdf.pdf>.
68 See, also, P. Zumbansen, 'Rethinking the Nature of the Firm: The Corporation as a Governance Object' (2012) 35 *Seattle University Law Rev.* 1469.
69 See Aubin, op. cit., n. 51; Kane and Lublin, op. cit., n. 51.

Table 3. The dynamics of boards in relation to stock price performance

Name	Date IPO	IPO Performance						Appointment Date of New Director	Expertise of New Director
		1-day	30-day	60-day	6 months	12 months	31 Dec 2012		
InterXion	28 Jan 11	6	14	4	12	10	83	Jun 11 Jan 12	Business Accounting
Epocrates	2 Feb 11	37	38	25	0	-35	-45	Mar 12	Business (also CEO)
Neophotonics	2 Feb 11	20	64	5	-36	-48	-48	Oct 12	Business
Pacira Pharma	3 Feb 11	0	-1	0	47	53	150	Jun 11 Jun 11	Business Business
BG Medicine	4 Feb 11	15	24	13	-2	-2	-67	Feb 12	General
Gevo	9 Feb 11	10	24	69	-13	-40	-90	Mar 12	PE/VC
AcelRx Pharma	11 Feb 11	-9	-37	-35	-26	-36	-15	Sep 11	Business
Fluidigm Corp	11 Feb 11	4	10	12	7	7	6	Mar 11 Apr 11	Business Business
Cornerstone OnDemand	17 Mar 11	41	32	49	-4	52	119	Apr 12	Business
ServiceSource	25 Mar 11	22	18	101	38	54	-42	Nov 12	Business
Zipcar	14 Apr 11	56	49	11	0	-27	-54	Jun 12	General
Boingo	4 May 11	-10	-26	-33	-43	-21	-44	Aug 11	Business

Company	Date						
RPX	4 May 11	26	51	51	−18	−11	−52
Vanguard Health Systems	22 Jun 11	0	−1	−23	−47	−54	−32
KiOR	24 Jun 11	0	1	−33	−30	−41	−57
HomeAway	29 Jun 11	49	53	38	−14	−19	−19
Horizon Pharma	28 Jul 11	2	−7	−10	−58	−30	−74
Ubiquiti Networks	14 Oct 11	17	30	39	129	−17	−19
ZELTIQ	19 Oct 11	19	8	−5	−57	−52	−64
Groupon	4 Nov 11	31	−5	−4	−50	−81	−76
Angie's List	17 Nov 11	25	21	16	3	−20	−8
Zynga	16 Dec 11	−5	−11	44	−44	−75	−76
Verastem	27 Jan 12	11	9	7	−3	—	−12
Ceres	22 Feb 12	14	22	14	−49	—	−65
Bazaarvoice	24 Feb 12	38	51	64	24	—	−22
CafePress	29 Mar 12	0	−11	−25	−52	—	−70
Merrimack Pharma	29 Mar 12	−14	4	−2	34	—	−13
Facebook	18 May 12	1	−21	−26	−38	—	−30

Date:

Apr 12
Oct 11

Jul 11
Jun 12
Aug 12
Dec 12
Mar 12
Oct 12
Sep 12
Jun 12

Feb 12
Nov 12
Jul 12
Sep 12
Nov 12

Aug 12
Apr 12
May 12
May 12
Jun 12
Jul 12

Nov 12

VC

Business
Finance
General
Business
Business
Business
Business
Business
Business
Finance
Accounting
Finance
General
Business
Business
(3x)
Business
Finance
PE/VC
Business
Business
Finance
Insider

143

general thesis that it makes good sense to add independent directors with economic and financial skills to the boards of companies with accounting problems. The accounting issues that Groupon experienced in their post-IPO era confirms this thesis. Thus, in order to immediately address the criticism of its financial reporting practices, Groupon appointed two new directors with extensive experience in the accounting and finance disciplines. What is more remarkable (and similar to the Apple story) is that companies that show a disappointing IPO performance often react with new appointments to the board of directors. In an effort to improve market acceptance and investor confidence, companies will usually appoint board members with specific market or sector expertise.[70] These findings are depicted in Table 3.

In fact, 62 per cent of VC-70 companies with a disappointing and declining IPO performance appointed one or more members with specific experience and skills to their boards in 2011 and/or 2012 (see the last two columns in Table 3). This percentage is significantly lower when companies show a positive or an improving IPO performance (20 per cent). Our results indicate that the boards of directors of the VC-70 companies do not operate insulated from the capital market and their investors. Moreover, if we for now assume (in line with the three-dimensional model of corporate governance) that the basis for generating an abundance of long-term investor interest is a compelling financial performance supported by future growth and a robust innovation pipeline, it is evident that the companies' potential and intentions are closely linked to the composition of the board of directors. It is noteworthy that the appointment of new directors with specific business expertise often has a positive affect on IPO performance in the months following the appointment. Conversely, it appears that a continuing declining IPO performance (and thus a failed attempt to reverse a company's growth and profitability perspectives) increases the pressures (from the capital markets) to seriously consider a corporate restructuring. In the cases of the car-sharing company ZipCar and healthcare company Epocrates, the continuing underperformance resulted in the firms being acquired by Avis and Athenahealth respectively.

(d) The role of the chairman and CEO

In this sub-section we consider whether the roles of chairman and CEO should be separated. Consistent with prior research that has analysed different types of board structure in terms of the firm's risk oversight

---

70 The conclusion that the composition of the board of directors is dynamic and should be adapted easily to new challenges supports Bebchuk's view that board members should be appointed for a one-year term (and are up for re-election every year). See L.A. Bebchuk, A. Cohen, and C.C.Y. Wang, 'Staggered Boards and the Wealth of Shareholders: Evidence from a Natural Experiment' (2010), at <http://ssrn.com/abstract=1706806>.

Table 4. Who is the chairman?

Who?	Percentage (on 31 December 2012)	IPO Performance (31 December 2012)		
		Average	Max.	Min.
Chairman = Founder + CEO	27%	22%	363%	−76%
Chairman = CEO	23%	−24%	71%	−74%
Chairman = Founder	13%	23%	155%	−76%
Chairman = Former VC/CEO	20%	12%	150%	−90%
Chairman = Outsider	17%	−22%	98%	−86%

responsibility, the answer would be in the affirmative. In practice, however, the one-person CEO-chairman model may be the preferred way of working since it avoids disharmony, conflicts, and time-consuming ambiguous leadership issues.[71] Table 4 indicates that the one-person model is the preferred model in VC-70 companies.[72] The results in Table 2 also show that the model is also frequently employed by the FT-40 companies.

However, if we again link the board leadership models to the IPO performance of the VC-70 companies, we come to a surprising conclusion. Note that the 'separation of CEO and chairman' model is extremely powerful if the founder or an experienced venture capitalist takes the chairman position. Based on the above discussion, this view is in line with an analysis of the FT-40 companies where more than 75 per cent of the boards of directors have either combined the role of CEO and chairman or have appointed an insider (former CEO, founder or family member) as chairman of the board.

A GROWTH-ORIENTED CORPORATE GOVERNANCE FRAMEWORK

Our results provide evidence that suggests that corporate governance should not focus solely on reducing principal-agent problems. This raises the question whether solely paying attention to agency issues could crowd out entrepreneurship in listed companies. For instance, not only does a focus on the principal-agent problems encourage over-regulation in listed companies, but it also makes organizations bureaucratic and resistant to economic and technological change. To the extent that corporate governance has an important role to play in promoting entrepreneurship and innovation in listed

71 See Bowen, op. cit. n. 42.
72 It should be noted, however, that 40 per cent of the companies that incorporated the one-person model also appointed a lead director to balance the power within the boardroom.

145

companies, it is time to redirect the corporate governance debate in Europe and beyond to the importance of board dynamics. The implication is that well-balanced boards can dedicate more time to strategy and the development process of innovative products and markets.

In this context, it is significant to note that the relatively 'young' companies in the FT-40 (that were established after 1970, such as Google, Apple, and Amazon) were founded and are listed in the United States (see Figure 3). Why do we not find these young listed companies in Europe? Several explanations have been put forward such as access to capital, the entrepreneurial mindset, and the experience and connectivity of advisors and intermediaries. However, other explanations have been advanced as well. Here, it should be noted that most listed companies in the United States employ the Delaware General Corporation Law, which allows managers and shareholders to set up an organizational structure that best meets their special business needs as a growth company. In this respect, it is remarkable that the United States FT-40 companies tend to deviate from the pre-defined (and widely accepted) corporate governance regime. This observation appears to support the argument that a sound corporate governance model should include more flexibility to companies by emphasizing minimum standards and disclosure requirements.[73] In the European context this is even more imperative given the very limited ability of any member state to play the role Delaware has in the United States, due to significant tax and company law barriers.[74]

However, once we focus specifically on the organization of the board of directors, it is striking that the American FT-40 companies employ a one-tier board system. A comparison of legal frameworks around the world indicates that the organization and structure of the board of directors is best seen in terms of a spectrum of possible oversight and advice functions. At one end of the spectrum is Japan's traditional statutory auditor system (the *Kansayaku* system). Listed Japanese companies are generally required to implement a board of statutory auditors, consisting of at least one auditor. Large companies must have at least three auditors. The function of the auditors is largely limited to monitoring the board's compliance with legal provisions and reviewing the financial statements. At the other end of the spectrum, we find the Anglo-American one-tier board system. A one-tier board consists of both executive and non-executive independent directors. Although certain powers are usually delegated to board committees, such as a nominating and corporate governance committee, an audit committee, and a compensation committee, the board as a whole is responsible for the decisions it makes based on the input of the committees. In theory, one-tier boards (in which

---

73 See P. Whitehead, 'Better Boards: 'Too Much Time Is Spent on Pay' *Financial Times*, 30 October 2013.
74 J.A. McCahery and E.P.M. Vermeulen, 'Does the European Company Prevent the "Delaware Effect"?' (2005) 11 *European Law J.* 785.

146

Figure 3. Incorporation date and location of the FT-40

Date of Incorporation

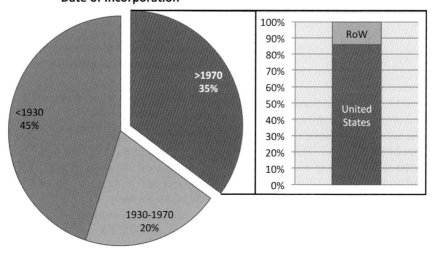

independent directors interact directly with executive managers, particularly the CEO) are well equipped to contribute to and support the planning and implementation of a company's strategy, without ignoring their oversight responsibilities. Two-tier systems, which are common in civil law countries in Europe and Asia, can be found near the mid-point of the spectrum. In two-tier systems, the control of management is the responsibility of a separate supervisory board.[75] The separation arguably puts more emphasis on the monitoring and oversight function of the board.

In light of the success of the 'young' high-growth companies in the United States, the formal convergence towards the Anglo-American one-tier board is not unexpected. As we have seen, the three-dimensional model offers an explanation for this. Here it should be noted that active and experienced board members often prefer one-tier board systems to two-tier systems.[76] Indeed, the more direct interaction with executive management and involvement in determining business strategy and growth targets appear to be attractive characteristics of the one-tier board. It should therefore come as no surprise that the legal frameworks of the respective jurisdictions in Europe increasingly facilitate the establishment of a one-tier board. This trend, largely inspired by the Statute for the European Company, explicitly

75 See C. Jungmann, 'The Effectiveness of Corporate Governance in One-Tier and Two-Tier Board Systems – Evidence from the UK and Germany' (2006) 3 *European Company and Financial Law Rev.* 426.

76 See, also, Y. De Jong and J. Woudt, 'Kees Storm' *Financieele Dagblad*, 13 April 2013.

147

allows firms to select a one-tier system.[77] In sum, we expect that growth-oriented companies will increasingly opt into the one-tier board system in Europe.

CONCLUSION

Something is profoundly wrong with the way we currently think about the structure and functioning of the board of directors. In particular, policy makers and regulators seem to believe that a more regulatory approach in this area will enhance the monitoring performance and accountability of the appointed directors. This belief is based on the assumption that directors will better serve the long-term interests of the company if they can embrace rules and regulations that offer them clear guidance about the best way in which to discharge their duties to investors and other stakeholders.

Ironically, the recent financial crisis has also led to studies that indicate that the excessively formal one-size-fits-all approach to the duties and tasks as well as the composition of the board of directors has turned – particularly non-executive – directors into 'toothless', unproductive, and irrelevant watchdogs who are sometimes destructive to business growth. Over-regulation makes companies bureaucratic and short-term oriented. Strict adherence to the corporate governance framework would then lead to companies not being able to reach their growth potential.

Mindful of this, high-performance and high-growth companies appear to take an 'ignored' dimension into account when structuring and organizing their boards of directors: the prospect of sustainable business growth and value creation. To show this, we analysed the board composition of seventy venture-capital-backed companies that were involved in IPOs on United States stock markets between 2011 and the first half of 2012 (VC-70 companies) and showed that venture capitalist (independent) directors continue to play a dominant role in the further development of the recently listed companies. We argued that this should come as no surprise in light of their continued stake in these companies which is largely due to lock-up provisions. Interestingly, however, we observed that certain venture capitalists remain on the boards of the companies, ensuring a continuation of the research and development intensity and innovation output. This also explains why we found on average one venture capitalist/investor on the board of the top forty of the world's largest companies in the Financial Times Global 500 2012 list (FT-40 companies). This number would be even higher if we also included board members who have an advisory role at venture capital funds.

---

77 See W.W. Bratton, J.A. McCahery, and E.P.M. Vermeulen, 'How Does Corporate Mobility Affect Lawmaking? A Comparative Analysis' (2009) 57 *Am. J. of Comparative Law* 347.

This brings us to the importance of board diversity. Again our data showed that age and gender diversity are linked to diversity in expertise. We found that while the average age of directors in FT-40 companies is significantly higher than VC-70 companies, they have also served longer on the board. We suggested that board members are usually recruited from networks of existing board members, which often consist of people of the same gender and age group. It is interesting to see that female independent directors appear to add more diversity in expertise and skills, which arguably contributes to a company's growth and innovation potential. We also found that the FT-40 companies tend to take gender diversity more seriously than the VC-70 companies. The latter result is consistent with the view that the more mature FT-40 companies are more sensitive to the policy and media attention regarding gender diversity than the companies that have just completed their IPOs.

In terms of the other characteristics of board members, we found evidence that most companies in our data have boards that consist of members not only with general management and leadership expertise, which is usually provided by the presence of other CEOs or former CEOs, but also include financially literate people (accountants, CFOs or former CFOs). In particular, we indicated that a significant number of board members hold academic positions, particularly in the area of biotech, medicine, and engineering. This is a rather general observation of the VC-70 companies. However, we showed that this also holds true for the FT-40 companies where 35 per cent of the analysed boards of directors appointed one or more academics. In our firm-level analysis, we observed that most scientists are appointed to the boards of directors of companies that operate in uncertain or fast-moving and highly competitive markets. That is, a more than average number of board members with specific business expertise can be found in companies that operate in the more volatile and unpredictable sectors, such as cleantech, internet, and biotech.

Interestingly, our analysis of the VC-70 companies indicated that the composition of the board of directors is dynamic. An underperforming IPO often results in the appointment of new directors with the specific experience, expertise, and skills necessary to refocus on growth and restore investor confidence. To be sure, the new directors sometimes replace venture capitalists that slowly but surely sell their stakes in the company. However, we observed that industry veterans and pioneers are often added to boards to deal with immediate governance and growth challenges. In many cases, these leadership changes contribute to the growth and performance of the companies.

Finally, we explored the question whether the roles of the chairman and CEO should be separated. Our analysis revealed that the one-person CEO-chairman approach is the preferred model in both the VC-70 companies and the FT-40 companies, since this may avoid disharmony, conflicts, and time-consuming leadership issues. More strikingly, we observed the separation of

149

CEO and chairman when the founder, an experienced venture capitalist or other insider, takes the chairman position.

Overall, to make further progress in this area, policy makers and regulators should be careful in deriving conclusions about the most effective structure and composition of corporate boards. The composition of the board of directors is firm-specific and varies across life-cycle stages, sectors, regions, countries, and cultures. The board of directors is 'fluid' in that it should change over time according to evolving markets and shifting business strategies and practices. In the aftermath of the financial crisis we have the chance to avoid – or at least minimize – the regulatory debate regarding the monitoring and oversight role of the board of directors. Indeed, the focus on sustainable growth and value creation has led to new insights that may prove hard to ignore in future corporate governance discussions and reforms. EU policy makers should take advantage of such new breakthroughs, if they wish to develop a competitiveness-enhancing governance framework.

Appendix A

VC-70 Companies

AcelRx Pharmaceuticals	Gevo	ServiceSource
Angie's List	Groupon	International
Audience	HomeAway	Skullcandy
Bazaarvoice	Horizon Pharma	Solazyme
BG Medicine	Imperva	Splunk
Boingo	Infoblox	Supernus
Brightcove	Intermolecular	Pharmaceuticals
CafePress	InterXion Holding	Synacor
Carbonite	Invensense	Tangoe
Cempra Pharmaceuticals	Jive Software	Tesaro
Ceres	KiOR Inc	The Active Network
Chemocentryx	LinkedIn	Tranzyme
Clovis Oncology	Merrimack Pharma	Ubiquiti Networks
Cornerstone OnDemand	Millenial Media	Vanguard Health
Demand Media	Neophotonics	Systems
Demandware	Pacira Pharmaceuticals	Verastem
Ellie Mea	Pandora Media	Vocera
Endocyte	Proofpoint	WageWorks
Emphase Energy	Proto Labs	Yandex
Epocrates	Renewable Energy	Yelp
Exa	Group	ZELTIQ Aesthetics
ExactTarget	Responsys	Zillow
Facebook	RPX Corp	Zipcar
Fluidigm	Sagent Pharmaceuticals	Zynga
Fusion-io	ServiceNow	

150

FT-40 Companies

Abbott Laboratories
Amazon.com
Ambev
Anheuser-Busch Inbev
Apple
AT&T
BASF
British American
   Tobacco
China Mobile
Cisco Systems
Coca-Cola
Comcast
General Electric
GlaxoSmithKline

Google
IBM
Intel
Johnson & Johnson
LVMH
McDonald's
Merck
Microsoft
Nestle
Novartis
Oracle
PepsiCo
Pfizer
Philip Morris
   International

Procter & Gamble
Qualcomm
Roche
Samsung Electronics
Sanofi
SAP
Siemens
Toyota Motor
Unilever
Verizon
   Communications
Vodafone Group
Wal-Mart Stores

JOURNAL OF LAW AND SOCIETY
VOLUME 41, NUMBER 1, MARCH 2014
ISSN: 0263-323X, pp. 152–71

Developing Two-tiered Regulatory Competition in EU Corporate Law: Assessing the Impact of the *Societas Privata Europaea*

MARTINA ECKARDT* AND WOLFGANG KERBER**

Since the Centros *ruling in 1999, Europe has evolved a two-tiered system of corporate laws. This opens up the possibility of some horizontal regulatory competition between the corporate laws of the member states. Following a draft regulation on the European Private Company (SPE), an additional legal form tailored to the needs of small and medium-sized enterprises (SMEs) is being proposed. We analyse whether such a supranational European legal form can be recommended from the perspective of the economic theory of legal federalism. We present a general theoretical framework for studying centralization/harmonization versus the decentralization of legal rules and regulations in regard to corporate law in the EU. Our analysis of the empirical evidence on horizontal regulatory competition and the advantages or disadvantages of such an additional legal form for SMEs shows clearly that it might render many benefits, compared with the existing situation of only (partial) horizontal competition.*

INTRODUCTION

Some 20.7 million small- and medium-sized enterprises (SMEs) in the EU account for 99.8 per cent of all the companies established in the EU. These SMEs employ 67 per cent of the workforce and provide nearly 60 per cent of

* Andrássy University Budapest, Pollack Mihály tér 3., H-1088 Budapest, Hungary
martina.eckardt@andrassyuni.hu
** University of Marburg, Am Plan 2, 35032 Marburg, Germany
kerber@wiwi.uni-marburg.de

The authors thank the editors of the *Journal of Law and Society* for valuable comments and suggestions. An earlier version of this article is part of the *Festschrift* for the seventieth birthday of Christian Kirchner, Humboldt University, Berlin: W. Kaal, M. Schmidt, and A. Schwartze (eds.), *Festschrift zu Ehren von Christian Kirchner Recht im ökonomischen Kontext* (2014).

152

the gross value added.[1] Unsurprisingly, given their importance to the single market, SMEs are on the political agenda at EU level. The Small Business Act, implemented in 2008, identified a number of obstacles for SMEs and introduced an Action Plan, which was revised in 2012.[2] One of the key proposed initiatives was the introduction of the European Private Company (*Societas Privata Europaea*, 'SPE'). The intention of the SPE was that it should complement already existing supranational legal forms like the European Economic Interest Grouping ('EEIG') introduced in 1985, the European Company (*Societas Europaea*, 'SE') introduced in 2001, and the European Cooperative Society (*Societas Cooperativa Europaea*, 'SCE') introduced in 2003 as a private cooperative company with a legal personality.

The SPE's particular advantage is that it is tailored to the needs of SMEs doing business internationally throughout the EU single market. Some 40 per cent of SMEs are involved in import, export or foreign direct investment.[3] Additionally, on average, about 2 per cent of all SMEs in the EU invest abroad, which amounts to around 500,000 enterprises.[4] However due to their size, SMEs have additional challenges when doing business abroad. It was these challenges that the SPE was designed to address. However, the process of introducing the SPE has come to a standstill. No agreement could be reached on a draft regulation of the SPE during the Hungarian Council Presidency in 2011, although most of the points of disagreement between the different actors involved had been successfully removed by that point.[5] The EU Commission no longer sees completing the SPE legislation as a priority in its revised Action Plan, but instead intends to explore other possibilities for facilitating the cross-border activities of SMEs.[6]

The question we focus on in this article is whether the introduction of an additional European legal form for limited liability companies is legitimate

---

1 P. Wymenga, V. Spanikova, A. Barker, J. Konings, and E. Canton, *EU SMEs in 2012: at the Crossroads. Annual Report on Small and Medium-sized Enterprises in the EU, 2011/ 12* (2012) 15, at <http://ec.europa.eu/enterprise/policies/sme/facts-figures-analysis/ performance-review/files/supporting-documents/2012/annual-report_en.pdf>.

2 European Commission, '"Think Small First" – A "Small Business Act" for Europe' (COM(2008) 394 final); European Commission, 'Action Plan: European Company Law and Corporate Governance – a Modern Legal Framework for More Engaged Shareholders and Sustainable Companies' (COM(2012) 740 final), at <http://eur-lex.europa.eu/LexUriServ/LexUriServ.do?uri=COM:2012:0740:FIN:EN:PDF>.

3 European Commission, *Internationalisation of European SMEs – Final Report* (2010) 46, at <http://ec.europa.eu/enterprise/policies/sme/market-access/files/ internationalisation_of_ european_smes_final_en.pdf>.

4 id., p. 10.

5 For details, see the papers in *The European Private Company – Societas Privata Europaea (SPE)*, eds. H. Hirte and C. Teichmann (2013), especially P. Hommelhoff and C. Teichmann, 'Societas Privata Europaea (SPE) – General Report' 1. See, also, R. Lewis and A. Buzdrev, 'The European Private Company: Entrepreneurial Flexibility and the Practicalities of National Law' (2012) 3 *International J. of Business and Social Science* 63.

6 European Commission, op. cit., n. 2, pp. 12 ff.

from the perspective of the economic theory of legal federalism. To this end, we analyse the current situation which, after *Centros* in 1999[7] and the cases that followed it, already facilitates some degree of horizontal regulatory competition between national legal forms. Based upon these results, we ask what the advantages and disadvantages of an additional legal form at the EU level will be. Our emphasis thus is less on a discussion of the specific pros and cons of the draft statute of the European Private Company. It is focused on the more fundamental question of whether introducing an additional European form of a limited liability company makes sense at all, given that there is already a certain free choice of legal forms from different countries through the effect of decisions of the European Court of Justice (ECJ) based on freedom of establishment treaty provisions.

This article is structured as follows: in the second section we present a general theoretical framework for analysing the problem of centralization/harmonization versus decentralization of legal rules and regulations in regard to corporate laws within the European Union. This includes the possibilities of horizontal and vertical regulatory competition in a two-tiered legal system. As such, it provides a clear framework for assessing the potential impact of this proposal. The third section analyses the results of empirical studies about the extent of horizontal regulatory competition which we already experience in regard to legal forms of limited liability companies within the EU. Based upon these results, the fourth section analyses the possible benefits but also problems of the introduction of such an additional European legal form. The last section concludes that based on our analysis the introduction of an additional legal form for SMEs might render many benefits without considerable disadvantages when compared with the existing situation of only (partial) horizontal competition between the legal forms of the member states.

A TWO-TIERED SYSTEM OF CORPORATE LAWS

Companies are characterized by one or more persons pooling their assets with the ultimate objective of gaining a profit from joint production. This implies a common-pool problem. Decision-making rights and control mechanisms are necessary to coordinate the joint use of the pooled assets and the resulting profits (or losses). Asymmetric information and principal-agent problems between the company owners and its other stakeholders (like creditors, employees, management, and so on) lead to moral hazard and adverse selection problems. Due to contingencies and general uncertainty, the writing of complete contracts is prohibitively costly. Accordingly, corporate laws offer different legal forms with special property rights, decision-

---

7 *Centros Ltd* v. *Erhvervs- og Selskabsstyrelsen* (Case C-212/97) 9 March 1999.

making rules, and information and disclosure rights to mitigate the resulting governance problems. Thus, it contributes to reducing the agency and transaction costs of team production.[8]

By choosing a legal form, firms can choose between different sets of rules for their governance. Different legal forms (as, for example, public limited liability companies, private limited liability companies, and so on) offer appropriate solutions for different kinds of companies and their needs. Corporate laws can be described as a combination of a set of mandatory rules and facilitative law. Mandatory rules are necessary to deal with market failure problems and the need to achieve further objectives. This is the regulatory dimension of corporate law rules. However, company law at its core is primarily a facilitative law. In that respect, it usually provides a broad legal scope for designing the constitutions of firms, but also offer a set of default rules for standard solutions. Within the EU, all member states offer sets of different legal forms with a combination of mandatory rules and facilitative law. Due to different legal traditions, there has been a wide variety of these national legal forms. This holds especially true for the specific private limited liability companies legal forms for SMEs, that we are dealing with in this article.

Although there is some consensus from an economic perspective about the most efficient legal solutions in regard to a number of firm-related issues, other key questions have not found a satisfactory answer yet.[9] This is because in many or indeed most jurisdictions there are additional objectives pursued by corporate law other than economic efficiency. The experience of serious failures in corporate governance over time indicates that so far, we have not yet developed optimal legal rules for companies. In our view, regulatory competition might be an important mechanism that could contribute to the development of better legal solutions for the governance of firms.[10]

To analyse the advantages and disadvantages of an additional supra-national European legal form for SMEs, we use the theoretical framework of legal federalism. It allows for legal rules on different levels of a multi-tiered system of jurisdictions. It analyses the optimal vertical allocation of regulatory and facilitative law within such a multi-tiered system of law from an economic perspective. In the following, we apply the framework of a two-tiered system of corporate laws for SMEs, that is, that both the member

---

8 A.A. Alchian and H. Demsetz, 'Production, Information Costs, and Economic Organization' (1972) 62 *Am. Economic Rev.* 777; J. Armour, H. Hansmann, and R. Kraakman, 'What is Corporate Law?' in *The Anatomy of Corporate Law. A Comparative and Functional Approach*, eds. R. Kraakman et al. (2009, 2nd edn.) 1; M. Eckardt, 'Der Einfluss der Unternehmensrechtsform auf die Internationalisierung von kleinen und mittleren Unternehmen' in *Der Donauraum in Europa, Andrassy Studien zur Europaforschung, Vol. 1*, eds. E. Bos et al. (2012) 125.

9 Kraakman et al., id.

10 K. Heine and W. Kerber, 'European Corporate Laws, Regulatory Competition and Path Dependence' (2002) 13 *European J. of Law and Economics* 43.

states and the EU can provide legal forms for SMEs. In doing so, competence rules are very important for such a two-tiered system of legal rules. They determine to what extent firms can choose between the corporate laws and the legal forms they provide within this two-tiered system (choice of law by firms). Additionally they determine how problems are solved in the case of conflicts between different corporate laws (conflict of laws rules; jurisdictional issues). These rules are essential for the working of the entire two-tiered system, because they decide on the possibility and extent of horizontal and vertical regulatory competition between different legal forms for SMEs.

The economic theory of legal federalism offers a number of criteria for assessing what the optimal degree of centralization or decentralization of legal rules should be.[11] These criteria run as follows:

(i) One group refers to different types of costs, like static economies of scale, information and transaction costs, externalities, costs through inconsistencies of the legal order and through distortions of competition (barriers to trade), which usually tend to favour a centralized provision of legal rules.

(ii) Heterogeneity between member states in regard to the problems that are solved by corporate laws as well as to different objectives (preferences) supports arguments for more decentralization.

(iii) Decentralized knowledge as well as the need for innovation and adaptability of corporate law solutions are important arguments for a decentralized provision and for experimentation with company laws.

(iv) Political economy problems (rent-seeking behaviour as well as high political transaction costs) provide arguments both for centralized and decentralized solutions.

(v) Strong legal traditions with long-established corporate law solutions in the member states lead to powerful path-dependence arguments and point to the necessity to take into account the historical status quo favouring the established decentralized legal forms.

(vi) Assessing the advantages and disadvantages of possible regulatory competition processes, which might be triggered within a decentralized system, also provides essential information for deciding between centralized and decentralized solutions.

In the United States, state-level corporate law has provided one of the most important examples of regulatory competition, which also triggered the first controversy regarding whether such competition entails beneficial or

---

11 R. Van den Bergh, 'Towards an Institutional Legal Framework for Regulatory Competition in Europe' (2000) 53 *Kyklos* 435; W. Kerber, 'European System of Private Laws: An Economic Perspective' in *The Making of European Private Law*, eds. F. Cafaggi and H. Muir Watt (2008) 64.

harmful results.[12] In the ensuing general discussion, it turned out that, on the one hand, regulatory competition can lead to better regulations through enhancing efficiency, faster adaptation, and more innovations of legal rules as well as less negative welfare effects through rent seeking. However, these potential advantages can be counterbalanced by a number of negative effects. The most important ones are higher information and transaction costs as well as race-to-the-bottom problems, which might lead to a too low level of regulations, especially in regard to the mandatory dimension of legal rules. Another problem is that a dynamic process of regulatory competition might not emerge at all, for instance, because of a lack of sufficient incentives for politicians or jurisdictions to engage in it. The overall result of both the theoretical and empirical research on regulatory competition is that it depends on the particular field of law and a number of specific circumstances whether, on balance, regulatory competition will have positive effects or not.[13] An important additional insight is that the institutional framework under which regulatory competition takes place has a crucial influence on what kind of regulatory competition emerges and what its overall outcome is. Choice-of-law and conflict-of-law rules as well as rules governing the mobility of firms are of utmost importance in this respect.[14]

Three main types of allocation of regulatory powers can be derived from the empirical experience with two-tiered regulatory systems like the European Union, as well as from theoretical analysis. To some extent these pure types can be combined and mixed, leading to hybrid forms. In the following, we present these types in regard to company law and discuss their main characteristics.

Full harmonization or perfect centralization (type 1) of corporate laws is the simplest form. It implies that only one uniform set of legal forms for firms exists for all member states in the EU. SMEs would not be able to choose between the different legal forms for private limited liability companies from different member states. However, they would be able to use the same legal form throughout the whole EU. In addition to that, the same mandatory rules would apply to all SMEs within the EU. In this way, any regulatory competition would be eliminated. An analysis based on the theory of legal federalism would show a number of advantages, but also large problems in comparison to more decentralized solutions. Harmonization has been the dominant form in a number of other legal fields in the EU, for example, in

---

12 L Bebchuk, 'Federalism and the Corporation: The Desirable Limits on State Competition in Corporate Law' (1992) 105 *Columbia Law Rev.* 1435; R. Romano, *The Genius of American Corporate Law* (1993).

13 J.-M. Sun and J Pelkmans, 'Regulatory Competition in the Single Market' (1995) 33 *J. of Common Market Studies* 67; K. Heine, *Regulierungswettbewerb im Gesell-schaftsrecht. Zur Funktionsfähigkeit eines Wettbewerbs der Rechtsordnungen im europäischen Gesellschaftsrecht* (2003); Kerber, op. cit., n. 11.

14 H. Muir Watt 'Choice of Law in Integrated and Interconnected Markets: A Matter of Political Economy', (2003) 9 *Columbia J. of European Law* 383; Kerber, id.

large parts of consumer law. In respect of corporate laws, however, a full harmonization or centralization approach seems unrealistic in the foreseeable future due to the significant variety present in existing corporate laws.

A *pure decentralization approach without direct regulatory competition* (type 2) is one of the opposite types. SMEs would only be able to choose from corporate laws at the member state level; at the same time, however, they would have to be established according to the corporate law of the member state in which they were doing business. If a firm wants to be recognized as a legal entity in another member state, it has to establish there in one of the member states' legal forms. This means (i) that a firm cannot migrate with its legal form to another member state, and (ii) that there is no direct freedom of choice of corporate laws between member states. Therefore, there is no direct regulatory competition between these laws. However, that is not the full picture: investors are free to choose in which member state they want to establish their firm (mobility of capital) and do business and, as such, there is still some indirect regulatory competition between different corporate laws through locational (that is, inter-jurisdictional) competition. In this case investors can only choose between a whole package of public goods, regulations, and taxes by choosing between different locations. Accordingly, the competitive pressure in regard to the specific corporate law, for example, for SMEs, is very weak. In other fields of regulation, this solution is well known within the EU as the principle of the country of destination. Historic-ally in corporate law, the conflict-of-laws rules have been the traditional 'real seat' or 'incorporation' doctrines, which were prevalent in the EU until the *Centros* decision in 1999 and subsequent rulings undermined their applicability and effect.[15] By doing so, the ECJ has taken a step, in the context of corporate mobility, in the direction it took in the *Cassis de Dijon* jurisprudence regarding the 'country of destination' and 'country of origin' principles in respect of natural persons' mobility in the EU.[16]

A *pure decentralization approach combined with free choice of law and direct regulatory competition* (type 3) is the other, opposite type, compared with a full harmonization approach. Here, too, only the member states offer legal forms with limited liability for SMEs. But the firms can choose freely between these national corporate laws. This implies (i) the freedom to choose between all national corporate laws when starting a business, and also (ii) the possibility of doing business with the legal form of one member

---

15 See, for example, *Cartesio Oktató és Szolgáltató bt* (Case C-210/06, 16 December 2008).

16 A. Wiśniewski and A. Opalski, 'Companies' Freedom of Establishment after the ECJ *Cartesio* Judgment' (2009) 10 European Business Organization Law Rev. 595. For a more nuanced account of the complex legal situation in the EU in regard to corporate law, see M. Schaper, *Selektion und Kombination von Gesellschaftsformen im institutionellen Wettbewerb. Typenvermischung und hybride Rechtsformen im europäischen und US-amerikanischen Wettbewerb der Gesellschaftsrechte* (2012).

state throughout the whole EU as well as to migrate with an already established legal form to other member states. In its pure theoretical form, this implies that all legal forms with limited liability for SMEs compete directly with each other in the EU. The partial replacement of traditional conflict of law rules in the EU through the jurisprudence of the ECJ can be interpreted as a transition in the direction of this third main approach of pure decentralization with free choice of law and direct regulatory competition. This form is – to a large extent – practised in the United States, where only the individual states offer corporate laws, while firms can choose between these laws without being restricted as to where they do business within the country. In the United States, empirical research in regard to competition between corporate laws tends to support the advantages of regulatory competition. Significantly, the evidence found does not support race-to-the-bottom concerns.[17] Nevertheless, Europe is not the United States, and this type of allocation of regulatory powers has raised concerns in the EU as to whether the ensuing process of regulatory competition between corporate laws from the member states might lead to a race-to-the-bottom problem.

In addition to these pure types of allocation of regulatory powers in a two-tiered system of legal rules, there exist also hybrid forms. They are combinations of the three pure types discussed so far.

Minimum harmonization constitutes an important group of such a hybrid form. At the central level, minimum rules are established, which all legal rules and regulations on member state level have to fulfil. Beyond these minimum rules, member states are allowed to enact rules with higher regulatory standards. In regard to corporate laws, this would imply that the EU would enact certain minimum standards. If the standards of the minimum rules are very high, then this solution is very close to full harmonization, whereas very low minimum standards render such a solution very similar to a pure decentralization approach. Such a minimum harmonization with the possibility of stricter national standards can come in two variants. In the first, the regulated entities have to comply with the stricter domestic regulations, that is, this is a combination of harmonization (type 1) with decentralization according to the host country principle (type 2). This would imply that the member state can enforce its higher national standards within its territory, because in regard to these rules no direct competition takes place. However, there is also a second variant, which we can observe in other regulatory fields in the EU (like, for example, product regulation). In this case member states can enact higher regulatory standards in their national laws than the EU minimum rules. However, due to the application of the home-country rule, only domestic firms have to comply with these higher regulatory standards, whereas firms from other member states need only comply with their home-country rules. This leads to direct regulatory competition and

17 R. Romano, 'Competition for State Corporation Law' in *The New Palgrave Dictionary of Economics and the Law, Vol. 1*, ed. P. Newman (1998) 364.

159

does not allow the particular member state to enforce its higher standards within its own territory. This second variant of minimum harmonization is therefore a combination of harmonization (type 1) with decentralization, free choice of law and direct regulatory competition (type 3).

Partial harmonization is another hybrid form of harmonization and decentralization, in which one part of the relevant legal rules for corporate governance are harmonized, while other parts are left to the national legislators. This might be an appropriate solution, if there are serious concerns about race-to-the-bottom problems in regard to specific aspects of corporate law without eliminating direct regulatory competition in regard to all other rules of the respective legal form. Hybrid forms resulting from a *mixture of the two types of pure decentralization with and without free choice of law* (type 2 and type 3) are also possible: for example, in general, firms might be free to choose between different legal forms with limited liability from different member states and use them within the entire EU. However, in respect of certain issues, for example, co-determination, they have to comply with the domestic rules of the host country. As a result, in regard to most aspects of corporate law, direct competition among the legal forms from different member states is possible, with the exception of certain explicitly defined issues. Other complex hybrid forms might be *mixtures of all three main types*: one part of corporate law rules might be harmonized (type 1), another part might be under direct competition through free choice of law (type 3), whereas some governance issues require compliance with the specific domestic rules of the host country (type 2).

So far, however, we have not taken into account the additional possibility of *choosing between corporate laws at the EU level and at the member state level*, leading to the possibility of vertical regulatory competition. In fact the proposal of the SPE aims at such a solution. In addition to the 27 private limited liability company statutes of the member states, firms would be able to choose the SPE as an additional European option and use it within the entire EU. In its pure form, without rules about minimum and partial harmonization, the provision of such a European legal form is primarily only the provision of a twenty-eighth legal form that competes with all the other national legal forms. However, other examples of additional European options for legal rules (such as optional European contract law rules) have shown that a European provision of optional legal rules might lead to special advantages, but also to specific problems, which can differ considerably from those of a pure horizontal regulatory competition. Especially important here are path-dependency problems and dangers of a monopolization of the European solution in the long run.[18]

---

18 Regarding vertical regulatory competition in corporate law, see K. Röpke and K. Heine, 'Vertikaler Regulierungswettbewerb und europäischer Binnenmarkt – die Europäische Aktiengesellschaft als supranationales Rechtsangebot' (2005) 56 *Ordo Yearbook of Economic and Social Order* 157.

Based upon such a theoretical framework with a two-tiered system of corporate laws in the EU, the above mentioned economic assessment criteria from the theory of legal federalism could be used for analysing which of these different types and hybrid forms are optimal from an economic perspective, both with regard to the extent of centralization or decentralization and to the extent and form of regulatory competition. The experience with other fields of law shows that sophisticated combinations of centralized and decentralized rules, with a perhaps limited degree of direct regulatory competition, might be a particularly promising solution for dealing with the manifold trade-offs between the advantages and problems of (de)centralization and regulatory competition.[19] This article does not attempt such a complex analysis in regard to limited liability corporate law, although this could lead to valuable insights. In the following, we only analyse the advantages and disadvantages of the introduction of a twenty-eighth legal form for limited liability companies for SMEs, compared with the current legal situation in which SMEs can already choose between the different legal forms of the member states.

HORIZONTAL REGULATORY COMPETITION BETWEEN LIMITED LIABILITY CORPORATE LAWS IN THE EU: THE EMPIRICAL EVIDENCE

This section presents the available empirical knowledge about the extent and intensity of the already existing horizontal regulatory competition between the 27 different legal forms for private limited liability companies of the member states. Since the *Centros* jurisprudence of the ECJ, free choice of different legal forms, and therefore direct regulatory competition, has become easier. This jurisprudence was therefore an important step from the former pure decentralization approach without direct regulatory competition (type 2) to the pure decentralization approach with direct regulatory competition (type 3). The crucial question, however, is whether this has led to a process of horizontal regulatory competition – independent of the question of its benefits or problems. In that respect, to what extent SMEs with their specific problems respond to differences between the legal forms of different member states, and whether member states have incentives to compete for incorporations of companies by modifying their legal forms, has to be analysed.

Kirchner et al. discuss different direct and indirect costs on the part of companies which might decrease the potential for horizontal regulatory

---

19 For example, see W. Kerber and S. Grundmann, 'An Optional European Contract Law Code: Advantages and Disadvantages' (2006) 21 *European J. of Law and Economics* 215, regarding the optional European contract law.

competition in the EU.[20] The main types are mobility costs, switching costs, and transaction costs. Costs resulting from different, that is, unfamiliar legal and adjudication systems, as well as costs resulting from the need to establish under a foreign language, are seen as additional factors potentially decreasing the working of horizontal regulatory competition.[21] This holds in particular when it comes to SMEs which are characterized by a general shortage of managerial resources and are rather limited in their potential to exploit scale economies. In addition to the costs of setting up a company under a foreign legal system, the on-going costs of complying with a member state's regulatory regime also have to be taken into account.[22]

For a fully effective process of regulatory competition, it is also necessary that member states strive to offer new or improved forms of corporate laws, that is, at least some member states must have incentives to modify their legal forms in order to attract additional companies to establish under their rules. Franchise taxes paid by the companies to the respective state of incorporation and successful lobbying by local lawyers specializing in corporate law are key factors in the United States evidence.[23] However, in the EU, such franchise taxes are prohibited and, so far, there is no empirical evidence on the lobbying impact of law firms specialized in corporate law. Nevertheless, we also observe in the EU a number of reforms of national private limited liability corporate laws over the last few years, which may be motivated by concerns about the international competitiveness of national law.[24] Accordingly, for the time being, it is an open question as to what exactly motivates member states to modify their legal forms so as to attract both start-ups and companies incorporated under a 'foreign' legal form to establish under their corporate law regime.

20 C. Kirchner, R.W. Painter, and W. Kaal, 'Regulatory Competition in EU Corporate Law After Inspire Art: Unbundling Delaware's Product for Europe' (2005) 2 *European Company and Financial Law Rev.* 159.
21 J. Armour, 'Who Should Make Corporate Law? EC Legislation Versus Regulatory Competition' (2005) 58 *Current Legal Problems* 369; W. Bratton, J. McCahery, and E. Vermeulen, 'How Does Corporate Mobility Affect Lawmaking? A Comparative Analysis' (2009) 57 *Am. J. of Comparative Law* 347; M. Gelter, 'The Structure of Regulatory Competition in European Corporate Law' (2005) 5 *J. of Corporate Law Studies* 247; E. Kieninger, 'The Legal Framework of Regulatory Competition Based on Company Mobility: EU and US Compared' (2004) 6 *German Law J.* 741; L. Klöhn, 'Supranationale Rechtsformen und vertikaler Wettbewerb der Gesetzgeber im europäischen Gesellschaftsrecht. Plädoyer für ein marktimitierendes Rechtsform-angebot der EU' (2012) 76 *RabelsZ* (*Rabel J. of Comparative and International Private Law*) 276.
22 M. Becht, C. Mayer, and H. Wagner, 'Where Do Firms Incorporate? Deregulation and the Cost of Entry' (2008) 14 *J. of Corporate Finance* 241.
23 Bratton et al., op. cit., n. 21; Gelter, op. cit., n. 21; Kieninger, op. cit., n. 21; Klöhn, op. cit., n. 21.
24 See C. Teichmann, 'Modernizing the GmbH: Germany's Move in Regulatory Competition' (2010) 7 *European Company Law* 20 (regarding reforms of the German *GmbH*).

However, even if no dynamics are triggered on the supply side, it would suffice if companies respond to the existing differences in legal form among member states. By a pure selection effect, the average quality of the legal forms in use in the EU would improve. If all SMEs choose those legal forms which they deem best for them through free choice of law, the 'market shares' of the superior legal forms would increase and those of inferior ones be reduced. In addition to that, through the combination of legal forms from different member states, new hybrid forms of private company laws can emerge. One prominent example is the *Limited & Co. KG* as a new combination of the United Kingdom private company limited by shares with the German *Kommanditgesellschaft ('KG')* as an alternative legal form to the well-known German *GmbH & Co. KG*. The result is a new hybrid form, which is different from both the German and the English form.[25] Such inventions of new legal forms through the combination of several already existing national forms is one possible outcome of horizontal regulatory competition through pure choice by firms, which does not require any active competition by the member states.

However, there is some evidence that member states do indeed compete for companies to establish under their corporate law, for example, in regard to minimum capital requirements. This is shown by the manifold differences as well as changes in the minimum capital requirement (MCR) for private limited liability companies within the EU.[26] In 2011 the average MCR was €7,000 with the median €3,000. However, in five countries only €1 has to be paid as MCR, while the highest MCR is €35,000. Since 2003, MCRs have been reduced in ten member states. In some – like Austria – such a reform is currently on the political agenda. In addition, some countries have introduced new legal forms for start-ups. For example, in 2009, Germany introduced the *Unternehmergesellschaft* with a €1 MCR to supplement the *Gesellschaft mit beschränkter Haftung (GmbH)*, the German private limited liability company, as a low-cost alternative for start-ups.[27]

There is empirical evidence in the German context that companies indeed react to cost differences resulting from differences in MCR when deciding in which member state to establish. The MCR in Germany is €25,000, while the British MCR and the German *Unternehmergesellschaft* MCR are only €1.[28] According to data from the German business register (*Gewerberegister*) from 2005 to 2012, on average 4,700 companies registered each year as a British

---

25 For a detailed analysis of its benefits and problems, see Schaper, op. cit., n. 16, pp. 268–303.

26 For details and additional references, see M. Eckardt, 'The European Private Company: Do We Need Another 28th Private Legal Form in the EU? On Regulatory Competition of Corporate Law' (2012) 20 *Estnische Gespräche über Wirtschaftspolitik* 39.

27 Teichmann, op. cit., n. 24.

28 Eckardt, op. cit., n. 26.

private company limited by shares in Germany, with a peak of 8,643 in 2006. With the introduction of the German *Unternehmergesellschaft*, the number of newly registered British private companies limited by shares dropped significantly by 38 per cent from 2008 to 2009, with a further decreasing tendency from 2010–12. Compared to that, the *Unternehmergesellschaft* has proved to be a success. In 2012 only 1,496 companies registered as British private companies limited by shares, which is only about one third of its average between 2005 and 2012. In contrast to that, 15,344 businesses registered as an *Unternehmergesellschaft*, which amounts to 17 per cent of all companies newly registered as a *GmbH*.[29] Bratton et al. have found similar evidence present for the Netherlands, where companies reacted to the relatively high MCR of €18,000 in a similar way.[30]

In addition to reductions in MCR in recent years, member states have also been concerned with reducing other costs resulting from their legal forms as well as administrative procedures for start-ups. Between 2007 and 2012 the overall costs of starting a new business changed in 16 of the 27 member states, declining by 27 per cent from an average of €485 to €353. Over the same period, the time required for performing all the necessary administrative tasks of establishing a company (that is, of setting up a new legal entity) declined by 52 per cent from 11 to 5 days on average. This is due to reforms undertaken by 15 of the 27 member states.[31] These reforms might be motivated at least in part through the raised awareness of these cost issues for SME brought about by the Small Business Act.[32]

There is also some econometric evidence available confirming these descriptive findings. Becht et al. analyse whether the ECJ's decisions on freedom of establishment for companies indeed led to a migration of companies to member states with lower costs of establishing.[33] They use a data set of all limited liability companies newly established in the United Kingdom between 1997 and 2005, based on the central business register. With the information available, they distinguish between domestic Ltds and non-domestic Ltds, the latter being companies which are established under United Kingdom corporate law as Ltds, but intended to have their principal place of business outside the United Kingdom. As a proxy for classifying such non-domestic Ltds they use the state of residence of a company's

---

29 For more details, see M. Eckardt, 'The Societas Privata Europaea (SPE) – Could it Promote the Internationalization of SMEs?', Andrássy Working Paper no. 27 (2012), at <http://ssrn.com/abstract=2307429>.

30 Bratton, op. cit., n. 21.

31 Own calculations based on data from European Commission, '2007 Country by Country assessment – overview table', at <http://ec.europa.eu/enterprise/policies/sme/files/support_measures/start-ups/onestop2006_en.pdf> and '2012 Country by Country assessment – overview table', at <http://ec.europa.eu/enterprise/policies/sme/business-environment/files/2012-country-fiches_en.pdf>.

32 European Commission, op. cit. (2008), n. 2.

33 Becht et al., op. cit., n. 22.

directors. In this way, they get a sample of 2.14 million limited liability companies, with 78,000 non-domestic firms established between 1997 and 2005 in the United Kingdom. One third of these are German limited companies, that is, they have directors residing in Germany. By applying difference-in-difference tests they find that after *Centros* there was a significantly stronger inflow of establishments from other EU member states than from non-EU member states in the United Kingdom. Additionally, there was a significantly higher number of establishments from EU member states with high setting-up costs, particularly in respect of MCR. Thus, according to Becht et al., horizontal regulatory competition is operating in the EU.[34]

A similar series of studies by Hornuf and Braun et al. confirm these trends.[35] They used a difference-in-difference approach for analysing the causal impact resulting from reforms in statutory rules concerning minimum capital requirements. Their studies take into account reforms in France, Germany, Hungary, Poland, and Spain between 2003 and 2008. Applying the same methodology as Becht et al.,[36] they found that a reduction in minimum capital requirements leads to a significant increase in new establishments in the respective country.

Econometric studies for the United States confirm the finding that the cost of establishment matters. By using ordinary least squares, Häusermann found that differences in establishment fees between states in the United States significantly affect the number of limited liability companies found in a state.[37] His study uses state-level data from 2004 to 2009. In addition, there is some, but not uniform, evidence that differences in substantive law and in adjudication also play a role for SMEs in where to establish, as is the case for publicly-held companies.[38] Gevurtz analysed the motives a company has for choosing a state to establish itself in that is not its principal business location.[39] By performing a qualitative analysis based on 50 interviews with private attorneys, he found that Delaware was chosen due to its superior legal infrastructure and because it had advantages in the eyes of majority owners or managers of limited liability companies. Furthermore, there is

34 id.
35 L. Hornuf, *Regulatory Competition in European Corporate and Capital Market Law: An Empirical Analysis* (2012); R. Braun, H. Eidenmüller, A. Engert, and L. Hornuf, 'Does Charter Competition Foster Entrepreneurship? A Difference-in-Difference Approach to European Company Law Reform' (2013) 51 *J. of Common Market Studies* 399.
36 Becht et al., op. cit., n. 22.
37 D. Häusermann, 'For a Few Dollars Less: Explaining State to State Variation in Limited Liability Company Popularity' (2011), at <http://ssrn.com/abstract=1879430>.
38 J. Dammann and M. Schündeln, 'Where are Limited Liability Companies Formed? An Empirical Analysis' (2010), at <http://ssrn.com/abstract=1633472>; B. Kobayashi and L. Ribstein, 'Delaware for Small FRY: Jurisdictional Competition for Limited Liability Companies' (2011) *University of Illinois Law Rev.* 91.
39 F. Gevurtz, 'Why Delaware LLCs?' (2012), at <http://ssrn.com/abstract=1998427>.

some evidence that horizontal regulatory competition for private limited liability companies, mostly SMEs, does not lead to a dominant market share for a single state in the United States, which is in contrast to the findings for publicly-held companies.[40]

At least based on limited empirical studies, a preliminary assessment of the empirical evidence about horizontal regulatory competition in regard to limited liability company laws for SMEs within Europe shows that different costs of establishment matter to SMEs. Importantly it indicates that a considerable number of firms seem to use the possibilities of a free market in choice of law. In turn, member states also seem to engage in regulatory competition by modifying and improving their legal forms. This is somewhat puzzling as their incentives are much more unclear since there seem to be no direct pecuniary incentives, like franchise fees in the United States. Therefore, we can conclude that the *Centros* jurisprudence that legally enabled the transition to the pure decentralization approach with direct regulatory competition (type 3) indeed triggered a process of regulatory competition between the corporate laws of member states. However, despite this evidence, we cannot assume that a dynamic and smoothly working regime of horizontal regulatory competition between the national legal forms yet exists. There are still serious legal problems as well as considerable (migration) costs due to the differences in languages and national legal systems.[41] In the next section we consider the role the SPE might play in overcoming these problems.

THE EUROPEAN PRIVATE COMPANY (SPE): ADVANTAGES AND DISADVANTAGES

According to the draft statute of the EU Commission, the European Private Company is a new legal form for a private limited liability company with a legal personality.[42] SMEs within the EU could choose it in addition to the already existing 27 national legal forms for private companies. It is especially designed to promote SMEs doing business across borders within the EU. According to the literature on the internationalization of SMEs and

---

40 Gelter, op. cit., n. 21; M. Kahan and E. Kamar, 'Price Discrimination in the Market for Corporate Law' (2001) 86 *Cornell Law Rev.* 1205; M. Kahan and E. Kamar, 'The Myth of State Competition in Corporate Law' (2002–3) 55 *Stanford Law Rev.* 679; M. Manesh, 'Delaware and the Market for LLC Law: A Theory of Contractibility and Legal Indeterminacy' (2011) 52 *Boston College Law Rev.* 189.

41 For general assessments of (the possibility of) regulatory competition in Europe, see Heine and Kerber, op. cit., n. 10; Kirchner et al., op. cit., n. 20; Bratton et al., op. cit, n. 21; Schaper, op. cit., n. 16; Klöhn, op. cit., n. 21.

42 Council of the European Union, 'Proposal for a Council Regulation on a European Private Company – Political agreement'(23 May 2011) Interinstitutional File 2008/0130 (CNS) at <http://register.consilium.europa.eu/pdf/en/11/st10/st10611.en11.pdf>.

166

on the economics of corporate law, the following aspects are important for an internationalization-friendly legal form for SMEs.[43] First, it should be inexpensive, requiring few resources for establishment and for meeting its regular tax and accounting obligations. Second, it should provide secure ownership rights, including limited liability so as not to endanger the parent company by doing business internationally. In addition, it should also provide secure property rights for creditors so as to reduce problems of getting access to outside finance and to lower extra risk charges. Third, it should reduce principal-agent problems due to information asymmetries. This holds for business partners, customers, and foreign authorities to whom the company statute should provide clear information about the company. Fourth, information and consultation costs for SMEs about legal and administrative questions should be low, which requires a relatively simple legal form. Fifth, competence rules should exist so that it can be decided easily and at low costs whether EU, the home or the host country legal rules apply in any particular case.

The SPE draft regulation comprises 48 articles, which are grouped in ten chapters with three annexes.[44] Its structure follows the life cycle of a company, stating property rights, decision-making rights, information rights as well as competence rules for the main stakeholders, that is, for owners, management, employees, creditors, and the public. Eckardt has argued that the proposed SPE statute is well suited to fulfill the role of an internationalization-friendly legal form for SMEs. Nonetheless, there might be some complications regarding co-determination regimes practiced in certain member states such as Germany but these would only concern enterprises with 500 or more employees. So, the draft SPE regulation seems to provide a viable legal form for the typical SME with fewer than 250 employees.[45] All in all, the SPE is a relatively simple legal form: on the one hand, it gives the owners broad scope for individual and flexible regulation of the articles of association; on the other, it contains a number of competence rules, where it states when the law of the country of establishment has to be applied. This increases legal certainty, which is a prerequisite for its successful implementation.[46] To what extent would the introduction of the SPE change the overall regime of corporate laws in Europe in regard to private limited liability companies? Since the proposed statute does not imply any kind of minimum or partial harmonization of existing national legal forms, it remains basically a decentralization approach with direct regulatory competition (type 3), supplemented by the SPE as an additional offer at EU level (pure vertical competition). It is dominated by free choice of law

43 See Eckardt, op. cit., n. 29, with additional references.
44 Council of the European Union, op. cit., n. 42.
45 Eckardt, op. cit., n. 29.
46 For a detailed discussion on specific issues of the SPE, see the papers in Hirte and Teichmann, op. cit., n. 5, and Lewis and Buzdrev, op. cit., n. 5.

through the firms, albeit limited to some extent by specific aspects where the country of establishment applies. The fact that there are no convincing arguments for harmonization is a very positive aspect of the Commission's draft statute, and remarkable in view of widespread harmonization efforts in many other legal fields in Europe.

To analyse the potential advantages and disadvantages of such an additional legal form in comparison to the current situation, we apply the assessment criteria from the economic theory of legal federalism from the second section. Since the introduction of the SPE would allow SMEs to choose between a larger set of legal forms for their private limited liability company, it seems to be hard to argue that extending choice might have any negative effects. SMEs remain free to use member-state domestic legal forms, and utilize their familiarity with these legal forms and the advantages of the cumulative experience of these well-established corporate law traditions (dynamic economies of scale). Since SMEs might have very different expectations of corporate law rules due to different business models and governance problems, a new and different legal form might better fulfil the demands of at least some SMEs. Additional options can increase efficiency and innovativeness. As a consequence, decentralized firm-level knowledge of the best corporate law arrangement and the need for innovative and adaptable approaches to corporate structures for small dynamic firms both favour increased competition between legal business forms. However, the SPE is more than an additional option: the specific advantages of the SPE as a legal form especially designed for doing business simultaneously in several member states of the EU will have a lot of specific advantages for those SMEs with a clear internationalization strategy. Since it can be used easily throughout the EU and would likely be known as the only European legal form in all member states, the SPE will lead to a reduction of information and transaction costs for establishing firms and doing business in the entire EU. Economies of scale and scope in regard to setting up companies as well as in regard to the costs associated with their regular duties can be realized. Reputation effects might also be very important for SMEs from member states with otherwise less familiar or less trusted legal forms. Both the cost advantages mentioned above and these reputation effects, which reduce costs for the trading partners of SMEs in the legal form of the SPE, imply lower barriers of entry within the EU and therefore easier market access. In that respect, the introduction of the SPE as an additional new legal form might fill a specific, so far unfulfilled, market demand. This is also positive in regard to the assessment criteria heterogeneity as well as innovation and adaptability. Therefore, we would argue that one can expect additional benefits from regulatory competition through the introduction of the SPE.[47]

47 See, also, Hommelhoff and Teichmann, op. cit., n. 5, pp. 13–15.

What kind of problems might arise with the introduction of this additional legal form? There might be problems due to path-dependency effects.[48] In the law and economics literature, it is a well-known fact that the quality of new laws depends on the extent of their application and adjudication. Therefore, a lot of experience with the SPE and a large number of court decisions are necessary before the new legal form achieves the same level of precision and legal quality as the limited liability company laws already well-established in the member states. Thus, a critical-mass problem emerges, which results from dynamic economies of scale. If the SPE is not used by a minimum number of firms, then it might never become sufficiently competitive in terms of legal quality. As a consequence, the SPE might fail in the market of legal forms for SMEs. But such a result would not worsen the situation compared to the current one. However, the opposite kind of problem might arise in the long run: the SPE might become so successful that it becomes the dominant legal form for SMEs in the EU. As a result, most other national limited liability legal forms for SMEs would be obsolete and thus regulatory competition would be eliminated. Both these types of problems are well known and discussed in regard to other fields of law, in which optional European legal rules have been proposed.[49] Whereas the critical mass problem might become relevant, it is less likely that the SPE would become the dominant legal form for SMEs in the EU. Since most SMEs are doing business only in domestic markets, it can be assumed that they would still use the national legal forms. In any case, it might be important for safeguarding regulatory competition that – in the long run – member states retain the right to introduce new legal forms.

Another concern is that regulatory competition might lead to race-to-the-bottom problems. Such problems can only emerge from the mandatory part of the new legal form, not from its – much more important – facilitative part. However, a small risk of race-to-the-bottom problems does already exist with respect to the current horizontal regulatory competition between the legal forms of different member states. The introduction of the SPE as an additional option would not increase it significantly, although it cannot be excluded that some mandatory rules of the SPE might lead to lower standards than the regulatory standards of the limited liability company laws prescribed in some member states. An already existing solution to this problem is that, in regard to certain governance issues, national legal systems require the application of the host-country rule. Although we would have, in general, free choice of law – and thus direct regulatory competition – between all legal forms available, there would be exceptions regarding certain issues, which would still be solved by applying the domestic (host-

---

48 See Heine and Kerber, op. cit., n. 10, regarding path dependency effects in corporate law.
49 For example, European contract law: Kerber and Grundmann, op. cit., n. 19.

country) rules.[50] Therefore, well-designed competence rules could take account of such race-to-the bottom problems.

However, these problems hint at a more general difficulty. Company laws always work within the context of a number of other sets of legal rules (such as tax law, accounting and auditing rules, securities law). Since many of these complementary laws are not harmonized within the EU, there might always be difficult interface problems, if legal rules from different member states are combined, either as legal forms from other member states or the SPE. This might lead to legal inconsistencies and thus to conflicts – resulting in manifold cost problems. However, with free choice of law, these kinds of problems already exist in the current situation. The introduction of the SPE will not increase them. On the contrary, a wide diffusion of the SPE throughout the EU might lead to more standardized interface solutions and therefore contribute to a reduction of such interface problems. A more critical problem in regard to the consistency of the resulting company law might emerge because all legal questions regarding the SPE have to be adjudicated on by national courts. The absence of an integrated European court system might lead to different decisions about the SPE in different member states. This would endanger the development of a uniform jurisprudence in regard to the SPE and cast doubt on the advantages of a uniform European legal form for SMEs. Solving this problem might be crucial for the success of the SPE in the long run.

CONCLUSIONS

Since *Centros* and subsequent rulings, the regime of corporate laws in Europe has evolved in a fundamental way. Although it is rather incomplete and imperfect, a two-tiered system of corporate laws has emerged. This two-tiered system is characterized by a considerable degree of free choice of law. This opens up the possibility of some horizontal regulatory competition between the company laws of the member states. An important additional development is the introduction of new legal forms at the EU level, such as the European Corporation (SE) and the European Cooperative Society (SCE), which can be chosen in addition to the national legal forms. Since these legal forms refer extensively to national company law rules, they provide only to a small extent a real alternative to the national legal forms such as, for example, the German *Aktiengesellschaft*. In that respect, there is scepticism about the degree of vertical competition in regard to these supranational legal forms. In contrast to this, the proposal regarding the European Private Company (SPE), would allow for much more vertical

---

50 As regards employee participation rights or the restructuring, winding up, and nullity of a SPE, see Council of European Union, op. cit., n. 42.

competition between such a European legal form and the national ones.[51] Therefore, in regard to limited liability companies, a two-tiered system would emerge based upon a decentralization approach with direct horizontal and vertical competition without any harmonization efforts.

Our analysis of the advantages and problems of the introduction of such an additional legal form for SMEs shows clearly that it might render many benefits without considerable disadvantages when compared with the existing situation of only horizontal competition between the legal forms of the member states. The summary of the empirical studies about the current state of horizontal regulatory competition in the third section suggests that firms do indeed respond to cost differences resulting from different legal forms by migrating to member states with less 'expensive' legal forms. Moreover, member states react to such movements by modifying and improving their legal forms, too. Therefore, horizontal regulatory competition in regard to limited liability company law seems to be working already. However, its extent and intensity seems rather weak still. The introduction of an additional European legal form for SMEs, such as the SPE, can be expected to reduce information and transaction costs and spur further regulatory competition. As a result, its advantages of more efficiency and innovation can be reaped. The risks associated with such an additional legal form – for example, race-to-the-bottom problems – seem to be quite small or even, in our view, negligible. The strongest concerns refer to the problem that the SPE, as any new legal form, has in overcoming a critical-mass problem in the form of attracting a minimum number of applications, and solving the various difficulties of matching the many complementary legal rules of the different national legal systems. This includes, in particular, its uniform adjudication by the national court systems.

51 Schaper, op. cit., n. 16, pp. 165–7.